HOW AMERICAN MEDIA PRESENTS CRISIS OF SINO-US RELATIONS

LIU WEN

authorHOUSE®

AuthorHouse™
1663 Liberty Drive
Bloomington, IN 47403
www.authorhouse.com
Phone: 833-262-8899

Published by AuthorHouse 10/23/2020

ISBN: 978-1-6655-0487-4 (sc)
ISBN: 978-1-6655-0486-7 (e)

Library of Congress Control Number: 2020920626

Print information available on the last page.

CONTENTS

CHAPTER 6 **MEDIA PRESENTATIONS OF THE CRISES IN SINO-U.S. RELATIONS AND U.S. DECISION-MAKING ON CHINA**...................... **179**

CHAPTER 1

INTRODUCTION

SECTION 1. QUESTIONS REGARDING THIS RESEARCH

Why This Research Topic?

In today's world, China-U.S. relations are generally recognized by politicians and scholars of the two countries as the most important bilateral relationship, and one that exerts the greatest influence on world politics. More than thirty years since the People's Republic of China and the United States established their diplomatic relations, the relationship has experienced much vicissitude. In areas of politics, economy, society, culture, environment and so forth, China and the United States have both common interests and many differences. The United States' China policy has thus shown paradoxical and sometimes vacillating characteristics. While the U.S. engages and works with China, it has always tried to contain and balance against her.

The separation of the three branches of the U.S. government and its pluralistic political system means that the making of American foreign policy entails a wide range of participants and multiple determining factors. The President with cabinet officials leading various departments including the State Department, and the United States Congress are direct participants. In addition to policies delineated by the Constitution, the

Executive Branch, and the Legislative Branch, interest groups, mass media, and public opinion also have powerful influences on foreign policy.[1]

The news media is considered the "fourth power" in addition to the three branches of U.S. government. It plays a crucial part in American politics. With regards to the making and practicing of U.S. foreign policy towards China, media coverage has on one hand enriched the American public's understanding of China, forming China's national image in the public eye, on the other hand, the media impacts agenda-setting and narratives in decision-making through using different content, forms and tones in reporting China affairs.[2] Media reporting is thus inexorably variable in determining the development of Sino-U.S. relations.

Since the cold war, the world has undergone fundamental changes. America has become the world's only superpower. Its need to team with China against the Soviet Union no longer exists. National interests, new global strategic objectives, domestic politics, debates on whether China is a friend or foe – all these have put America's China policy on a shifting pendulum with containment and engagement on each end.[3] The Sino-China relations has thus experienced much turbulence in its complicated and difficult development. There has been cooperation in multiple fields, but also crises from time to time, bred by frictions and conflicts.

As the world's biggest developed country and developing country, the U.S. and China are major powers which have a vast impact on global affairs. Both countries object to foreign interventions in their internal affairs and foreign policy. According to American political scientist Glenn H. Snyder, any core issues in international politics manifest themselves in times of crises.[4] The crises between China and the U.S. have exposed the two's conflicts of interests and posed severe challenges to the relations. The risks and uncertainties amidst the crises, with their unique, crucial, and urgent nature are a sure recipe of news

---

[1] Gu Yaoming, *American Media in My Eye* (Beijing: Xinhua Publishing House, 2000), 199-203.

[2] Xi Laiwang, *Analyses of America's Decision-Making and China Policy* (Beijing: Jiuzhou Book Publishing House, 1999), 121.

[3] Han Yugui, *Sino-US Relations After the Cold War* (Beijing: Social Sciences Literature Press, 2007), 13.

[4] James E. Dougherty and Robert L. Pfaltzgraff, *Contending Theories of International Relations* (Philadelphia: Lippincott, 1971)

coverage by media of both countries, leading to high-profile, fast, and comprehensive coverage.

American scholar Christopher Jespersen has argued that any study into China-U.S. relations should take into consideration the press, which start the debates on China policy in the first place.[5] During the past crises, the mass media has played multiple roles; it has been the information disseminator, public opinion shaper, and problem solver.[6] Amid the unique tension in the course of a crisis, the press is not only an important channel through which governments and the people acquire information, it also assumes the role of diplomacy when it sets agenda, explains policies, and expresses attitudes: shaping the future of the major power relations.

It is therefore of great significance that we study news coverage by the American media during crises between China and the U.S. within the scope of international communication and international relations. Through analysis of the media's impacts on the crisis process and bilateral ties, as well as discussions of the "media factor" in U.S. crisis response and its formulation of China policy, this work contributes to the theoretical understanding on the interplay between American media and foreign policy making. It also has important implications as China tries to gain the power for shaping discourse in international crisis communication and improve her national image in the eye of the American public through influencing the American media.

Subject of Study

Research question

The intersection of international communication and international relations, especially the relationship between news coverage and foreign policy, has been an important and hotly debated area of study for the

---

[5] Christopher Jespersen, *American Image of China* (United States: Stanford University Press, 1996), XIX.
[6] Gao Xiaohong and Sui Yan, ed., *International Crisis Communication* (Beijing: Communication University of China Press, 2011), 3.

students of international communication in China and abroad. Foreign policy is a key part of a country's global strategy. "It sets a country's fundamental and guiding principles in dealing with international affairs, foreign relations and diplomatic activities."[7] Diplomacy is an important way for a country to establish and develop foreign relations and achieve its foreign policy objective. Diplomatic activities are also important news items for media organizations of different countries. Coverage of foreign news informs foreign policy-making and is part of a country's diplomatic processes.[8]

The exact role the news media plays in the making of American foreign policy and diplomatic measures is debated among scholars in China and the U.S., with no certain dominant viewpoint. However, there has been consensus among politicians, scholars, and media practitioners about the media's participation in American politics and its influence on the country's foreign policy processes. As renowned American scholar Theodore White observes, in the U.S., unless the press readies the minds of the public, there can be no success in any major congressional legislations, foreign adventures, diplomatic activities, or major social reforms.[9]

With the end of the Cold War also came to the end of the Sino-American consensus in coping with the Soviet Union's threats. The strategic foundation of the Sino-U.S. relationship was thus fundamentally shaken. In finding a consensual view on China, China-U.S. relations, and the position and role of China in the U.S. global strategy, America has come a long, contentious, and arduous way. In this process, the American media has played a significant part in the bumpy road of the changing bilateral ties. Media coverage on China has on one hand influenced the cognition and viewpoints of the American government and public on China. On the other hand, the press has indirectly engaged in the formulation and implementation of America's policy on China.

This book originally intended to present and analyze two decades

---

[7] Zhang Jiliang, *Introduction to International Relations* (Beijing: World Affairs Press, 1989), 76.

[8] Liu Xiaoying. *International Journalism: Ontology, Methods and Functions* (Beijing: China Radio and Television Press, 2010), 266.

[9] Li Daojiu, *American Government and American Politics* (Beijing: China Social Sciences Press, 1990), 149.

of the American media's coverage on China on a macro level since the end of the Cold War, studying how China and China-U.S. relations have been reported and how this media coverage has impacted the making and implementation of U.S. foreign policy on China. However, due to the lengthy span of the historical period, it is difficult to analyze the vast amount of materials and samples in a limited amount of time. Therefore, with feasibility in view, this book focuses on the crises that occurred between the two countries and studies the characteristics and patterns of U.S. media reporting during the crises. It also attempts to explore how this coverage has impacted the American public's attitudes towards China, making the press an indirect force in creating American foreign policy.

Scope of research

Determining timeframe. Before further exploration, the timeframe of this study needs to first be delineated. That is, when did the Cold War end? What is the hallmark of its end? Contending answers have been raised by Chinese and foreign scholars. Some argue that the Cold War ended when Mikhail Gorbachev, then President of the Soviet Union, spoke at the United Nations General Assembly announcing to abandon the communist ideology. Some believe the Cold War came to an end when East Europe drastically changed and especially when the wall fell down in Berlin in December 1989. Some assert that it was the disintegration of the USSR after the August Coup of 1991.[10] Still, many scholars have regarded the two to three years between the late 1980s and early 1990s as the end of the Cold War. Professor Chu Shulong of American studies has marked the 1989 summer political unrest in Beijing as the beginning of post-Cold War Sino-U.S. relationship.[11] Since the purpose of this study is within the framework of Sino-U.S. relations, and because there has already been much research into the

---

[10] Tao Wenzhao, *American Policy on China after the Cold War* (Chongqing: Chongqing Publishing Group, 2006), 1.
[11] Chu Shulong, "Sino-U.S. Relations Since the End of the Cold War," in *China and the United States—Opponents or Partners,* ed. Liu Xuecheng and Li Jidong (Beijing: Economic Science Press, 2001), 25.

1989 incident, this book narrows down the timeframe of its study to the years between 1990 and 2015.

The end of the Cold War ushered international relations into a new era. But at the time, due to the difficulty to accurately define this era and the lingering legacy of the Cold War, scholars have used the term "Post-Cold War Era" to describe the new zeitgeist of world politics.[12] After the 9/11 attack, American politicians and scholars believed in the coming of another new era, and thus coined the notion of the "Post-Post-Cold War Era".[13] With the hit of the 2008 Financial Crisis, some Chinese scholars came to believe that the American model of development has been severely undermined, and that it was difficult for the post-Cold War international order led by the U.S. to continue. With the changes in the fundamentals of the international community, the scholars pronounced the demise of the "Post-Cold War Era".[14] Nevertheless, the idea of "Post-Post-Cold War Era" and the belief that the "Post-Cold War Era" has ended have been subject to contentious debates in China and abroad. Moreover, the legacies of the Cold War remain today with the international order still led by the West, the alliance and competition of major powers, and the issues of Russia's relationship with the West. Thus, this book still uses the term "Post-Cold War Era" in reference to the developmental stage of international relations since the end of the Cold War.

The choosing of news media. The United States is the birthplace for the modern-day news media industry. At the time of writing, the U.S. has over 1600 daily newspapers, 110,000 radio stations, 1202 commercial television stations licensed by the Federal Communications Commission, and 360 non-commercial TV stations.[15] Even though

---

[12] Liu Debin, "Speculation and Judgment of 'Post-Cold War Era'," *Journal of Social Science of Jilin University*, no. 4 (2002): 35-41.

[13] Richard N. Haass, "Defining U.S. Foreign Policy in a Post-Post-Cold War," Remarks to Foreign Policy Association April 2002, accessed September 12, 2020, https://2001-2009.state.gov/s/p/rem/9632.htm.

[14] Jiao Shixin and Zhou Jianming, "The End of the Post-Cold War Era and its Significance to China," *World Economy and Politics*, no. 12 (2009): 40-46.

[15] Li Liangrong, *Contemporary Western News Media* (Shanghai: Fudan University Press, 2010), 46-47.

many Americans today tend to turn to TV or the Internet as their number one news sources, for most people print media is still the main way for information, and digital media for entertainment.[16] Besides, due to the long time span between 1990 and 2015, in view of research feasibility and the easiness of gathering and possessing data from newspapers, this book chooses China-related coverage by *The New York Times* for the sample of analysis. The Times is a mainstream American news organization which is highly influential and representative of American society.

The New York Times has a reputation of being the "newspaper of record", and is regarded as America's best mainstream newspaper on international coverage. As one State Department official says, "The first thing we do is read the newspaper – *the* newspaper – *The New York Times*. You can't work in the State Department without reading *The New York Times*."[17] In 2010, the Pew Research Center for the People & the Press conducted a survey through television interview; The result shows for more than 70% of frequent *New York Times* readers, their purpose is to get "latest news and headlines, in-depth reporting, entertainment, or interesting views/opinions",[18] defining the newspaper's function as an information provider. (see fig. 1.1)

---

[16] Doris A. Graber, *Mass Media and American Politics*, 7th ed. (Washington, D.C.: Congressional Quarterly Press Inc., 2006), 5.

[17] Doris A. Graber, *Mass Media and American Politics* (Washington, D.C.: Congressional Quarterly Inc., 1993), 362.

[18] "Americans Spending More Time Following the News," Pew Research Center for the People & the Press, September 12, 2010, accessed September 29, 2020, https://www.pewresearch.org/wp-content/uploads/sites/4/legacy-pdf/652.pdf.

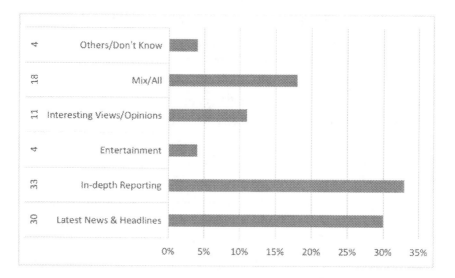

Figure 1.1 Survey by Pew Research Center for
the People & the Press in June, 2010.[19]

Most U.S. media organizations claim their coverage as being impartial, objective and non-partisan, but in reality, virtually all have certain biases. For example, the Washington Post is thought to have a bias towards the Democrats, the Wall Street Journal towards the Republicans, and *The New York Times* is considered middle-of-the-road.[20] These different biases are the reason why U.S. news coverage on Sino-U.S. relations has appeared to be multi-faceted. For a long time, the international coverage of *The New York Times* has been regarded to have a high degree of objectivity, authoritativeness, and influence. In view of the sufficient representativeness of the Times' China coverage among mainstream U.S. media and the hypothesis that the newspaper can to some degree reflect the China reporting strategies of mainstream American media, this book has chosen the paper's news coverage

---

[19] "Americans Spending More Time Following the News," Pew Research Center for the People & the Press, September 12, 2010, accessed September 29, 2020, https://www.pewresearch.org/wp-content/uploads/sites/4/legacy-pdf/652.pdf.
[20] Tao Wenzhao, *American Policy on China after the Cold War* (Chongqing: Chongqing Publishing Group, 2006), 366.

covering China, and the Sino-U.S. relations since the end of Cold War, especially coverage during crises, as the research sample.

It has to be pointed out that the word *coverage* has a wider meaning than *news* or *reports*. It includes both news reports and opinions. In the United States, various news media, especially newspapers, have a clear differentiation between reports and opinions. About 97% of daily newspapers have at least one opinion column. Big national and world-famous papers usually have two whole pages for opinions.[21] News reports are fact-based and emphasize truthfulness and objectivity, while opinions may have different perspectives with editorials penned by the newspaper's own staff representing the views of the paper, and also writings by independent writers, columnists, and readers. Newspapers showcase their objective and impartial stance through an open opinion section, while the commentators seek to lead the public opinion through influencing readers' views. This book seeks to analyze the impact of news coverage in crisis times on the crisis processes and Sino-U.S. relations, therefore opinions are also included in the research sample as important study materials.

Crises and crisis incidents. Crises are haphazard situational changes that pose severe challenges to the basic values and operation principles of a certain organizational system, so much so that the decision maker must make choices under high time constraints and uncertainties.[22] In international relations, crises are severe conflicts between at least two sovereign countries which could lead to war,[23] usually only in military or political nature. Crises are situations or states which do not equal crisis incidents. International crisis incidents are a special state in the conflict process. Left unresolved, conflicts could morph into wars or cause major changes to international relations.

---

[21] Li Liangrong, *Contemporary Western News Media* (Shanghai: Fudan University Press, 2010), 247-248.

[22] Gao Xiaohong and Sui Yan, ed., *International Crisis Communication* (Beijing: Communication University of China, 2011), 9.

[23] Glenn Herald Snyder and Paul Diesing, *Conflict Among Nations: Bargaining, Decision-Making and System Structure in International Crises* (New Jersey: Princeton University Press, 1977).

The reason why crisis incidents between China and the U.S. are selected for research are three-fold. First, crises are rooted in long-term conflicts of national interests. The crisis incidents between China and the U.S. essentially manifest the core issues between the two countries and cause deep impacts on their relationship. Second, even though the high level of investment of media organizations into covering international crisis incidents do not necessarily yield equivalent returns, such incidents nevertheless are hotly covered by media organizations in the world, which see these times as important opportunities to showcase their missions. Lastly, the media is a special form of communication in its coverage of international crisis incidents, with its work constrained by on-the-ground conditions of each country, however, the coverage also has major influence or even changes the direction of international relations. During crisis times, decision makers of each country heavily rely upon information, thus studying media coverage on crisis incidents is conducive in understanding the relationship between media and foreign relations.

SECTION 2. LITERATURE REVIEW

A literature review lays the foundation of academic research. Through reading and analyzing literature, the historical development and current status of the research question can be understood, avoiding the regurgitation of existing research. Second, literature review helps to find the problems and loopholes within existing research and thus identifies new frontiers to deepen and extend one's own research. There are three dimensions of the research questions of this book. First, international news and politics, namely, looking at international news from a foreign relations' point of view and studying the relationship between media and foreign policy. Second, American media and diplomacy, especially with regard to the interplay between American media coverage and U.S. policy towards China. Third, foreign news coverage by American media, including coverage on China by *The New York Times*.

This book's literature review was conducted by: 1) Retrieving Chinese-language related studies, including academic monographs, books, and journal papers, through the National Library of China's collection catalogue and the China Knowledge Network (CNKI); 2) Retrieving relevant studies done outside China, mainly academic monographs and papers, through the National Library of China's foreign-language literature library, the mass communication and applied foreign language database in the EBSCO database retrieval system, as well as the Cambridge Journals Online (CJO) system, and so on.

International News and Politics

Studies by foreign scholars

On the website of the National Library of China, the foreign-language literature collection catalog was searched. Keywords of "international journalism and politics", "international news and politics", and "media and international politics" each returned five, six, and fifteen monographs, respectively. Excluding the overlapping results, there are currently only eighteen foreign monographs on the subject of "International News and Politics". (See fig. 1.2)

Figure 1.2 Foreign-language literature collection catalog at National Library of China.

When searching for "media and international relations", "journalism and international relations", and "media and foreign policy", the number of monographs found was forty-eight, nine, and ten, respectively. After removing duplicate and irrelevant results, there are currently forty-five foreign-language monographs with the theme of "media and foreign policy" in the system. There were six duplicate results with the search results under "international news and politics".

In addition, in the Cambridge Journals Online (CJO) system purchased by the Communication University of China Library, searches using the keywords "media and foreign policy" for English-language journals outside China showed that since 1998 there have been hundreds of related papers published every year in various journals.

The discipline of international relations is an important approach towards studying international news. This book's ultimate purpose is to discuss how the American media's China and China-U.S. relations coverage impacts America's China policy and Sino-U.S. relations. Therefore, the relationship between media and foreign affairs, especially the relationship between the American media and the U.S. government's foreign policy is treated as this book's focus area.

Walter Lippmann can be said to be one of the pioneers in the study of the relationship between media and foreign policy. As early as the 1920s when TV media had not yet flourished, Lippmann argued in his book *Public Opinion*[24] that media coverage on foreign affairs will affect the cognition of the public on the world, and that this cognition is the major source of public opinion. *Public Opinion* was the genesis of the study on media and foreign policy. After the Second World War, studies on media's political impact slipped into a nadir. More than a few scholars believed that the media had little impact on politics.[25] Additionally, most of the research was on media's impact on domestic politics, with few studies in international affairs.

Bona-fide study into how the media influences foreign policy began in the 1960s. With the deepening of globalization and rapid development of communication technologies, media and foreign policy

---

[24] Walter Lippmann, *Public Opinion* (New York: Harcourt, Brace and Company, 1922).

[25] W. Lance Bennett, *News: The Politics of Illusion* (New York: Longman, 1988)

became increasingly linked. The field became a major realm of research in the study of international news and politics.

In 1960, renowned American political scientist Gabriel A. Almond put the elite groups that influence American foreign policy making into four categories in his book *The American People and Foreign Policy*.[26] Namely: 1) Political elites: party leaders, high-level government officials and elected lawmakers; 2) Executive elites, especially foreign affairs and service departments; 3) Interest elites, including various groups and representatives of private entities with interests related with foreign policy; 4) Media elites, including decision makers and news gatekeepers in mass media. The media focuses on and influence certain foreign affairs items. Although without government authorization, media plays an important role in the making of foreign policy.[27]

In 1963, American scholar Bernard C. Cohen released his empirical work *The Press and Foreign Policy*.[28] The book discusses several topics including journalists and their work, the relationship between journalists and government officials, the relationship between media and policymakers, government utilization of the media, and relations between the public and foreign policy. In his book the Two-Steps Theory was raised. The first "step" is when media influence opinion leaders, who in turn influence the government in the second "step". Cohen argues that the press is a political actor of major influences,[29] and that it connects the government with audience members concerned about international affairs. According to Cohen the media plays three roles in foreign policy making – as the observer of foreign policy news, the participator in foreign policy making, and the medium for foreign information. Cohen also finds that the media at the time had strong connections with the American government's foreign policy sector – at most times the press supported the government's foreign policies and

---

[26] Gabriel A. Almond, *The American People and Foreign Policy* (New York: Frederick A. Praeger, 1960).

[27] Gabriel A. Almond, *The American People and Foreign Policy* (New York: Frederick A. Praeger, 1960), 268.

[28] Bernard C. Cohen, *The Press and Foreign Policy* (Princeton: Princeton University, 1963).

[29] Bernard C. Cohen, *The Press and Foreign Policy* (Princeton: Princeton University, 1963), 140.

was in a harmonious partnership with the government. The press exerts impact in two ways. First, it informs and explains the government's foreign policy. Second, it questions, critiques and supervises decision makers on behalf of the public, thus engaging in foreign policy making.[30] This work of Cohen is seminal for the study on the relationship between the media and governmental foreign policy.

The year 1967 saw the release of American journalist James Reston's book *The Artillery of the Press: Its Influence on American Foreign Policy*,[31] which stresses the role of journalists, who, according to Reston, should be more active in news gathering, as well as exposing, critiquing and holding American foreign policy accountable. In 1968, American scholar Arthur S. Hoffman discussed the different ways international media communicates in open and closed countries, in his *International Communication and the New Diplomacy*.[32]

In 1971, Columbia University professor Roger Hilsman, who served as Assistant Secretary of State under the Kennedy Administration, categorized the American political power into three layers. At the center sit the President, his advisors and staff, presidential appointees of officials, the Congress and other administrative staff. The second layer comprises interest groups, the press and television. Constituencies and public opinion make up the third peripheral sphere.[33]

In 1972, American international relations scholar Richard Meritt put forward his three-fold model of international communication in *Communication in International Politics*.[34] He identified the government, non-government actors, and culture as the three channels

---

[30] Abbas Malek and Krista E. Wiegand, "News Media and Foreign Policy: An Integrated Review," in *News Media and Foreign Relations: A Multifaceted Perspective*, ed. Abbas Malek (United States: Greenwood Publishing Group, Incorporated, 1996), 5.

[31] James Reston, *The Artillery of the Press: Its Influence on American Foreign Policy* (New York: Harper & Row, 1967).

[32] Arthur S. Hoffman, ed., *International Communication and the New Diplomacy* (Bloomington: Indiana Univ. Pr., 1968).

[33] Roger Hilsman, *The Politics of Policy Making in Defense and Foreign Affairs* (New Jersey: Prentice-Hall, Inc., 1971).

[34] Richard Meritt, *Communication in International Politics* (Urbana: University of Illinois Press, 1972).

of international communication, further laying the foundation of the study of international political communication.[35] In 1978, the great international relations scholar Karl W. Deutsch in *The Analysis of International Relations*[36] established a five-layer system in a country's foreign policy making. From top to bottom they are: social and economic aristocracy, political and government system, mass media, public opinion communication network, and the general public. The mass media is positioned in the third layer, with its importance just below the aristocracy and government.

The year of 1984 saw the release of Andrew Arno and Wimal Dissanayake's *The News Media in National and International Conflict.*[37] The two authors treated the mass media as the originator of international conflicts, and that the key to resolve domestic and international conflicts also lies in the press. The book looked into the conflicts between the United States and Iran, India and Pakistan, and the United States and China, exploring the roles of and influences of three forms of media: the newspaper, radio, and television in the processes.

The 1990s witnessed an increasing body of research into the relationship between media and foreign policy. In 1991, in the *Mass Media and American Foreign Policy: Insider Perspectives on Global Journalism and the Foreign Policy Process*[38] edited by American scholar Patrick O' Heffernan, case analysis and interview of decision makers were used with both quantitative and qualitative methods, to establish a theoretical model of how the mass media influences foreign policy, and vice versa. Heffernan pointed out that the news media is a timely and highly-efficient source of information in the making of foreign policy, and that the decision maker is even sometimes more influenced by news coverage than information obtained through official government

---

[35] Tatsuo Urano, *Introduction to International Relations Theory*, trans. Liu Suchao (Beijing: China Social Sciences Press, 2000), 233.

[36] Karl W. Deutsch, *The Analysis of International Relations* (Englewood Cliffs, N.J.: Prentice-Hall, 1978).

[37] Andrew Arno and Wimal Dissanayake, ed., *The News Media in National and International Conflict* (Boulder: Westview Press, 1984).

[38] Patrick O'Heffernan, *Mass Media and American Foreign Policy: Insider Perspectives on Global Journalism and the Foreign Policy Process* (New Jersey: Ablex Publishing Corporation, 1991).

channels. This book captured the research results at Massachusetts Institute of Technology between 1977 and 1988, filling the gap between empirical and theoretical research.

The year 1997 saw the coming of *News Media and Foreign Relations: A Multifaceted Perspective*[39] edited by Abbas Malek, renowned international communication scholar at Howard University. This important and noteworthy book offered a comprehensive query into the media-foreign policy relationship. It is a collection of both theoretical papers and case studies. Based on the analysis of the divisions existing in previous research on the relationship between media and foreign policy, the book showed that issues including foreign policy culture, decision-making process, national security, public opinion and interest groups, trade and culture, and modern communication technologies need to be taken into consideration. In the book, the role of media in the implementation of policies by the state was also analyzed from the angle of sociology.

The same year saw *Politics and the Press: The News Media and Their Influence*[40] edited by American scholar Pippa Norris. It is collection of papers on the relationship between media and politics and contains the works by researchers from the John Shorenstein Center of Harvard University on the influence and role of media on government decision-making bodies, including the relationship between media and foreign policy. It was an early discovery and analysis of the contemporary characteristics and changes in the relations between international news and politics. There is a section in the book devoted specifically to how TV news affects the country's foreign policy. For example, CNN's news programs have influenced the foreign policy and actions taken by the United States against countries such as Bosnia, Somalia, and Zaire, in terms of humanitarian assistance or withdrawing troops, etc. Steven Livingston concluded that the interests of the media and the potential impact it exerts varies widely depending on different diplomatic issues

---

[39] Abbas Malek, ed., *News Media and Foreign Relations: A Multifaceted Perspective* (United States: Greenwood Publishing Group, Incorporated, 1996).
[40] Pippa Norris, ed., *Politics and the Press: The News Media and Their Influence* (United States: Lynne Rienner Publishers, 1997).

and foreign policies; therefore, analysis should be conducted on a case-by-case basis.[41]

In his book *The CNN Effect: The Myth of News, Foreign Policy and Intervention*[42], the well-known scholar Piers Robinson offered convincing analysis that after the Cold War, on international issues such as those with Iraq, Bosnia, Somalia, Rwanda, and Chechnya, the media's field coverage of these crises created invisible but enormous pressures on the U.S.'s diplomatic activities and diplomatic decision-making. As a result, the U.S. government often had to take actions that seemed hasty and inconsistent with its national interests, in order to not be seen by the public as weak, indecisive, and not adhering to international humanitarian principles.

In terms of government's foreign policy, scholars hardly deny that the media is an important force that can influence public opinion, which in turn influences foreign policy decision-making, but opinions are divided on the breadth of the media's influence on public opinion and the depth of media involvement in the making of foreign policy. However, still some other scholars, when observing the relationship between news and politics from the media angle, conclude that the press does not have a decisive influence on foreign policy decisions, and sometimes even the opposite is true.

As early as the 1970s, Herbert J. Gans discovered that the media was in fact reluctant to play the role of a supervisor, one that criticizes and opposes the government. The reason is that most journalists hail from the middle class and that they share common social values with those in power. Therefore, the media tends to support and please the elite class, especially those who are most powerful.[43]

American scholar W. Lance Bennett's highly representative monograph *News: The Politics of Illusion*[44] was published in 1983. Bennett

[41] Steven Livingston, "Beyond the 'CNN' Effect: The Media-Foreign Policy Dynamic," in *Politics and The Press: The News Media and Their Influences*, ed. Pippa Norris (United States: Lynne Rienner Publishers, 1997), 291-314.

[42] Piers Robinson, *The CNN Effect: The Myth of News, Foreign Policy and Intervention* (New York: Routledge, 2002).

[43] Herbert J Gans, *Deciding What's News: A Study of CBS Evening News, NBC Nightly News, Newsweek, and Time* (United Kingdom: Vintage Books, 1980).

[44] W. Lance Bennett, *News: The Politics of Illusion* (New York: Longman, 1988).

discussed the interrelationship between media and politics from a brand new and unique perspective, exposing in a profound way the operation and problems of the American news and political system. Bennett argues that the government, the media and the public have the following relationship in the political process. First, government departments use the media to construct simple and clear images and symbols that are ideologically and culturally popular; afterwards, journalists will look for tension-filled, theoretical angles, toe the safest political line, and emphasize the middle-of-way ideology and the official rhetoric; finally, the public at the passively receiving end either block all political speech or reinforce their existing prejudices, thus finally completing the news communication process.[45] Lance Bennett's main argument is that news does have an impact on politics, but the politics reflected in news reports is only the façade of facts. It is because politicians are becoming more and more skilled in manipulating the media, and the media, operating under the force of the market, finds it more and more difficult to ensure objectivity. A few years later, Bennett once again emphasized in another paper that the characteristic of media coverage of international news is that they are consistent with the country's foreign policy.[46]

Simon Serfaty stated in *The Media and Foreign Policy*[47] that the main role of the news media is not to exert a key influence in the center of foreign policy decision-making, but to pass important information to the public and provide feedback from the public to the authority. However, when the discussion of foreign policy overflows from the core decision-making level of the government to public domain, the role of the media will be amplified. Edward S. Herman and Noam Chomsky in *Manufacturing Consent: the Political Economy of the Mass Media*[48], analyzed the defects in the scope in international news choices and

---

[45] W. Lance Bennett, *News: The Politics of Illusion* (New York: Longman, 1988), 176.

[46] W. Lance Bennett, "Toward a Theory of Press-State Relations in the US," *Journal of Communication* 40, no. 2 (Spring 1990)
: 103-125.

[47] Simon Serfaty, ed., *The Media and Foreign Policy* (New York: St. Martin's Press, 1990).

[48] Edward S. Herman and Noam Chomsky, *Manufacturing Consent: the Political Economy of the Mass Media* (New York: Pantheon, 1988).

their causes, and argued that the mainstream media would emphasize, magnify, or ignore and even fabricate certain facts in line with the interests of the elite - indeed, the press can be described as an extension of the state propaganda machine.

In *Debating War and Peace: Media Coverage of U.S. Intervention in the Post-Vietnam Era* [49]Jonathan Mermin analyzed American media's coverage of several foreign intervention operations, such as the invasions of Grenada and Panama, during the Reagan and Bush administrations. Mermin argues that even after the Vietnam War, the media has yet to be able to focus on a certain foreign policy matter without a clear definition and position by the government.

In her book *Mass Media and American Politics*[50], Doris A. Graber analyzed the sources of news and argued that media and the government have a close relationship, in that the government is the media's main source of information. Graber proposed that because most government officials believe that the media has some important political power, governments in almost every country in the world try to control and manipulate the media, even during peacetime. Graber believes there is no media organization that is completely outside the control of the government and society, although such control may be informal and obscure. Politicians usually pay close attention to agenda setting by the media and its possible impact. They will make every effort to arrange and organize an event, so that the media reports favorably, and to hinder any potential negative reports. In addition, Graber believes that American reporters will follow these three principles when reporting international news: first, taking the position of the United States and the American people; second, being consistent with the foreign policy of the government; third, being consistent with the American public's general mindset of the world.[51]

---

[49] Jonathan Mermin, *Debating War and Peace: Media Coverage of U.S. Intervention in the Post-Vietnam Era* (New Jersey: Princeton University Press, 1999).

[50] Doris A. Graber, *Mass Media and American Politics* (Washington, D.C.: Congressional Quarterly Press Inc., 2006).

[51] Doris A. Graber, *Mass Media and American Politics* (Washington, D.C.: Congressional Quarterly Press Inc., 2006), 101.

Studies by Chinese scholars

Domestic Chinese scholars started paying attention to international journalism and politics in the 1990s. The research has been in the following three areas: first, mass communication and international relations - mainly theoretically exploring the mutual influence mass communication and international relations have on one another; second, global communication and soft power – from the angle of global communication analyzing the source of a country's soft power and ways to promote it; third, national image research - exploring the influence and constructive force media international news coverage has on national image. This book mainly involves the literature in the field of mass communication and international relations, especially relevant research results in the relationship between media and foreign policy.

On find.nlc.cn of the National Library of China, when searching for the Chinese-language keyword *Chuanboyuguojiguanxi*, or *communication and international relations*, there were 46 monographs, of which there were only about ten books closely related to communication and international relations.

Mass Communication and International Relations,[52] edited by Professor Liu Jinan, is a groundbreaking work in the field of mass communication and international relations. Liu discusses the role and influence of media on international relations, covering different medium forms: print media, international radio, satellite TV, the Internet, and news agencies. Liu believes that there is a natural connection between mass communication and international relations, and that the former has closely followed and actively participated in the matters of the latter right from the onset.[53] The book summarizes several ways in which mass media influences diplomacy, namely: 1) channeling the international community's attention on certain specific global issues; 2) altering traditional sources of information for foreign affairs and thus increasing the complexity of international relations; 3) through coverage

---

[52] Liu Jinan, *Mass Communication and International Relations* (Beijing: Beijing Broadcasting Institute Press, 1999).

[53] Liu Jinan, *Mass Communication and International Relations* (Beijing: Beijing Broadcasting Institute Press, 1999), 2-3.

on foreign affairs increasing government attention, thus speeding up the decision-making process; 4) being used by the government as a tool for carrying out foreign policy.[54]

In *Perspective of Media in International Relations,*[55] Zhang Guizhen specifically explores the relationship between mass communication and foreign policy. She points out that the mass media is first used as a tool to promote foreign policy, and its impact on foreign policy is mainly manifested in policy formulation and implementation. That is to say, mass media may exert influence on the kind of policy to be introduced, what is included in a policy, and to what extent the policy can be implemented, etc.[56]

In *The Visible Hand: Media in International Events*[57] edited by Zhao Xuebo, some quintessential major international matters are used as research cases, including the Vietnam War, the Gulf War, the Kosovo War, the "China Threat Theory", the prisoner abuse scandal, etc., with the goal to analyze the impact and role of media coverage in the entire process: the beginning, the middle and the end of international events. The author argues that with today's highly developed mass media, most of the time we cannot even tell whether an international event is one affected by news media, or whether it is a media event in itself.[58]

International Relations and Global Communication[59] is a collection of papers edited by Professor Chen Weixing, discussing global communication from different angles such as international relations, geopolitics, war on terrorism, and cultural exchanges. In the article "Mass Communication, Restricted by International Relations", author Zhang

---

[54] Liu Jinan, *Mass Communication and International Relations* (Beijing: Beijing Broadcasting Institute Press, 1999), 189-191.

[55] Zhang Guizhen, *Perspective of Media in International Relations* (Beijing: Beijing Broadcasting Institute Press, 2000).

[56] Zhang Guizhen, *Perspective of Media in International Relations* (Beijing: Beijing Broadcasting Institute Press, 2000), 208-210.

[57] Zhao Xuebo, *Visible Hands: Media in International Events* (Hefei: Hefei University of Technology Press, 2007).

[58] Zhao Xuebo, Preface to *Visible Hands: Media in International Events* (Hefei: Hefei University of Technology Press, 2007), 1.

[59] Chen Weixing, ed., *International Relations and Global Communication* (Beijing: Beijing Broadcasting Institute, 2003).

Guizhen believes that the restrictive effects of international relations on mass communication are mainly through restricting content provision for news reports, channeling the direction for mass communication, influencing reporting methods, restricting the properties of mass communication and so on.[60] Zhao Xuebo's "Research on the Influence of Mass Communication on International Relations" summarizes the impact of mass communication on international relations, namely: setting focus points, accelerating pace, increasing transparency, and expanding the participants of international relations.[61]

Related research works in this field also include: *Infiltration and Interaction: Radio, Television and International Relations* edited by Yang Weifen (Beijing Broadcasting Institute Press 2000 Edition), *Mass Communication in International Wars* edited by Liu Jinan, Zhou Jihua and Duan Peng (Beijing Broadcasting Institute Press, 2004), *Media Politics* by Li Hong, Li Min, et al. (Communication University of China Press, 2006), *Contemporary World Political Economy and Media* by Zhao Hongyan (Communication University of China Press, 2008), Zhou Yuhao's *Power and Game: International Political Communication in the Information Age* (Communication University of China Press 2008 Edition), Liu Hu's *National Interest and Media's International Coverage* (Jinan University Press 2009 Edition), Liao Weimin's *Rise and Fall of Nations: Research on the Dynamic Mechanism of Communication* (Communication University of China Press 2011 Edition), etc.

In addition, there are a number of quintessential papers on mass communication and international relations. Feng Cunwan argues in his article "Modern International Communication and International Relations"[62] that the impact of modern international communication on international relations lies in: promoting the formation of a holistic world view, facilitating changes in international relations, and challenging

---

[60] Zhang Guizhen, "Mass Communication, Restricted by International Relations," in *International Relations and Global Communication,* ed. Chen Weixing (Beijing: Beijing Broadcasting Institute, 2003), 29-47.

[61] Zhao Xuebo, "Research on the Influence of Mass Communication on International Relations," in *International Relations and Global Communication,* ed. Chen Weixing (Beijing: Beijing Broadcasting Institute, 2003), 67-80.

[62] Feng Cunwan, "Modern International Communication and International Relations," *World Economy and Politics,* no. 12 (1999): 40-44.

national sovereignty. Zhao Xuebo and Zhai Huixia demonstrate four reasons leading to the tangling of relations of media and diplomacy in their "The Philosophical Foundation of the Combination of Media and Diplomacy"[63]: First, the transmission of information is the main role of the news media, and diplomacy is precisely the field with a heavy concentration of information; second, the media has the mission of supervising society; third, diplomatic decision-making should be open and democratic; fourth, citizens have the right to know the information in the public domain and the process, content, and results of the government performing its duties. Sun Lu proposes in "A Preliminary Interdisciplinary Approach to Communication and International Relations"[64] that due to the fact that journalism and international relations are both social sciences, and a large amount of research materials in journalism and communication come from the field of international relations, interdisciplinary research can be conducted and common research paradigms gradually formed, in the sharing of materials and data, research methods, concepts and theories.

In recent years, there have been papers studying the relationship between the Chinese media's international news reports and foreign policy which are also worth noting. For example, Jiang Changjian and Shen Yi's "Mass Media and the Making of China's Foreign Policy"[65] combs through the changing history of the government's media management policies since the founding of the People's Republic of China, and argue that the historical changes have had new impact on the interactions between mass media and China's foreign policy. Jiang and Shen argue that the roles of the media in the making of China's foreign policy are mainly: 1) the "mouthpiece" of the party and government, 2) the "microphone" of the intellectual elite to express opinions, 3) the "arena" for policy debate, 4) the "accelerator" that puts

---

[63] Zhao Xuebo and Zhai Huixia, "The Philosophical Foundation of the Combination of Media and Diplomacy," *Modern Communication*, no. 4 (2005): 109-111.

[64] Sun Lu, "A Preliminary Interdisciplinary Approach to Communication and International Relations," *Journal of Hubei University of Science and Technology*, no. 2 (2013): 98-99.

[65] Jiang Changjian and Shen Yi, "Mass Media and the Making of China's Foreign Policy," *International Observation*, no. 1 (2007): 43-50.

pressure in order to speed up the decision-making response, and 5) a "safety valve" for the public to vent their dissatisfaction with some countries' policies on China.

Also on this subject are books such as Jin Hao's *"People's Daily* and China's Diplomacy: Analysis and Interpretation of the 'International Forum' column (1994-2006)"[66], Tao Ye's "Analysis of the Interplay Between Domestic Media and China's Foreign Policy Decisions"[67], Han Xu's "On the Influence of Internet Media on China's Foreign Policy Decisions"[68], Liu Yin's "Interactions of Media, Diplomacy and National Interests—A Comparative Study of the *People's Daily*'s Coverage on the Gulf War and the Iraq War"[69], Yang Yang's "Research on the Relationship Between China's International News Coverage and Foreign Policy— Taking Xinhua News Agency as an Example"[70], and Chen Yinhua's "Media and China's Diplomacy-*Global Times* and *People's Daily* in Sino-U.S. Relations"[71], etc.

U.S. Media Coverage and American Policy toward China

Research by foreign scholars

In the foreign language literature collection at the website of the National Library of China, the keywords of "American Media and China Policy", "Media and China-Us Relations" and the like were

---

[66] Jin Hao, *"People's Daily* and China's Diplomacy: Analysis and Interpretation of the 'International Forum' Column (1994-2006)" (Master's thesis, Fudan University, 2008).

[67] Tao Ye, "Analysis of the Interplay Between Domestic Media and China's Foreign Policy Decisions" (Master's thesis, China Foreign Affairs University, 2009).

[68] Han Xu, "On the Influence of Internet Media on China's Foreign Policy Decisions" (Master's thesis, China Foreign Affairs University, 2011).

[69] Liu Yin, "Interactions of Media, Diplomacy and National Interests—A Comparative Study of the *People's Daily*" (Master's thesis, Xiamen University, 2011).

[70] Yang Yang, "Research on the Relationship Between China's International News Coverage and Foreign Policy—Taking Xinhua News Agency as an Example" (PhD diss., Communication University of China, 2012).

[71] Chen Yinhua, "Media and China's Diplomacy: *Global Times* and *People's Daily* in Sino-US Relations" (PhD diss., Communication University of China, 2014).

searched respectfully. The results showed that there were no English-language monographs, but there were a number of relevant journal papers and doctoral books. To today there has been a fairly rich body of foreign research on the relationship between the U.S. media and U.S. foreign policy, but there are few monographs devoted to studying the relationship between U.S. media coverage and U.S.'s China policy, most of the body of research in this topic are in the forms of journal articles, conferences, papers, and books. However, in academic monographs that study Sino-U.S. relations, U.S. foreign policy, U.S. media culture, and U.S. media international news coverage, there are usually sections that discuss the role and impact of U.S. media coverage in U.S.-China relations.

Ezra Vogel believes that with the end of the Cold War, the United States lost an outright hostile rival, and "no consensus remained to counterbalance either the appeals of special interest groups or the images projected by the media, both of which gained greater prominence in the ensuing policy vacuum."[72] Kenneth Lieberthal affirms that the media is an important factor affecting U.S. policy toward China. He argues negative media coverage made China into a political symbol in the U.S., affecting Sino-U.S. relations. He suggested that when American presidents handle China affairs, they should create a favorable atmosphere of public opinion and curb one that is not conducive to decision-making.[73]

When evaluating the impact of the media on foreign policy, some American scholars believe that after the Cold War the United States lost its opponent, and thus its foreign policy was formulated by its reaction to the "impulse" of the media and the "image" the media creates.[74] Henry Kissinger said that if the news media can promote or push forward a

---

[72] Ezra F. Vogel, "How Can the United States and China Pursue Common Interests and Manage Differences?," in *Living with China: U.S./China Relations in the Twenty-first Century*, ed. Ezra F. Vogel (United Kingdom: W.W. Norton, 1997), 17.

[73] Kenneth Lieberthal, "Domestic Forces and Sino-U.S. Relations," in *Living with China: U.S./China Relations in the Twenty-first Century*, ed. Ezra F. Vogel (United Kingdom: W.W. Norton, 1997).

[74] James Schlesinger, "Quest for a Post-Cold War Foreign Policy," *Foreign Affairs*, published in Winter 1992, accessed September 24, 2020, https://www.foreignaffairs.com/articles/1992-01-01/quest-post-cold-war-foreign-policy.

foreign policy, then we may have to accept the fact that they will also make the implementation of a certain policy much more difficult.[75] The unusually active moves by the media often forced the U.S. government to respond passively, especially in military interventions overseas and changes in attitudes toward China.

Since the focus of this study is on American media coverage in Sino-U.S. relations, foreign scholars' empirical research and case analyses on U.S. media coverage of China and Sino-U.S. relations are the key literature that this book focuses on.

Wenjie Yan analyzed the image of China presented by *The New York Times* from 1949 to 1988 and found that the newspaper was consistent with the changes in the U.S. policy toward China over the past 40 years[76]; Alexander Liss reached the same conclusion after analyzing coverage on China by four American daily newspapers: *The Washington Post, The New York Times, The Los Angeles Times,* and *The Wall Street Journal,* from the year of 2000 to 2002[77].

The year 1993 saw University of Minnesota's Tsan-Kuo Chang's work *The Press and China Policy: The Illusion of Sino-American Relations (1950-1984).*[78] It is a quantitative analysis of the mainstream U.S. media's coverage on China between 1950 and 1984, exploring the relationship between the media, public opinion, and the U.S. government's China policy. The author found that: a) Although American media's coverage has always sustained a critical tone toward China's policies, its commentaries have always supported the Sino-U.S. relationship; b) newspapers' news reports on the U.S. policy on China have not had an impact on public opinion, but their commentaries on Sino-U.S. relations have had a great influence on public opinion; C) during the ups and downs of Sino-U.S. relations, newspaper editorials clearly supported

---

[75] Patrick O'Heffernan, *Insider Perspective on Global Journalism and Foreign Policy Process: Mass Media and American Foreign Policy* (Norwood, N.J.: Ablex Publishing Corporation, 1990), 37.

[76] Wenjie Yan, "A Structural Analysis of the Changing Image of China in the New York Times from 1949 through 1988," *Quality and Quantity* 32, no. 1 (1998): 46-62.

[77] Alexander Liss, "Images of China in the American print media: A survey from 2000 to 2002," *Journal of Contemporary China* 12, no. 35 (2003): 299-318.

[78] Tsan-Kuo Chang, *The Press and China Policy: The Illusion of Sino-American Relations (1950-1984)* (New Jersey: Ablex Publishing Corporation, 1993).

the government's handling of China's issues, and this remains the same throughout different stages of the relations.[79] However, the portrayal of Sino-U.S. relations which the U.S. media participates in constructing is very different from the real situation. After being filtered by the opinions of policymakers, it can only be called "media reality" at best.

Yanmin Yu believes that the U.S. media often adopts an attitude supporting the government's position in the foreign policy formulation process. Yu bases his argument on the American media's barrage of attacks on China's human rights, intellectual property rights, arms sales, and the Taiwan Missile Crisis during the Clinton Administration. Yu argues that the President of the United States and his administration have agenda set for media coverage, and media coverage has in turn further affected public opinion. Yu believes that the main reasons why the media caters to the government's position lie in: first, the American press is deeply affected by mainstream domestic ideology and is natural anti-communist; second, the American press from a national interest point of view does worry that China's rise poses a threat to the U.S.'s dominant position in the world, fearing that this will break the existing international political landscape and regional balance of power.[80]

Robyn S. Goodman looked through a total of 1,177 news reports and editorial articles on Sino-U.S. relations in *The New York Times and The Washington Post* from 1985 to 1993, and compared them with 399 government publications in the same period. Her analysis reveals that the two newspapers' coverage on Sino-U.S. relations during the post-Cold War period were less dependent on the government and more independent than they were before the end of the Cold War.[81]

In addition, Neil Wu Becker conducted a content analysis of news

---

[79] Tsan-Kuo Chang, *The Press and China Policy: The Illusion of Sino-American Relations (1950-1984)* (New Jersey: Ablex Publishing Corporation, 1993), 218-219.

[80] Yanmin Yu, "Projecting the China Image: News Making and News Reporting in the United States," in *Image, Perception and the Making of U.S.- China Relations,* ed. Hongshan Li and Zhaohui Hong (Maryland: University Press of America. 1998), 43-72.

[81] Robyn S. Goodman, "Prestige Press Coverage of Us-China Policy During the Cold War's Collapse and Post-Cold War Years: Did a Deteriorating Cold War Paradigm Set the Stage for More Independent Press Coverage?," *International Communication Gazette* 61, no. 5 (1999): 391.

reports on major events in Sino-U.S. relations between 1949 and 1989, and tested the interdependence between the media and the government.[82] Xigen Li compared reports on Sino-U.S. relations in *The New York Times* and *People's Daily*, and analyzed the influence exerted by national interest factors;[83] Jonathen Goldstein compared the differences in the U.S. media coverage of past and contemporary China and the changes in China's image in the American media;[84] C.C. Lee explored the interactive relationship between media and politics on China issues.

Research by domestic scholars

Chinese academics have written extensively on the relationship between China and the United States after the end of the Cold War and American media coverage on China, but there are few monographs that combine the two for a systematic enquiry. Through the "Wenjin" search of the National Library of China website, the only current monographs by Chinese scholars on U.S. media and Sino-U.S. relations are He Ying's *American Media and China's Image (1995-2005)*[85] and Qiao *Mu's Dragon in the Eagles' Eyes: American Media's China Coverage and Sino-U.S. Relations,*[86] and both works are the expanded and deepened versions on the author's original doctoral books.

In *American Media and China's Image (1995-2005),* He points out the social class attributes and limitations of the American media from a Marxist point of view. From a constructivist school of thought, he argues that the relationship between China and the United States after

---

[82] Neil Wu Becker, "China and United States Press from 1949-1989: Critical Events Foreign Policy Analysis" (PhD diss., San Jose State University, 1999).

[83] Xigen Li, "Effect of National Interest on Coverage of United States-China Relations: A Content Analysis of the New York Times and People's Daily, 1987-1996" (PhD diss., Michigan State University, 1999).

[84] Jonathan Goldstein, ed., Jerry Israel, ed., and Hilary Conroy, ed., *America Views China: American Images of China Then and Now* (Bethlehem: Lehigh University Press. 1991).

[85] He Ying, *American Media and China's Image (1995-2005)* (Guangzhou, China: Nanfang Daily Press, 2005).

[86] Qiao Mu, *Dragon in the Eagles' Eyes: American Media's China Coverage and Sino-US Relations* (Beijing: CPC Central Party School Press, 2006).

the Cold War is explained with the notion of Lockean Culture, with two powers in a state of competition. He sifts through cases including the 1999 U.S. bombing of the Chinese embassy in Belgrade, the China-U.S. Aircraft Collision Incident of 2001, and the "China threat theory", and analyzes the theoretical roots, internal logic and patterns behind American media's negative coverage of China after the Cold War. The author argues that the negative media coverage of China by U.S. media is both a functional issue and a structural issue, reflecting the interplay between U.S. journalists and U.S. ideology, values, public opinion of the two countries, and U.S. national interests. U.S. media's negative coverage on China follows an inherent thinking patterns, which is not much affected by the ups and downs of Sino-U.S. relations, but instead produces an important impact on Sino-U.S. relations, especially in the U.S. policy toward China.[87]

In *Dragon in the Eagles' Eyes: American Media's China Coverage and Sino-U.S. Relations,* Qiao Mu examines the changes, causes, and effects of U.S. media's coverage of China and Sino-U.S. relations between 1990 and 2001. Qiao argues the "Cold War thinking" and the re-emphasis of ideology after the Cold War are the background of the negative media coverage by the U.S. media, while the American journalistic ideas and its own attributes are the specific reasons for its negative tendency in covering China. Through analyses of the "Li Wenhe" case, the 2001 "China-U.S. Plane Collision Incident" (known in the U.S. as the Hainan Island Incident) and the Taiwan Question, the book concludes that the media's influence on Sino-U.S. relations is sometimes a "weathervane", setting the agenda before or during the implementation of policy and diplomacy. The media is also sometimes a "post-mortem" with its follow-up coverage and reactions, commenting on and leading public opinion in Sino-U.S. relations. The ups and downs of Sino-U.S. relations are certainly related to the negative influence of the U.S. media, but its roots also lie in the U.S. government's China policy and the American society's cognition of China's development.[88]

---

[87] He Ying, *American Media and China's Image (1995-2005)* (Guangzhou, China: Nanfang Daily Press, 2005), 235-237.

[88] Qiao Mu, *Dragon in the Eagles' Eyes: American Media's China Coverage and Sino-US Relations* (Beijing: CPC Central Party School Press, 2006), 224.

The impact of U.S. media coverage on U.S. policy toward China has always been a hot issue of high concern to many experts in Sino-U.S. relations. In the book *U.S. Policy to China and the Taiwan Issue*,[89] Su Ge extensively reviews the coverage of U.S. media on the Taiwan issue, and analyzes the restrictive effects of U.S. media, Congress, and interest groups on America's policy towards China. Wang Jisi, focusing on the policy-making of America's China policy, examines the policy debates in the United States caused by ideas disseminated by the U.S. media after the Cold War.[90] Jin Canrong summarizes the characteristics, political role, and diplomatic influence of U.S. news media.[91]

Fan Shiming's *Public Opinion and News Media's Impact on the Domestic Environment of U.S. Policy on China in the 1990s* and Pan Zhigao's *Analysis of the Image of China in The New York Times from 1993 to 1998* are quintessential doctoral books on American media and Sino-U.S. relations. The two works are systematic and cogent, and are often referenced in this field of research. Fan Shiming focuses on theoretical analysis, with references from works on international politics and communication. He regards the media as part of public opinion, discussing the impact of public opinion on the decision-making environment of the United States, and analyzes the relationship between public opinion and U.S. policy toward China through case studies of American media's coverage on the Taiwan issue. Pan Zhigao, on the other hand, conducts a statistical analysis of U.S. media's coverage on China during the post-cold-war period from 1993 to 1998, specifically through examining *The New York Times*, discussing China's image as presented by American media.

---

[89] Su Ge, *U.S. Policy to China and the Taiwan Issue* (Beijing: World Affairs Press, 1998).

[90] Wang Jisi, "U.S. Policy Toward China at the End of the Century—Background Analysis and Basic Judgment," in *Cross-Century Sino-American Relations*, ed. Zhao Baoxi (Shanghai: Oriental Publishing House, 1999).

[91] Jin Canrong, "Supervisors Lacking Supervision—American News Media and Their Political Role," *World Knowledge*, no. 24 (1997): 16-17.

International Crisis Communication

Research by foreign scholars

On the website of the National Library of China, the search using keywords "international crisis and communication" returned only two results that completely met the search criteria. One is *Case Studies in Crisis Communication: International Perspectives on Hits and Misses*[92] edited by Amiso M. George and Cornelius B. Pratt, selecting cases from a dual perspective of society and culture, involving politics, economy, environment, health, social management and other fields. It surmounts to a level of a textbook of international crisis communication case studies. The other is *Louder Than Words: Tacit Communication in International Crises*[93] by John Arquilla, who believes that clear and unambiguous information transmission is a necessity for peacefully resolving international crises. And the success of negotiation, containment, and other enforcement strategies cannot be achieved unless mutual trust be established by the two sides through clearly communicating each other's signals.

In addition, through the CJO Database, the search of keywords "international crisis and communication" for relevant foreign English-language journal papers found 107 eligible results.

The research of international crisis communication can be traced back to the early 20th century, as a branch of crisis communication with a special scope. Early researchers mainly focused on the communication behavior and phenomena amid diplomatic conflicts and wars. Since the onset of the Cold War, relevant research began to focus on major international cases such as the Cuban Missile Crisis. Since the beginning of the 21st Century, with global public issues like environmental pollution, climate change and energy shortages gradually becoming a hot topic in

---

[92] Amiso M. George and Cornelius B. Pratt, ed., *Case Studies in Crisis Communication: International Perspectives on Hits and Misses* (New York: Routledge, 2012).

[93] John Arquilla. *Louder Than Words: Tacit Communication in International Crises* (U.S.: Rand, 1993).

international politics, research in international crisis communication has also paid more attention to the public domain.

Judging from the above search results, there are currently few monographs on international crisis communication by foreign scholars, and the number of academic papers is also small. More research results are found in the two fields of international crisis management and crisis communication.

Regarding the definition of the concept of "international crisis", foreign scholars' views are mainly divided into three schools, defined each from the unit role level, the system/structure level and a comprehensive level.[94] Representatives works that define the crisis at the unit role level include Charles F. Hermann's *Criss in Foreign Policy: A Simulation Analysis*,[95] and *International Crises: Insights from Behavior Research*[96] and Michael Brecher's *Studies in Crisis Behavior.*[97] They argue the characteristics of crisis situations are mainly found in threats made to high priority high-value targets, high probability of military confrontations, and limited response time.

The representative scholars and works that define crises from the system/structural angle include Oran R. Young's *The Intermediaries: Third Parties in International Crises*,[98] and Glenn Herald Snyder and Paul Diesing's *Conflict Among Nations: Bargaining, Decision-Making and System Structure in International Crises.*[99] The authors think that the main characteristics of crises are manifested in the change of the interaction mode and intensity between states, reduced stability of the system, and increased possibility of violence. In addition, some scholars

---

[94] Qiu Meirong, "Review of International Crisis Research," *European Studies*, no. 6 (2003): 86.

[95] Charles F. Hermann, *Crises in Foreign Policy: A Simulation Analysis* (Indianapolis: Bobbs-Merrill, 1969).

[96] Charles F. Hermann, ed., *International Crises: Insights from Behavior Research* (New York: Free Press, 1972).

[97] Michael Brecher, *Studies in Crisis Behavior* (New Jersey: Transaction Books, 1978).

[98] Oran R. Young, *The Intermediaries: Third Parties in International Crises* (Princeton NJ: Princeton University Press, 1967).

[99] Glenn Herald Snyder and Paul Diesing, *Conflict Among Nations: Bargaining, Decision-Making and System Structure in International Crises* (New Jersey: Princeton University Press, 1977).

define crises from a comprehensive angle looking at the process and structure, arguing that a crisis is a fundamental change in the interactive process of normal relations between countries, which may affect the structural variables of the system. This camp's main flag bearers include Russell J. Leng and J. David Singer, with their *Militarized International Crises: The BCOW Typology and Its Applications.*[100]

Crisis communication is a sub branch of the research in crisis management. From the perspective of communication, crisis communication covers and uses inductive reasoning to explore the mode, function and effects of communication during the crisis process, with the help of relevant theories of communication.[101] The following are some important findings achieved: First, Steven Fink's research paradigm of "Stage Analysis Theory" divides the crisis into different stages, including the latent period, the acute onset, the spreading period, and the final resolution period. Thus, crisis communication can be effectively studied with each period's own characteristics in view. The latent period is unnoticeable, but it is also the easiest stage to deal with effectively; the acute emergency period is the stage where crisis incidents explode within a short duration, but the most destructive power, the spreading period, is long and offers the opportunity to reflect on crisis causes and make reparations. The entering of the resolution period means that the impact of the crisis has been eliminated, and relevant plans need to be formulated to prevent similar crises from recurring.[102]

Second, William L. Benoit's "Image Strategy Theory" argues that reputation or public image is a very valuable and important asset that needs to be safeguarded strategically, and that any social organization should do its best to protect its reputation and enhance its image. Based on this assessment, Bennett proposes strategies and tactics on how to restore one's image, which has wide practical implications for handling

---

[100] Russell J. Leng and J. David Singer, "Militarized International Crises: The BCOW Typology and Its Applications," *International Studies Quarterly* 29, no. 2 (1988): 155-173.

[101] Gao Xiaohong and Sui Yan, ed., *International Crisis Communication* (Beijing: Communication University of China Press, 2011), 14-16.

[102] Steven Fink, *Crisis Management: Planning for the Inevitable* (United States: iUniverse, 2000).

various crisis events.[103] Third, Thomas A. Birkland's "Focal Point Event Theory" asserts that "Focal Point Event", that is, crisis events, have great impacts, and that they play significant roles in setting the public agenda, promoting policy discussions, and influencing government decisions. They can even promote introductions of relevant laws and regulations. "Focal Point Event" cannot directly change policies, but long-term media attention and coverage of focus events can promote better behaviors.[104] This theory is derived from the agenda-setting theory in communication and provides an alternative perspective for research in crisis communication.

At present, foreign scholars' research on international crisis communication is mostly within the framework of international politics, from the perspective of national actors or on the level of organizations/structures, discussing how the actor in crisis should communicate information, set agendas, and safeguard image during the crisis process. This type of research draws on the relevant theories in communication, but still belongs to the research category of international crisis management. Research results that explore the role, influence, and functions of mass media, especially news media's coverage on crises in the crisis process are relatively fewer in numbers.

Research by domestic scholars

On the website of the National Library of China, the search of keywords "international crisis communication" on the Chinese-language literature collection catalogue returned 37 results, of which five were monographs and the rest were master's degree theses. Of the five monographs, two are studies specifically devoted to media coverage on world financial crisis and cross-border communication. Therefore there are currently only three comprehensive research works by domestic scholars on international crisis communication, namely:

---

[103] William L. Benoit, "Image Repair Discourse and Crisis Communication," *Public Relations Review* 23, no. 2 (1997): 177-186.

[104] Gao Shiyi, "A Preliminary Study of Crisis Communication Research in the United States," accessed September 24, 2020, http://cul.cssn.cn/xwcbx/xwcbx_cbx/201402/t20140211_961352.shtml.

International Crisis Communication edited by Gao Xiaohong and Sui Yan (Communication University of China Press 2011 Edition), *Global Media Report II: Public Image and Crisis Management* edited by Li Xiguang (Fudan University Press 2005 Edition), and *International News and Crisis Communication in the Age of Anti-Terrorism* by Taiwan scholars Hu Fengying and Wu Fei (Taipei Xiuwei Information Technology Co., Ltd. 2006 edition).

The keywords "international crisis communication" were used to search journals and books on the Wenjin Search on the National Library of China's website as well as on the China National Knowledge Infrastructure (CNKI). The combined search results showed that there were less than a hundred domestic scholars' papers on international crisis communication, with most works on international financial crisis and specific cases, while comprehensive studies were few.

Domestic Chinese scholars' research on international crises and crisis communication began in the 1980s. *Modern International Crisis Research* edited by Pan Guang (China Social Science Press, 1989 edition) can be regarded as the first domestic academic monograph on crises. It is a comprehensive analysis of the major crisis events that occurred in the world at the time, mainly introducing different cases. Since the 1990s, Chinese academia has begun to pay more attention to crisis research, and has translated and introduced some research of Western scholars.

Global Media Report II: Public Image and Crisis Management is a collection of papers edited by Li Xiguang. It contains more than ten articles on questions of government image building in crisis events, international communication barriers and response strategies for the Chinese media, and crisis communication case studies, etc. The book is of high significance for reference in the study of international crisis communication. Taiwanese scholars Hu Fengying and Wu Fei, in their *International News and Crisis Dissemination in the Age of Anti-Terrorism*, attempt to summarize from the chaotic international crisis events the pattern of news processes in the anti-terrorism era. In view of international news and current affairs, the authors focus on the interactions between U.S. and Russian government actions and media coverage. The authors also argue that, for China, whether the government can trust the media to handle the relationship between news worthiness and national interests well is at the core of the issue for international crisis communication.[105]

International Crisis Communication, edited by Gao Xiaohong and Sui Yan, is a highly valuable academic monograph in this field. Starting with definitions and understanding of international crisis communication, the phenomenon of international crisis communication is analyzed, and the subject in communication, the operation mode and function are discussed. In addition, the book summarizes the patterns of international crisis communication. The authors argue that in international crisis communication, the media also partially participates in diplomacy, especially in the early stages of the crisis. Amid unclear prospects and complex situations, media coverage can play a role in communication information, clarifying positions, and leading agendas. Thus, the country's diplomatic decision-making can gain understanding and support, enhancing the legitimacy of its foreign policy.[106]

Relevant papers on international crisis communication by domestic scholars are also worthy of attention. In "Review of International Crisis Research"[107] Qiu Meirong, from the perspectives of crisis, crisis management, and crisis decision-making, reviews and comments on research on military security crises in international politics by Chinese and foreign scholars. Qiu believes that China's crisis research started late and lags behind, with one of the difficulties being in obtaining materials of national core decision-making materials such as archives in diplomatic activities. Zhou Yang's "International Communication Strategies in Incidents of Military Frictions—Taking the Sino-U.S. Ship Confrontation on the South China Sea as an Example"[108] summarizes the characteristics of the war of words in public opinions in the confrontation on the South China Sea, and accordingly

---

[105] Hu Fengying and Wu Fei, *International News and Crisis Communication in the Era of Anti-Terrorism* (Taipei: Showwe Taiwan, 2006), 4.

[106] Gao Xiaohong and Sui Yan, ed., *International Crisis Communication* (Beijing: Communication University of China Press, 2011), 72-73.

[107] Qiu Meirong, "Review of International Crisis Research," *European Studies*, no. 6 (2003): 85-99.

[108] Zhou Yang, "International Communication Strategies in Incidents of Military Frictions—Taking the Sino-US Ship Confrontation on the South China Sea as an Example," *Southeast Communication*, no. 11 (2009): 12-14.

proposes recommendations on how to improve the Chinese military's international communication strategies.

Zhou Qingan's "The Dilemma of International Crisis Communication: the Fukushima Nuclear Plant Accident"[109] analyzes the difficulties and the causes of difficulties in international crisis communication following the Fukushima nuclear accident in Japan, and proposes that the biggest difference between international crisis communication and domestic crisis communication is that the former's fundamental purpose is to protect national interests and enhance national image, with its reach inevitably extending into to the global political environment. Therefore, while it is necessary to keep one's own government at the heart, it is also important to be careful in communicating information and coordinating news releases with other countries. Zhang Jingjing, in "Mass Media and International Crisis Management"[110] conducts a case study on the involvement of American media in the crises of the Vietnam War crisis and "9.11" Attacks, and argues that in today's era, mass media has become a very important actor in international crisis management. How to use the media and maximize its effectiveness has become an issue demanding policymakers' attention and consideration when dealing with crises. Papers in this area include Zhao Xusheng's "On the International Crisis and Crisis Management in the Post-Cold War Period", [111]Zhu Chongfei's "Information Game Between China and the United States Amid Two Taiwan Strait Crises,"[112] and Hou Lijie's "Improving News Media's Communication Capacity in Crisis Communication,"[113] etc.

So far, as a special form of crisis communication, international crisis

---

[109] Zhou Qingan, "The Dilemma of International Crisis Communication: the Fukushima Nuclear Plant Accident," *International Communications*, no. 5 (2011): 15.

[110] Zhang Jingjing, "Mass Media and International Crisis Management" (Master's thesis, Shanghai International Studies University, 2005).

[111] Zhao Xusheng, "On the International Crisis and Crisis Management in the Post-Cold War Period," *Modern International Relations*, no. 1 (2003): 23-28.

[112] Zhu Chongfei, "Information Game Between China and the United States Amid Two Taiwan Strait Crises" (Master's thesis, Suzhou University, 2011).

[113] Hou Lijie, "Improving News Media's Communication Capacity in Crisis Communication" (Master's thesis, Hebei University of Economics and Business, 2015).

communication is still under researched by Chinese domestic scholars, who tend to focus on case studies and *ex post* analyses, lacking a complete theoretical system and a clear research path. This is apparently not in line with the changing development of international relations and China's strategic needs to cope with international crises.

As the two major powers in the world today, China and the United States have collided on major core issues of interest since the end of the Cold War. The number of various crises they have faced has increased significantly. Cooperation in coping with and managing international crises has become an important area and way of interaction in their bilateral relations.[114] This book builds on the current research status and seeks to meet practical needs. The hope is that with solid data analysis and in-depth theoretical discussions, through studying coverage of U.S. media in the events of a bilateral crises between China and the United States, and analyzing the impact the coverage had on the directions of crisis events and on U.S. foreign policy, new findings and knowledge could be achieved in this field. This book seeks to contribute a modest addition to the theoretical construction and research scope in the fields of international news and politics, international crisis communication, and Sino-U.S. relations, and so forth.

SECTION 3. THEORETICAL BASIS AND RESEARCH METHODS

Theoretical Basis

This book falls into the interdisciplinary study of international journalism and international relations. Thus, it is necessary to draw from theoretical achievements in both fields. Drawing from journalism theory, this book utilizes Gaye Tuchman's theory of news production, and examines the samples of American media coverage from the perspective of media organization, news framing and news production process, attempting to explain the causes and impacts of this news coverage. From the vantage point of international relations, this book utilizes the

---

[114] Yang Jiemian, *Broadening of International Crises and China-US Joint Responses* (Beijing: Current Affairs Press, 2010), 7.

international political and social construction theory articulated by Alexander Windt. Assuming that ideas and behaviors make up national identity and interests, the impact and role of international news on national foreign policy-making are explored.

News production theory

The research on the "production" of news emerged in the 1970s, and Gaye Tuchman is a flag bearer in the theoretical study of news production. Tuchman's book *Making News* was published in 1978. It depicts the complete process in which media organizations and news practitioners follow specific ideologies, values, and rules in a specific social context in producing news products.

The news production theory asserts that news is not discovered, but rather a product produced by editors and reporters in accordance with institutional procedures, work norms and common practices. Whether it is the assignment of reporting tasks or the choice of news sources, the selection criteria of news facts or the judging criteria of news worthiness, they are all the result of consultations among editors at meetings of the editorial department at large. The news media disseminates and standardizes knowledge while disseminating information by reporting social facts that news professionals think the audience wants to know or should know.[115]

News is "produced" by media organizations and news practitioners based on a network of time and space that they construct. This network is the "frame" of news. The news frame comprises a set of knowledge, norms and experiential system of editors and reporters about the objective world and social reality. Therefore, every news item they report unavoidably constitutes the recognition and repeated affirmation of the existing social system, order, ideology, values and legitimacy of the social status quo.

---

[115] Gaye Tuchman and Barbara W. Tuchman, *Making News: A Study in the Construction of Reality* (United Kingdom: Free Press, 1978).

Social constructivism in international relations

In the late 1980s and early 1990s, different schools of Western international relations theories competed in a debate on paradigms. Social constructivism in international relations emerged in this background, with Alexander Wendt being the most quintessential scholar of this school.

Constructivism in international relations is a theory on the interactions of system and structure. The theory asserts that the identity and interests of a country are not formed in a vacuum, but are constructed by an international system and structure and shaped by behaviors and ideas. Windt believes that in addition to having a material structure, the international political system is also a social construction.[116] The state is the main actor and decision-maker in the international system. There is a mutually constructive relationship between the behavior of the state and the social structure of international politics: the social structure of international politics influences the behavior of the state, which then builds the state's identity and core interests; on the other hand, the behaviors, value choices, and identity of the state also affect the formation, existence, and development of social structures of the international political system.

According to the social constructivism in international relations, the interests of the country are not set in stone, but are constructed through interactions with other countries. In constant interactions, countries come to identify each other's identities and also clarify and strengthen their own. When identity and core interests are clearly identified, states take actions consistent with their identity and interests.

Wendt also believes that the international community is constantly developing and advancing, with almost no possibility of regression. The high mortality rate in the Hobbesian culture prompted people to create Lockean culture. The risks of competition and violent tendencies caused by the Lockean culture then gave birth to people's yearning for the Kantian culture. Once a certain culture is internalized, it is difficult

---

[116] Qin Yaqing, *Rights, Institutions and Culture—A Collection of International Relations Theories and Methods* (Beijing: Peking University Press, 2005), 130.

to retreat to the past.[117] Hobbesian culture belongs in the past tense. Now is the period of Lockean culture. Kantian culture will become the main feature of the future international society.

Research Methods

This book adopts a combination of quantitative and qualitative research methods, mainly including: literature analysis, historical research, content analysis and case studies.

Literature analysis

This book begins with analyzing the interactions between post-Cold War U.S. media coverage and Sino-U.S. relations. This is done by sorting through domestic and foreign research on Sino-U.S. relations in the post-Cold War era, as well as the research on the U.S. policy system towards China, the American decision-making mechanism, their development, and influencing factors. The book reviews current domestic and foreign research on the relationship between U.S. media coverage and U.S. policy toward China, draws on relevant theories and research methods, summarizes research conclusions, and discovers their deficiencies and problems, laying the foundation for future research.

Historical research method

The research in this book involves a long timeframe. We need to review the development of Sino-U.S. relations and crisis events between the two countries in the more than 20 years after the end of the Cold War. This demands a historical research approach. Through in-depth research on existing historical data, building on the description, interpretation and analysis of relevant information, historical facts are to be revealed, internal patterns of events inducted, and history's impacts on current status discussed.

---

[117] Alexander Wendt, *Social Theory of International Politics* (United States: Cambridge University Press, 1999).

Content analysis method

Content analysis is most suitable for examining the media content on the record. It is advantageous in that it does not intervene with research subjects, its research process repeatable, and that it is safe and economical.[118] In this study, content analysis is used to investigate variables of volume, genre, topics, sources, biases, etc. of relevant coverage on *The New York Times* during Sino-U.S. crisis times in the post-Cold War era. The characteristics of the variables are summarized and compared with American foreign policy at the same times, looking for relationships and patterns.

Case study method

Case studies are conducted on several crisis events that significantly influenced the relations between the two countries in the post-Cold War era, such as the Third Taiwan Strait Crisis of 1996, "China-U.S. Plane Collision Incident" in 2001, and China's 2013 move to establish an Air Defense Identification Zone at East China Sea, etc. Analysis is done on the content, biases, sources of relevant *New York Times* coverage, which are compared with relevant U.S. policy documents and comments of U.S. decision-makers on media reports. The influence of media coverage on the development of events and U.S. foreign policy decisions is discussed.

Database of This Research

When selecting research samples, considering that all China-related coverage is to some extent a reflection of Sino-U.S. relations, and likely to directly or indirectly affect the relations, *all* 16,899 articles in *The New York Times* on China from 1990 to 2015 are chosen as the database for this study. The full-text *New York Times* articles are sourced from the ProQuest database purchased by East China Normal University.

---

[118] Earl R. Babbie, *The Practice of Social Research* (United States: Cengage Learning, 2013).

The sub-database of "New York Times" was found under the "News and Newspapers" section. Full texts of China-related *New York Times* coverage since 1990 can be downloaded using a keyword search.

The search method used for this book: enter the keyword "China", and the time range between January 1, 1990 and 2015 December 31, 2015, using the advanced search under the sub-database "New York Times" of ProQuest. (See fig. 1.3)

In addition, the quantitative measurement of Sino-U.S. relations in this study is based on the "Database on China Relations with Great Powers "[119] developed by the Institute of International Relations of Tsinghua University. The database features scores of Sino-U.S. relations from 1950 to 2014. The figures reflect the quality of the relations specific to each month.

Figure 1.3 Search for "China" in the sub-database "New York Times" of ProQuest.

---

[119] "Database on China Relations with Great Powers", Institute of International Relations of Tsinghua University, accessed September 25, 2020, http://www.imir.tsinghua.edu.cn/publish/iis/7522/index.html.

CHAPTER 2

PRESENTATION OF SINO-U.S. RELATIONS BY AMERICAN MEDIA AND ANALYSIS OF CRISIS EVENTS

Mass media's international news coverage and major events in international politics are often positively related in their patterns and trends amid the changing courses of events. International affairs that the media considers important and has long been paying attention to are also news items that the audience considers important and worthy of attention. The media's coverage of international news is not only transmission of facts and information, but also a process of persuasion and guidance of the target audience. News coverage may also be part of the process of international affairs and even affect the course of international relations, through leveraging the power of public opinion.

Some Chinese domestic scholars on Sino-U.S. relations and U.S. media coverage since the end of the Cold War concluded[120] that with the changing development of relations in this era, China coverage by U.S. media has also shown periodic changes: In the early and mid-1990s, China coverage in U.S. media was mainly negative, unbalanced

---

[120] Consequential scholars and works in this area include: Qiao Mu's *Dragon in the Eagles' Eyes: American Media's China Coverage and Sino-US Relations* (Beijing: CPC Central Party School Press, 2006); Qiao covers the period between 1990 and 2001; And He Ying's *American Media and China's Image (1995-2005)* (Guangzhou, China: Nanfang Daily Press, 2005); He covers the period between 1995 and 2005.

and hostile. This caused dissatisfaction among Chinese scholars, who accused U.S. media of "demonizing" China; "After the 9/11 terrorist attacks, the war on terror became the new focus of U.S. foreign strategy, and China coverage by U.S. media also changed significantly, with more objective and positive content. Through empirical research on U.S. media's China coverage, which is compared with structural changes in Sino-U.S. relations in the post-Cold War era, scholars came to believe that U.S. media's China coverage is influenced by the relationship between the two countries, their national interests, and foreign policies.

Fundamentally, the question of what role and influence China coverage by U.S. media plays in the development of Sino-U.S. relations is a study of communication effects. In the occurrence and course of major international affairs, the processes beginning from the onset of news coverage to the formation of public opinion, and from pressure of public opinion to the introduction of foreign policy, it is difficult to obtain a complete data chain and to use scientific research methods. Thus, research in this category can only reach conclusions through comparing and contrasting, content analysis, and logical reasoning.

Based on the above analysis, as well as considerations on feasibility and scientificity of the research, this study does not attempt to analyze and explain the impact of U.S. media's China coverage on the processes of Sino-U.S. relations, but rather compares and contrasts the characteristics of media coverage with the quality and trend of Sino-U.S. relationship at a given time, looking for similarities, differences, and correlations between their respective changing patterns, especially during events that have significant impacts on the bilateral relationship such as during international crises. The purpose of this chapter is to conduct a macro analysis of U.S. media's presentation of Sino-U.S. relations since the end of the Cold War, with *The New York Times* as an example; to sort out and analyze relevant concepts and theories of international crisis and the international crisis communication; to review post-Cold War crisis events that have significant impacts on China-U.S. relations, and explain why specific cases are selected for study in this book.

SECTION 1. PRESENTATION OF U.S. MEDIA ON SINO-U.S. RELATIONS IN THE POST-COLD WAR

Statistics and Overview of China-related Coverage in The New York Times

The American newspaper *The New York Times* was founded on September 18, 1851. It received the reputation of "Gray Lady" for its serious and solemn style. Due to its thorough coverage on major international and domestic news events, as well as its publishing of important official documents, treaties, political speeches, and presidential press releases, the *Times* is regarded as a national "newspaper of record", and is generally also seen as the most authoritative paper in the United States. The U.S. executive and legislative branches, embassies of various countries, and various social groups use the *Times*' daily news coverage as a general reference point. *The New York Times* has a close relationship with the U.S. government, especially the State Department. The paper is a leader among major American papers in its comprehensive and in-depth international news coverage. With regard to this study, *The New York Times* China coverage is fairly representative among its peers, and is of crucial research value.

Number and type of reports about China

The keyword "China" was searched in the subsection of "New York Times" of the PROQUEST database purchased by East China Normal University. The results were 17,679 articles of China-related coverage on *The New York Times* from 1990 to 2015. (See fig. 2.1)

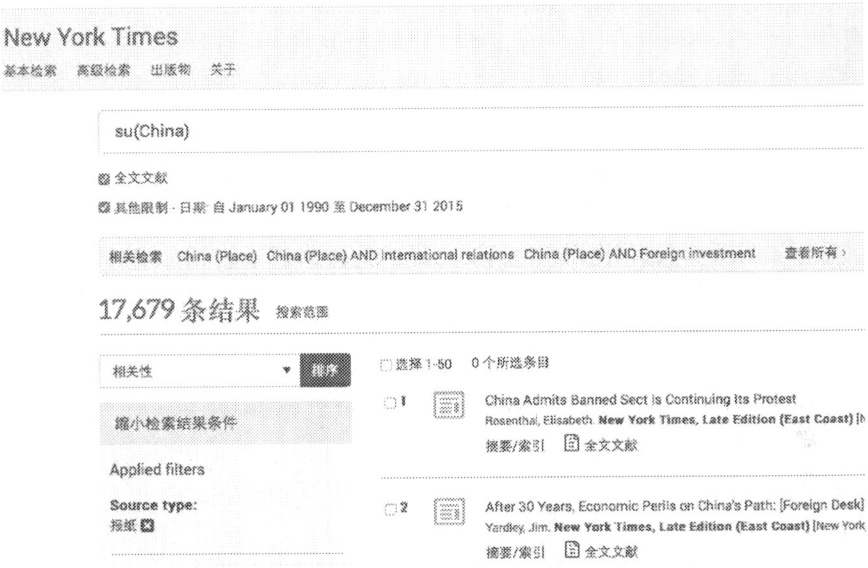

Figure 2.1 China-related coverage on *The New York Times* from 1990 to 2015

The search results page also showed distributions of "Document Type", "Subject", and the changing number of articles of coverage every year for twenty-six years. The author counted the number of articles on China from 1990 to 2015, and presents them in a table format. (see table 2.1)

Year	Number of articles	Year	Number of articles
1990	517	2003	532
1991	407	2004	536
1992	460	2005	719
1993	559	2006	599
1994	559	2007	638
1995	593	2008	920
1996	471	2009	635
1997	512	2010	766
1998	530	2011	576
1999	728	2012	922
2000	599	2013	1029

2001	606	2014	1058
2002	364	2015	1074
Total: 16899 articles			

Table 2.1 Annual number of china-related articles
in *The New York Times* from 1990 to 2015.

As seen in the table, the average number of China-related articles of coverage in *The New York Times* before 2011 was between 400 and 600. Among them, the number of articles in the four years of 1999, 2005, 2008, and 2010 is relatively large, all reaching more than 700; particularly the number in 2008 reached 920, the year when the 29th Summer Olympic Games was held in Beijing. Since 2012, China-related coverage has increased significantly. From 2013 to 2015, the number of articles each year exceeded 1,000.

In terms of the types of articles, the search results include not only news reports, commentaries, editorials, and feature articles, but also biographies, correspondence, corrections/withdrawals, obituaries, and other content. Given that this paper focuses on China-related coverage (including editorials, opinions, etc.) of *The New York Times* in the processes of Sino-U.S. relations, biographies, correspondence, corrections/retractions, obituaries and other types of articles are less relevant to this study - so they are excluded from the analysis, which resulted in a total of 16,899 valid articles. Among them, there are 13,886 articles of news, 755 editorials, 1,392 commentaries/reviews, and 866 articles/features. (see table 2.2)

Types of China-related Articles on *The New York Times*				
Type	News	Editorials	Commentaries	Articles/features
Number	13886	755	1392	866
Percentage	82.2%	4.5%	8.2%	5.1%
Total: 16899 articles				

Table 2.2 Types of China-related articles in *The New York Times*.

In American newspapers and periodicals, news reporting emphasizes objectivity and authenticity, while editorials are subjective and represent

48

the newspaper's position. It is also a tradition and a characteristic of *The New York Times* to strictly distinguish the content between news and commentaries, assigning them different sections.[121] Commentaries and column articles are from independent authors, with diverse views ranging from left to right of the political spectrum. Whereas editorials reflect the own views of *The New York Times*, written by the paper's own commentators, who critically comment on recent major events, attracting readers' attention and influencing readers' understanding of the news events.

As can be seen from table 2.2, among all types of articles related to China in *The New York Times* from 1990 to 2015, news reports accounted for the largest proportion, exceeding 80%. What follows are commentaries (8.2%), and articles/features (5.1%). The smallest number goes to editorials, accounting for only 4.5% of the total. It can be seen that in all the China-related articles on *The New York Times*, objective and neutral news reports, along with diverse commentaries and feature articles, comprise the main portion, with of articles representing the views of the newspaper having the least volume.

Distribution of topics of China-related coverage

While it is infeasible to read all the 16,899 Chinese-related articles in *The New York Times* from 1990 to 2015, search results of the "New York Times" sub-database of ProQuest are classified by their subject, drawing on the quantitative method used by today's relevant research for news coverage. Tailored to the purpose of this paper, the search results are divided into seven subjects: politics, international relations, economy, society, military, culture/sports, and science and technology. In other similar studies, "international relations" is usually regarded as a subordinate under "politics", but considering that the Sino-U.S. relations are an important reference variable in this study, "international relations" is considered as a separate subject for analysis.

In order to minimize arbitrariness in classification and to present as completely and comprehensively as possible the China-related coverage

---

[121] Liu Xiaoying, "Archives and Records: *The New York Times,*" *International Communications*, no. 4 (2009): 58-60.

of *The New York Times* since the end of the Cold War, a second level of classification is designed under the seven subjects. For example, articles in the field of "international relations" are categorized into "Sino-U.S. relations", "China's relations with other countries", "diplomatic activities", "foreign policies", "state visits", and "international sanctions". (see table 2.3)

Distribution of Topics of China-related Coverage on *The New York Times*				
Topics	Specific Content	Number	Percentage	Sum
Politics (3768 Articles)	Judicial and Criminal issues	757	4.48%	22.3%
	Political persecution and political dissenters	728	4.31%	
	Sovereignty and territorial issues	431	2.55%	
	News censorship	372	2.2%	
	Government	368	2.18%	
	State leaders	317	1.9%	
	Democracy/ Election	245	1.45%	
	Ethnic and religious issues	164	0.97%	
	Corruption issues	139	0.82%	
	Parties/ Party factions	97	0.57%	
	Reforms and reorganizations	87	0.51%	
	Others	63	0.4%	
International relations (3499 Articles)	China-U.S. relations	1564	9.25%	20.7%
	China's relations with other countries	1161	6.9%	
	Diplomatic activities	483	2.86%	
	Foreign policies	163	0.96%	
	State visits	75	0.44%	
	International sanctions	53	0.3%	

Economy (4224 Articles)	International trade	1552	9.2%	25%
	Investment and foreign investment	560	3.31%	
	Economic status and development trends	547	3.24%	
	Finance, securities, and currency	498	3%	
	Economic policy	250	1.5%	
	Smuggling	145	1%	
	Mergers and acquisitions	136	0.8%	
	Factory	118	0.7%	
	U.S. companies operating in China	109	0.65%	
	Oil industry	78	0.5%	
	Auto industry	73	0.43%	
	Most-favored-nation treatment	72	0.43%	
	Manufacturing	55	0.33%	
	Inflation	31	0.2%	
Society (2646 Articles)	Human rights issues	1124	6.65%	15.7%
	Protests, violence	655	3.9%	
	Major disaster	311	1.84%	
	Immigration, illegal immigration	160	0.95%	
	Aircraft crash and aviation safety	146	0.9%	
	Women	131	0.8%	
	Public health	119	0.7%	
Military (1409 Articles)	Defense and military power	290	1.72%	8.3%
	Nuclear weapon	249	1.47%	
	National security	235	1.39%	
	Espionage	216	1.28%	
	Arms control	132	0.78%	
	Arms sale	111	0.66%	
	Military aircraft	95	0.56%	
	Missile	81	0.48%	

Culture and sports	Olympic Games	367	2.2%	
	Athlete	240	1.4%	
	Tourism	148	0.8%	5.8%
(978 Articles)	Movie	115	0.7%	
	News media	108	0.64%	
Science and technology (375 Articles)	Internet	257	1.5%	2.2%
	Technology transfer	118	0.7%	
Total		16899	100%	100%

Table 2.3 Distribution of various topics of China-related articles in *The New York Times*.

As seen from the table, there are few articles under some specific categories, such as "inflation"(31) and "manufacturing"(55) in economy, and "international sanctions"(53) in international relations. They comprise only between 2% and 3% of the total number of the China-related articles in *The New York Times* from 1990 to 2015. Nevertheless, in this chapter, these articles are listed, counted, and analyzed in detail. On one hand, it is out of consideration for the accuracy and scientificity of the research that all content is classified as much as possible; on the other hand, this more entirely and comprehensively reflects the wide attention, and the focus and depth of that attention, of *The New York Times* as a quintessential mainstream U.S. media organization on various fields such as politics, economy, social development, culture, and technology in China since the end of the Cold War.

In order to more intuitively analyze and compare the distribution of different topics, the author uses pie charts to present the proportion and quantity of the seven subjects of politics, international relations, economy, society, military, culture/sports, as well as science and technology (see fig. 2.2). It can be clearly seen from the figure that the number of economic articles is the largest, with a total of 4224, accounting for 25% of all China-related articles. Clearly, *The New York Times* pays high attention to China's economic development. What follows is political and international relations articles – numbering 3768 and 3499 respectively, with each accounting for 22.3% and

20.7% of the total. It is worth noting that the number of articles in "international relations", as a sub-section separately from "politics" for research purposes, is similar to the sum of all other articles in "politics" combined. The number of articles in "international relations" is also larger than that of articles in "society". The strong focus of *The New York Times* on China-U.S. relations, China's status and activities in the international community is evident. The total number of articles on the three topics of "economy", "politics", and "international relations" account for 68% of all China-related articles in *The New York Times* from 1990 to 2015.

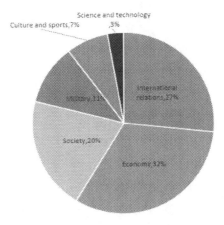

Figure 2.2 Distribution of Various Topics of China-related Coverage in *The New York Times*.

Topics in "military", "culture/sports", and "science and technology" are in relatively small numbers, each being 1,409, 978 and 375, accounting for 8.3%, 5.8% and 2.2% respectively of the total. In particular, "military" articles are fewer in number than articles in "economy", "politics", and "international relations". This reflects the changes in the international environment in the post-Cold War era and the relationship between China and the United States. The numbers of articles in the fields of "culture/sport", and "science and technology" rank the least. The number of "science and technology" articles, in particular, average less than fifteen per year in the twenty-six-year timeframe. The attention that *The New York Times* gives to China's culture, sports, and science and technology between 1990 and 2015 is low.

Among articles in "politics", most numerous are ones in judicial and criminal issues, as well as in political persecution and political dissidents. These include articles in criminal investigations, criminal trials, and political prisoners. This shows *The New York Times'* strong attention on China's political system and political order. This is followed by articles on sovereignty and territorial issues, and news censorship. It is worth noting that *The New York Times* also has a large number of articles on China's government, state leaders, as well as democratic and electoral issues, showing its concern about China's political system and democratic development. (see fig. 2.3)

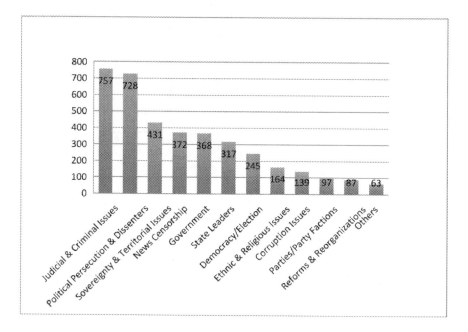

Figure 2.3 Distribution of articles in "politics" in
The New York Times from 1990 to 2015.

In the field of "international relations", *The New York Times* has the largest number of articles on the subsection "Sino-U.S. relations". Between 1990 and 2015, there are 1,564 related articles, accounting for nearly 10% of all China-related articles. This subsection contains the greatest number of articles among all subsections. Under "international relations", the second largest number of articles are on the relationship between China and other countries - as many as 1161 of them. (see fig. 2.4)

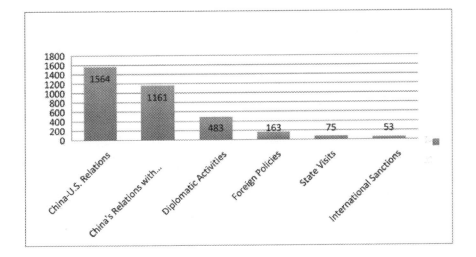

Figure 2.4 Distribution of articles in "international relations" in *The New York Times* from 1990 to 2015.

Among all the topics, articles in "economy" are the greatest in number as well as the most diverse in content. Among its subsections, the number of articles in international trade ranks first, with a total of 1552 articles, second only among its subsection peer of China-U.S. relations in the field of "international relations". International trade articles cover international trade policy, import and export, foreign exchange, etc., showing *The New York Times'* strong attention on China's performance in the development of foreign trade and its participation in global market competition. In addition, many articles were written on investment (including foreign investment), economic development status and trends, economic policies, finance, securities, currency, and so on. (see fig. 2.5)

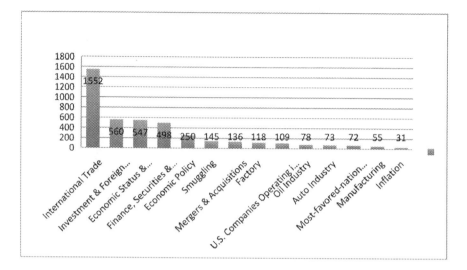

Figure 2.5 Distribution of articles in "economy" in
The New York Times from 1990 to 2015.

For articles in "society", *The New York Times* focuses mainly on negative issues. The largest number of articles are on human rights issues, with a total of 1124, accounting for 42.5% of all "society" articles. The reason may be that American media coverage of China is still affected by ideological factors even in the post-Cold War era. Secondly, there are many articles on protests, violence and major disasters, accounting for 36.5% of the total "society" articles. (see fig. 2.6)

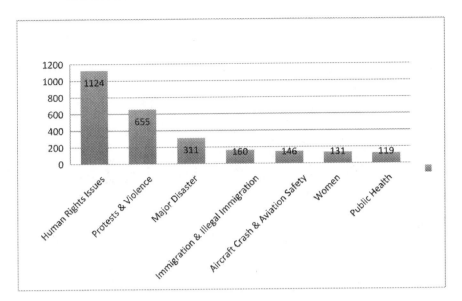

Figure 2.6 Distribution of articles in "society" in
The New York Times from 1990 to 2015.

In "military" articles, the largest volume is found in the subsection of defense and military forces. There are many articles on national security and espionage issues. Especially since the end of the Cold War, the U.S. media has repeatedly hyped up the "Chinese spy cases". The distribution chart also shows *The New York Times* is very concerned about weapons-related issues, including nuclear weapons, arms control, arms sales, military aircraft and missiles, with a combined number of articles accounting for 47.4% of the total "military" articles. (see fig. 2.7)

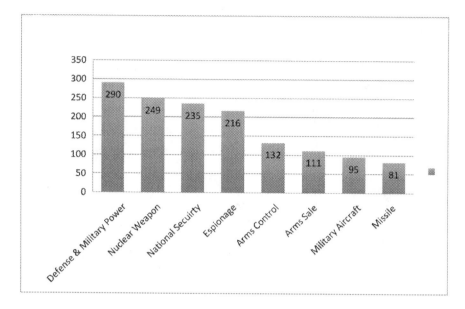

Figure 2.7 Distribution of articles in "military" in
The New York Times from 1990 to 2015.

The category of culture/sports includes the two fields: culture and sports. However, it can be seen that the number of sports articles greatly exceeds that of cultural ones. Articles on the Olympic Games - 367 of them - are the greatest in number in this category. The main reason is that the 29th Summer Olympic Games in 2008 were held in Beijing. Subsections in the culture field have more evenly scattered articles in tourism, movies and news media, with tourism having a few more articles than the other two. (see fig. 2.8)

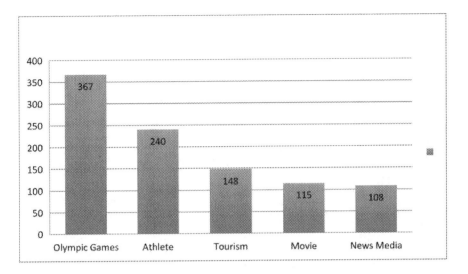

Figure 2.8 Distribution of articles in "culture/sports"
in *The New York Times* from 1990 to 2015.

There are only two subsections for the topic of "science and technology", namely internet development and technology transfer, with small numbers of articles of 257 and 118 respectively. This shows that between 1990 and 2015, compared with other topics, *The New York Times* paid less attention to the development of China's science and technology field, and that attention mainly focused on the Internet field. (see fig. 2.9)

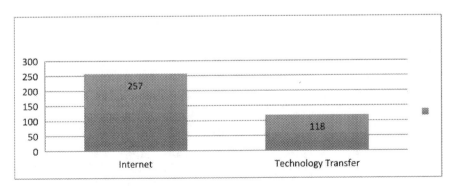

Figure 2.9 Distribution of articles in "science and technology" in *The New York Times* from 1990 to 2015.

The New York Times' coverage on China and Sino-U.S. relations

Based on the research sample obtained through keyword searches in the ProQuest database, with statistical analysis, subject classification and content analysis, we can deduce the main characteristics of all China-related articles in *The New York Times* from 1990 to 2015.

First of all, from a standpoint of the changing number of articles, before 2011, *The New York Times* had an average of 500 to 600 articles on China each year. The years of 1999, 2005, 2008, and 2010 had a particularly large number of articles compared with other years. Since 2012, the number of articles increased significantly, especially between 2013 and 2015 when the number of articles each year is more than 1,000. (see fig. 2.10)

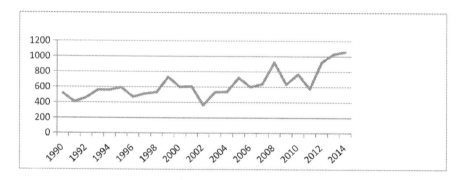

Figure 2.10 Distribution of China-related articles each year in *The New York Times* from 1990 to 2015.

Secondly, among all China-related articles, the ones on politics, international relations, economy, and society stand out in their volumes, with economy having the greatest number of articles. The number of articles in science and technology, and culture/sports is relatively small, far from the dominating topics. Furthermore, among all the topics, almost every field has subsections with a large number of articles and focused attention, such as articles on judicial and criminal issues, and political persecution and political dissidents in the field of "politics", articles on China-U.S. relations and China's relations with other countries in the field of "international relations", international trade in the "economy", and human rights issues in "society" articles.

In order to better understand the distribution characteristics of *The New York Times'* articles on China in terms of their volume and topic, and the reasons behind such distributions, it is necessary to analyze and explain changes in the international relations after the end of the Cold War, as well as the structure and characteristics of Sino-U.S. relations.

Characteristics of Sino-U.S. relations and structural changes

China-U.S. relations are the most important and complicated bilateral relations in the world. Since the establishment of diplomatic ties in 1979, Sino-U.S. relations have experienced many ups and downs, with some times of progress and others of set-backs. Since the end of the Cold War, along with the profound changes in the international landscape, and the growth and decline of power between the two countries, Sino-U.S. relations have continued to undergo new tests and challenges as they continue to move forward. The relationship presents the following characteristics:

First, cooperation and competition coexist. As the world's largest developed country and largest developing country, the United States and China have extensive common interests in the economy, trade, regional security, and many other global issues. In 2015, the bilateral trade volume reached U.S. $558.39 billion. The United States is China's second largest trading partner and largest export market, while China has surpassed Canada to become the United States' largest trading partner.[122] At the regional and global levels, the two sides have wide cooperation on issues such as counter-terrorism, nuclear non-proliferation, climate change, and financial security. However, with the continuous growth of China's overall national strength, especially its economic strength, and China's increasing influence in the international community, competition between China and the United States has

---

[122] "Year-End Roundup of Business Work in 2015, Section 16: Deepening Win-Win Cooperation: Sino-US Economic and Trade Relations," Ministry of Commerce of the People's Republic of China, accessed September 25, 2020, http://www.mofcom. gov.cn/article/ae/ai/201601/20160101245056.shtml.

become increasingly fierce. With the Obama administration's "Pivot to Asia" to strengthen its containment of China, worries and pessimism regarding the deterioration of the relations have appeared from time to time. However, the dual nature of cooperation and competition of the Sino-U.S. relations has not changed. American Sinologist David Shambaugh, once commented that the Sino-U.S. relationship cannot get too good or too bad, comparing it to an unbroken marriage in which the two giants cooperate and compete for a long time to come.[123] The author strongly concurs.

Second, Sino-U.S. relations are affected by the structure and mechanism of the international system. The anarchic and competitive structure of international politics has led to competition and mutual suspicion between the two countries; the balance of power, rise and fall of strengths, and common weaknesses of China and the United States have created a "structural interdependence" between them. As globalization continues to accelerate, there are more and more multilateral factors, as well as regional and global issues for the two countries, injecting increasing complexity into the Sino-U.S. relationship,[124] whose implications are no longer just bilateral but global.

Third, dealing with differences, and controlling competition are important challenges for China-U.S. relations. In the post-Cold War era, China and the United States have many common interests, but their differences cannot be ignored. Tao Wenzhao, an expert on China-U.S. relations, observes that there are three main types of differences between China and the United States: The first is the differences between their political systems and ideologies. This is the fundamental reason why human rights has become an important factor in the stability of Sino-U.S. relations and the constant attention U.S. media pays to political issues. The second is the disagreements over China's sovereignty and territorial integrity. These include issues such as the Taiwan question, the South China Sea disputes, separatist forces in ethnic regions, all of which concern China's core national interests and thus often cause tensions between the two countries. The third is disagreements over

---

[123] David Shambaugh, *China's Future* (Germany: Wiley, 2016)

[124] Tao Wenzhao, "How to Treat Sino-US Relations," *Contemporary World*, no. 8 (2015): 2-7.

other certain issues, including economic and trade disputes, and quarrels over responsibility sharing on issues including emission reduction and new energy. Among the aforementioned kinds of disagreements, the first type has existed for a long time. After the end of the Cold War, as China's opening-up accelerated and American society learned more about China, the harm and influence of these political and ideological differences on the relationship became increasingly limited. The problems in the third type are more specific, involve less scope, and are less difficult to deal with. Therefore, for Sino-U.S. relations, the second type of disagreement stands out as a key issue in the crisis management of the two countries.

The quality score of Sino-U.S. relations and the volume of media coverage about China

The author assumes that there is a certain degree of correlation between the changes in the number of China-related articles of *The New York Times* and the development of Sino-U.S. relations between 1990 and 2015. Thus attempts were made to observe and compare changes in the two matters. However, attaching numerical values to the bilateral relationship is a very specialized and difficult task. Fortunately, scholars at the Institute of International Relations of Tsinghua University already have given such scores in the Tsinghua University "Database on Relations between China and Great Powers". Using the method of quantitative research on international relations, specific scores are given to Sino-U.S. relations from 1950 to 2014. Different scores correspond to different statuses and levels of the relationship. (see fig. 2.11)

Spectrum of quality of bilateral relationship

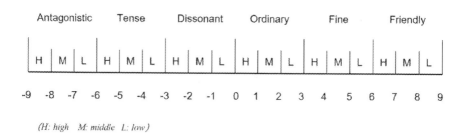

(H: high M: middle L: low)

Figure 2.11 Spectrum of quality of bilateral relationship.[125]

The user manual of the database clearly defines the terms for six different statuses for the relationship, namely: "antagonistic", "tense", "dissonant", "ordinary", "fine", and "friendly". When the relationship is "antagonistic", it means the countries are hostile to each other and publicly declare the other party as their strategic enemy; When the relationship is "tense", it means that it is still hostile, but there is no direct, large-scale military conflict; when the relationship is "dissonant", the relationship is defined as having greater animosity than amity, with more hostile policies adopted than amiable ones; an "ordinary" relationship is defined as one having more amity than animosity, with amiable policy seen in most areas; A "fine" relationship is defined as one that is amicable in nature, suggesting that the two sides are satisfied with the status quo, nevertheless there are still ostensible strategic differences on some issues; finally, a "friendly" relationship is defined as one that is friendly in nature, with the two having identical strategic positions in international politics and few differences. Researchers also tested the effectiveness of the measurement, proving it to be consistent with actual situations and able to objectively reflect historical facts. In view of its rigor and scientificity, this study directly uses the scores from the database for comparisons and analyses.

With regards to the measuring and calculations of bilateral

---

[125] "Database on China's Relations with Great Powers", Institute of International Relations of Tsinghua University, accessed September 25, 2020, http://www.imir. tsinghua.edu.cn/publish/iis/7522/index.html.

relations, the database details a strict and complex set of methods and procedures. While the author is not a professional in international relations, and Sino-U.S. relations per se is not the focus but only an important variable of this book, I will not regurgitate how the scores are calculated, but only make a brief explanation. That is, researchers use the official website of the Chinese Ministry of Foreign Affairs and the People's Daily as the main data sources for events relating to Sino-U.S. relations. They then assign scores to the events of the month according to the conflict-cooperation spectrum, and finally refine the scores in view of the general status of Sino-U.S. relations of the time prior to the event occurrence, reflecting the event's degree of impact on the relations. (see fig. 2.12)'

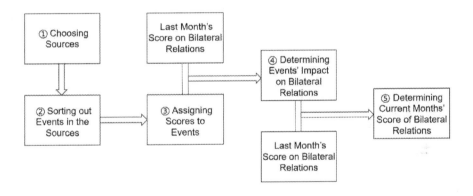

Figure 2.12 Process of quantitative measurement
of the bilateral relationship.[126]

According to this method and procedure, scores for the bilateral relationship specific to each month can be calculated. The time range of this book is from 1990 to 2015, but the database has calculated scores from 1950 to 2014. That is, as of the writing of this paper, the 2015 score has not yet been announced by the database researchers. However, to the extent of the research needs in comparing and analyzing the trend of China-U.S. relations against the distribution of *The New York Times*

---

[126] "Database on China's Relations with Great Powers", Institute of International Relations of Tsinghua University, accessed September 25, 2020, http://www.imir. tsinghua.edu.cn/publish/iis/7522/index.html.

China-related articles of the same period, the databases' China-U.S. relations scores of the twenty-five years from 1990 to 2014 are sufficient. (see table 2.4).

Month / Year	1	2	3	4	5	6	7	8	9	10	11	12
1990	-0.6	-0.8	-0.9	-0.9	-0.9	-0.9	-0.9	-0.9	-0.9	-0.9	-0.8	-0.7
1991	-0.7	-0.7	-0.7	-0.7	-0.7	-0.6	-0.6	-0.6	-0.6	-0.6	-0.6	-0.6
1992	-0.5	-0.5	-0.4	-0.4	-0.4	-0.4	-0.5	-0.5	-1.1	-1.1	-1.1	-1.0
1993	-1.0	-1.0	-1.0	-1.0	-1.0	-1.0	-1.0	-1.1	-1.2	-1.2	-1.0	-1.0
1994	-0.8	-0.8	-0.5	-0.3	-0.2	-0.2	-0.2	-0.1	-0.1	0.3	0.6	0.6
1995	0.6	0.4	0.6	0.6	0.1	-0.1	-0.2	-0.2	-0.2	-0.1	0.0	0.0
1996	0.0	0.0	-1.0	-1.0	-1.2	-1.0	-0.9	-0.9	-0.9	-0.9	-0.5	-0.3
1997	-0.3	-0.1	0.2	0.2	0.3	0.3	0.3	0.5	0.7	2.2	2.1	2.2
1998	2.2	2.2	2.3	2.3	2.5	3.1	3.1	3.2	3.3	3.2	3.2	3.1
1999	2.7	2.6	1.9	1.9	-0.3	-0.3	-0.2	-0.5	-0.3	-0.4	0.0	0.0
2000	0.2	0.1	0.1	0.1	0.1	0.2	0.2	0.2	0.3	0.3	0.4	0.4
2001	0.2	-0.2	-0.2	-0.8	-1.2	-1.2	-0.8	-0.8	-0.5	-0.4	-0.3	0.0
2002	0.0	0.2	-0.3	-0.2	-0.3	-0.1	-0.2	-0.2	-0.1	-0.1	-0.1	0.0
2003	0.2	0.5	0.5	0.6	0.4	0.3	0.5	0.5	0.5	0.8	0.8	1.3
2004	1.3	1.4	1.2	1.2	0.8	0.7	0.6	0.6	0.6	0.5	0.8	0.7
2005	0.7	0.2	0.2	0.2	0.2	0.2	0.3	0.5	0.6	0.6	0.7	0.6
2006	0.7	0.7	0.7	1.1	1.1	1.0	1.3	1.5	1.5	1.7	1.9	2.0
2007	1.9	1.9	1.8	1.8	1.8	1.6	1.3	1.4	1.4	1.2	1.2	1.4
2008	1.4	1.3	1.0	0.7	0.9	1.0	1.0	1.1	1.0	0.7	0.8	1.0
2009	1.1	1.0	0.6	0.5	0.4	0.8	1.2	1.2	1.2	1.2	1.6	1.7
2010	1.1	0.9	0.8	1.0	1.2	1.1	1.0	1.0	1.1	1.1	1.2	1.2
2011	2.0	2.0	2.2	2.0	2.0	2.1	2.1	2.1	1.8	1.8	1.9	1.9
2012	1.9	1.9	1.9	1.8	1.7	1.8	1.8	1.6	1.7	1.7	1.7	1.7
2013	1.7	1.7	1.8	2.0	2.0	2.1	2.1	2.2	2.3	2.3	2.3	2.3
2014	2.2	2.0	2.0	1.4	1.3	1.2	1.2	1.2	1.2	1.3	1.7	1.7

Table 2.4 Scores of Sino-relations from 1990 to 2014.[127]

---

[127] "Database on China's Relations with Great Powers", Institute of International Relations of Tsinghua University, accessed September 25, 2020, http://www.imir. tsinghua.edu.cn/publish/iis/7522/index.html.

Analyzing the data in the table above, we can find that the peak of Sino-U.S. relations since the end of the Cold War appeared from June to December 1998, with monthly scores exceeding 3.0. Throughout the twenty-five-year period, only this period saw scores reaching or exceeding 3.0, or the "fine" score. In view of the trajectory of Sino-U.S. relations, the main reason behind the stellar scores was the successful exchange of visits between the heads of state of China and the U.S. from 1997 to 1998. On June 25, 1998, the then U.S. President Bill Clinton paid a nine-day state visit to China. The two sides signed an economic and trade cooperation agreement worth nearly U.S. $2 billion. The two heads of state issued three joint statements and signed a joint-military-exercise agreement.[128] The visits yielded positive and constructive results, and led to significant improvement and progress in Sino-U.S. relations over a period of time thereafter.

On the other hand, also on the table are three low periods of China-U.S. relations, with scores equal to or lower than -1.0, pointing to a state of "dissonance". The first period was from September 1992 to December 1993, lasting one year and four months. It was a longest trough in our study timeframe, caused by a series of events. The events that had major impact on Sino-U.S. relations during the time mainly include the following: On September 2, 1992, then U.S. President George H. W. Bush announced the authorized sale of 150 F-16A/B fighter jets to Taiwan, provoking China's strong protest;[129] And on July 23, 1993, the United States for no reason accused China's "Yinhe" cargo ship of carrying dangerous chemicals, and interfered in the ship's normal commercial transportation activities.

The second down period was from March to June in 1996. China and the United States plunged into the "Taiwan Strait Crisis" sparked by Taiwan leader Lee Teng-hui's visit to the U.S. In March during the Taiwan's "presidential election", the People's Liberation Army conducted missile launch trainings on targeted areas in South China Sea and East

---

[128] Tao Wenzhao and He Xingqiang, *History of Sino-US Relations* (Beijing: China Social Sciences Press, 2009), 308-309.

[129] Liu Liandi and Wang Dawei, *The Track of Sino-US Relations—An Overview of Major Events Since the Establishment of Diplomatic Relations* (Beijing: Current Affairs Press, 1995), 344-345.

China Sea, as well as joint land-sea-air military exercises in the Taiwan Strait to show its determination for reunification.[130]

The third down period was from May to June in 2001, with a cause of the tension direct and clear: the "April 1st China-U.S. Plane Collision Incident over the South China Sea", also known as the "Hainan Island Incident". The two countries engaged in a political tug of war and delved into an impasse over whose fault it was, leading to a diplomatic crisis.

In order to more clearly and intuitively compare the changes in the scores of Sino-U.S. relations against the distribution of China-related articles in *The New York Times* between 1990 and 2014, the author draws two curves corresponding to the two sets of data, set in the same graph. The vertical axis on the left is the number of China-related articles of *The New York Times*, and the vertical axis on the right is the scores for the quality of China-U.S. relations. The horizontal values, which denote the time horizon, are shared by both curves. (see fig. 2.13)

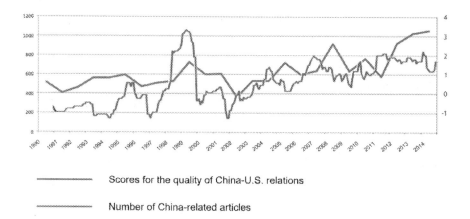

———————— Scores for the quality of China-U.S. relations

———————— Number of China-related articles

Figure 2.13 Scores of Sino-U.S. relations and numbers of China-related articles in *The New York Times* between 1990 and 2014.

Through observing the values and trends shown in the graph, we can find some certain correlations between the two curves:

First, overall the number of China-related articles in *The New*

---

[130] Tao Wenzhao and He Xingqiang, *History of Sino-US Relations* (Beijing: China Social Sciences Press, 2009), 296-297

York Times and the score of Sino-U.S. relations both reflect a rising trend. Moreover, since 2001, the two curves become significantly more correlated, moving nearly in tandem.

Second, prior to 2001, the China-U.S. relationship scores fluctuated sharply, and the relationship peaks appeared basically at the same time as the peak numbers of China-related articles of *The New York Times*, only differing in height.

Third, since 2012, the curve of Sino-U.S. relations remains relatively stable. In contrast, the number of articles on China in *The New York Times* has increased significantly.

Fourth, when the score of China-U.S. relations is low and the countries in a state of "dissonance", the number of China-related articles in *The New York Times* increases significantly. The two curves have a negative correlation.

Fifth, since 2001, the two curves showed a rhythmically correlative phenomenon. If the score of Sino-U.S. relations falls in that year, the number of articles on China in *The New York Times* would decrease the year after; conversely, if the former rises in a given year, the latter increases the following year.

What needs to be clear is that the correlation between the two curves is only a surface phenomenon. It cannot represent a causal relationship between the two, nor can it explain the mutual influence between the two. Nonetheless, in view of both the post-Cold-War-era U.S. policy on China and changes in Sino-U.S. relations, the patterns presented in the graph can still be explained and analyzed. In 2001, after the September 11 terrorist attacks, President George W. Bush declared that the United States had entered a state of war, listing counter-terrorism as the top priority. And China was no longer regarded as the main threat to the U.S. Since then, the common interests between China and the United States have expanded. The two actively cooperated in counter-terrorism and nuclear issues on the Korean Peninsula. The relationship between the two countries began to develop in a more stable direction.[131] Against such a backdrop of a major shift in U.S. strategy toward China, the score of Sino-U.S. relations and the number of articles on China in *The New*

---

[131] Tao Wenzhao, *American Policy on China after the Cold War* (Chongqing: Chongqing Publishing Group, 2006), 38-43.

York Times both started to show an overall significantly more upward trend, after a low in 2001.

In 2012, Barack Obama was successfully re-elected as U.S. president. The same year then Chinese Vice President Xi Jinping visited the United States and in November of the same year, was elected General Secretary of the Communist Party of China. The heads of state of the two countries have established good working relations and friendship through many meetings and exchanges. They have reached a consensus on jointly promoting a cooperative partnership, setting a positive and stable tone for the development of bilateral relations.[132] As China surpassed Japan as the world's second-largest economy, the development gap between China and the United States has rapidly narrowed, and the power balance between the two countries has changed. China's position in the American global strategy has become increasingly important. Since 2012, the number of China-related articles in *The New York Times* began to increase significantly, indicating its rising attention on China as a quintessential mainstream U.S. news organization.

In addition, it is noticeable that when the score of Sino-U.S. relations hits valleys, the number of *The New York Times* articles on China increases. This indicates that *The New York Times* pays more attention to crisis events such as disagreements and conflicts causing "dissonance" in Sino-U.S. relations. This is mainly due to the American journalism ethos that stresses the newsworthiness of bad news.

SECTION 2. INTERNATIONAL CRISIS THEORY AND REVIEW OF SINO-U.S. CRISIS EVENTS

Overview of International Crisis and
Crisis Communication Theories

Since the research object of this book is media coverage of crisis events in Sino-U.S. relations, it is necessary to first explain and distinguish the

---

[132] Jin Canrong and Liu Shiqiang, "Sino-US Relations since Obama Took Office," *American Studies*, no. 4 (2009): 39-50.

different major concepts of crisis, crisis events, international crisis, and international crisis communication, clarifying their connotations, key components, characteristics, and classifications.

Crises and crisis events

The word "crisis" is derived from the medical term "krinein" in ancient Greek, which means "a turning point in life and death". It is a critical moment for the patient's condition and determines whether the patient will start to recover, or deteriorate and face the risk of death.[133] In Chinese, "crisis" literally contains two meanings: "danger" and "opportunity". The definition of "crisis" in the Chinese dictionary *Ci Yuan* is: "a lurking woe."[134]

Modern crisis research began with the Cuban Missile Crisis in 1962. Early research focused on major events such as military conflicts and natural disasters, most of them being case studies. At this stage, Charles F. Hermann defined the crisis as a situation when decision makers are caught off guard, their fundamental goals are threatened, and the time to respond is very limited.[135] In the 1980s, research on crisis began to turn to the field of public relations, with the purpose of guiding governments and enterprises in managing and controlling crises. Laurence Barton argues that a crisis is a major event with potential negative impact and uncertainty, and that its repercussions may cause huge damage to organizations, members, assets, products, services and reputation.[136] Uriel Rosenthal defines a crisis as a serious threat to the basic values and code of conduct of a social system, and an event

---

[133] Phil Williams, Donald M. Goldstein, and Jay M. Shafritz, *Classic Readings of International Relations* (United Kingdom: Wadsworth Publishing Company, 1994)
[134] Commercial Press, *Ci Yuan Volume 1* (Beijing: Commercial Press, 1979), 434.
[135] Charles F. Hermann, ed., *International Crises: Insights from Behavior Research* (New York: Free Press, 1972).
[136] Robert Lawrence Heath, *Crisis Management for Managers and Executives: Business Crises, the Definitive Handbook to Reduction, Readiness, Response, and Recovery* (United Kingdom: Financial Times Management, 1998)

that demands key decision-making in a time-pressing and extremely uncertain situation.[137]

Thus, definitions of "crisis" given by scholars can be roughly divided into two categories, namely: "event theory", which considers a crisis to be a special event; and "state theory", which considers crisis to be a special state. In the author's opinion, a crisis is a sudden, uncertain and dangerous state change that demands quick response by decision makers. A crisis is fundamentally a "state". Thus, it is necessary to distinguish and analyze the different concepts of "crisis" and "crisis event".

Crisis events refer to all kinds of emergencies that occur urgently and unexpectedly. *Crisis events* pose potential threats or cause significant damage to society, organizations, etc. From a social and historical point of view, *crises* should be defined as a state and a process, an unspoken norm that accompanies the social, or organizational development process. *Crisis events*, however, are high-profile stages in the process of a crisis. They are the face of a crisis. Even if no *crisis event* occurs, a *crisis* may exist for a long time.

Therefore, a *crisis event* does not mean a *crisis*, but a special stage in a crisis process. In practical experience, many crises only clearly manifest themselves in the ongoing course of events.[138] According to American scholar Steven Fink, there are four stages in a crisis: the prodromal crisis stage, the acute crisis stage, the chronic crisis stage, and the crisis resolution stage.[139] Thus, the outbreak of a crisis event is the acute stage of crisis.

In the specific situation of the bilateral relationship between China and the United States, due to the long-standing differences in political system and ideology, competition in the economic realm, and divergence in core interests such as those in territory and sovereignty, crisis is a norm that has always accompanied the development of the relations. As

---

[137] Uriel Rosenthal and Michael T. Charles, *Coping with Crisis: The Management of Disaster, Riots and Terrorism* (Springfield: Charles C. Thomas, 1989).

[138] Gao Xiaohong and Sui Yan, ed., *International Crisis Communication* (Beijing: Communication University of China Press, 2011), 9-10

[139] Steven Fink, *Crisis Management: Planning for the Inevitable* (United States: iUniverse, 2000).

a result, friction and conflicts occur often between the two countries. Even if there are no *crisis events*, the *crisis* always lurks in the deep structure of the relationship: it is only a question of awareness and its proper management and control.

International crisis and international crisis communication

The first person to introduce the word "crisis" into the field of international politics is Thucydides of ancient Greece. He used the word "crisis" six times in his *History of the Peloponnesian War* to describe the critical turning points in nations' relations.[140] In the field of international relations, a crisis means a turning point for war or peace. The traditional and narrowly-defined meaning of *international crisis* refers to the crises in the relations between countries, especially those in political and military nature. Scholars mainly define *international crisis* from two different levels: national and international.

An international crisis from the national level can be approached from looking at the decision-making process in dealing with foreign policy crises. Scholars define crises at this level as a threatening tension that policymakers perceive. It is argued that only when policymakers become aware of it can a crisis be proved to exist.[141] Michael Brecher, for example, argues that international crises are three situations faced by a country's top policymakers, namely: threats to the fundamental values of a country's political system, the high probability of a breakout of hostile military operations, and external threats that only allow a short reaction time for decision-making.[142] Chinese scholar Hu Ping argues that an international crisis is a short-term political decision-making process when conflicts of interests among nations reach a certain stage.[143]

---

[140] Ding Bangquan, *International Crisis Management* (Beijing: National Defense University Press, 2004), 10.

[141] Xu Hui, *International Crisis Management: Theory and Case Analyses* (Beijing: National Defense University Press, 2011), 4.

[142] Michael Brecher, "State Behavior in International Crisis," *Journal of Conflict Resolution* 23, no. 3 (September 1979): 447.

[143] Hu Ping, *International Conflict Analysis and Crisis Management Research* (Beijing: Military Yiwen Press, 1993), 153.

The definition of an international crisis on the level of an international system is from the perspective of interactions between states, focusing on the changes or damages the crisis causes to the international system. For example, Glenn H. Snyder and Paul Diesing define an international crisis as a series of interaction processes between two or more sovereign states' governments during serious conflicts. Although no war has erupted in this process, the danger can be felt of a highly-likely war.[144] In addition, some domestic scholars define the international crisis as one in which two or more states are the main actors, in predominantly diplomatic and military realms.[145]

Chinese scholar Yang Jiemian believes that confining international crises to political and military fields no longer reflects the actual situation and research needs of the current international community. Therefore, Yang combines the two perspectives and defines the international crisis from a comprehensive view. He argues that an international crisis is "a series of diplomatic, political, security, economic, social, and health events that suddenly occur in international relations, cause serious conflicts of interests between actors, and if not resolved in time, may lead to various serious consequences, including war."[146]

In view of the different research perspectives on international crises and the practical needs of this research, the author leans towards the definition from the level of an international system. That is, to define an international crisis as a turning point in the relationships between states, for war or for peace. At this turning point, if the crisis-causing conflicts are not resolved in time, the crisis may escalate and even lead to war. The development of an international crisis is generally divided into four stages, namely: outbreak, escalation, easing, and end.

---

[144] Glenn Herald Snyder and Paul Diesing, *Conflict Among Nations: Bargaining, Decision-Making and System Structure in International Crises* (New Jersey: Princeton University Press, 1977), 455.

[145] China Institute of Contemporary International Relations, *Introduction to International Crisis Management* (Beijing: Current Affairs Press, 2003), 9.

[146] Yang Jiemian, *Broadening of International Crises and China-US Joint Responses* (Beijing: Current Affairs Press, 2010), 32.

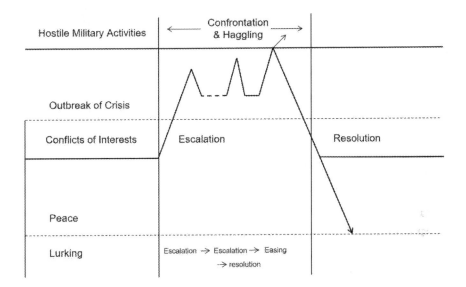

Figure 2.14 Different stages of international crisis process.[147]

For Sino-U.S. relations, a crisis means a situation where conflicts between the two countries in national interests have risen to such an extent that it poses a serious threat to the nature of the relationship, and may even cause hostile military actions. The main features of such crises are: first, at least one of the countries believes that their major interests, core values, and even survival are seriously threatened; second, the behavior or reaction of the two parties have caused conflicts to constantly escalate, forcing policymakers to react within a limited amount of time; third, different decisions will produce different results, but the possibility of military operations or even war is increased, and it is much greater than the possibility for peace; finally, the crisis between the two countries may not only cause the relationship to break down, but may cause a shocking wave to the international community, threatening the balance and stability of the international system.[148]

International crises are rooted in chronic differences and conflicts of

---

[147] Xu Hui, *International Crisis Management: Theory and Case Analyses* (Beijing: National Defense University Press, 2011), 10.

[148] Xu Hui, *International Crisis Management: Theory and Case Analyses* (Beijing: National Defense University Press, 2011), 6-8.

national interests, usually with an incubation period and can be traced and identified. When one party in the conflict tries to force the other to give in, or change the status quo in a way beneficial to its own and therefore causes the other party to feel a sense of crisis, who then reacts antagonistically, an international crisis may break out. Events or actions that may trigger an international crisis are as listed in table 2.5 below.

Action categories	Action examples
War of words	Verbal threats such as protests, threats, accusations, demands, etc.
Political actions	Subversion, diplomatic sanctions, severance of diplomatic relations, violation of treaties or agreements, etc.
Economic actions	Trade embargo, economic sanctions, nationalization of property, termination of economic assistance, etc.
Changes in the external environment	Changes in certain special weapon systems and offensive capabilities, changes in global or regional systems, changes in the legitimacy of international organizations, etc.
Domestic political changes	Incitement by media, new government assuming power, government downfall, coups, conspiring to sabotage, terrorism, assassination, unrest, demonstrations, strikes, arrests of sensitive persons, executions of sensitive persons, execution of martial law or military control, rebellion or mutiny, resistance or uprising, etc.
Non-violent military operations	Show of power, war drills, military mobilization, troop mobilization, military entering into offensive posture
Indirect violent actions	Insurgency in another country, violence against an allied or friendly country or affiliate
Violent actions	Border conflicts, limited military force crossing borders, invading sovereign airspace, sinking warships, sea and air emergencies, major targets being bombed, large-scale military offensives, wars

Table 2.5 Events or actions that may trigger an international crisis.[149]

Among the triggering factors of the crisis, media incitement is one domestic political change that causes crises. Thus, media can be both the main information disseminator during the international crisis as well as the triggering factor of crisis. The process in which media, through its coverage on international crisis, influences the interplay between the process and actors of the crisis, is international crisis communication. Because of their great newsworthiness, international crises often attract

---

[149] Xu Hui, *International Crisis Management: Theory and Case Analyses* (Beijing: National Defense University Press, 2011), 10.

extensive attention and coverage from global media. Thus, international crisis communication occurs.

After the Cuban Missile Crisis, the study of crisis communication has for a long time focused on international crisis events, with a major aim to provide a theoretical basis for Cold War policy. Since the end of the Cold War, with the acceleration of globalization and the development of communication technologies, the boundaries between domestic, regional and international crises have become increasingly blurred. A crisis event that occurs in one country may have its communication scope and influence extending to all corners of the world. Nowadays, since almost any crisis may develop into an international crisis, all research on crisis communication can be regarded as research on *international* crisis communication.[150]

Compared with crisis communication in the general sense, international crisis communication has the following characteristics: national governments and media organizations are the main communicators; main communication channels are transnational and global; the international community and international audiences are the communication target; and safeguarding national interests is the primary purpose. In the process of international crisis communication, the roles the media plays include information transmission and feedback, crisis agenda-setting and construction, early warning of a crisis event, as well as social mobilization and integration. To some extent, the media also assumes diplomatic functions such as interpreting government positions and policies.

The occurrence of international crisis itself alludes to the problem of information transmission and interpretation. The lack of effective information communication between states leads to the lack of mutual trust, which is one of the indirect sources of international crises.[151] The management and resolution of international crises cannot succeed without accurate, timely, sufficient and effective information communication. Therefore, the research and practice of international

---

[150] Gao Xiaohong and Sui Yan, ed., *International Crisis Communication* (Beijing: Communication University of China Press, 2011), 17.

[151] Zheng Wei, *International Crisis Management and Information Communication* (Beijing: Central Compilation & Translation Press, 2009), 23-28.

crisis communication is of great significance for safeguarding national interests, as well as striving for the power of shaping discourse and a proactive role in international crises.

Crisis in Sino-U.S. Relations

Examining U.S. media's China coverage in the framework of Sino-U.S. relations has recently become a hot topic for scholars in international relations and international journalism. The main purpose of its research is to find out the relationship between news media coverage and governments' foreign policy decisions. This is an ambitious research task, involving not only a large number of materials and texts, but also interdisciplinary application and innovation of research methods. The procedures, process, and timespan of such a query is far beyond the scope of a doctoral book. Therefore, the author narrows down the study to crisis events in Sino-U.S. relations. This is on one hand out of concern for feasibility and operability. On the other hand, it is because of the importance and specialty of crisis events in international relations.

Glen Snyder argues that crisis is microscopic international politics, and that core issues in international politics can be epitomized in international crisis.[152] These issues include not only a series of issues such as conflicts, negotiations, use of force and threats of use of force, and deterrence between countries, but also institutional and ideational differences such as power structure, core interests, values, and foreign policy decisions. Crises between China and the United States are often caused by some unexpected events, and mirror the core interests, fundamental disagreements, and outstanding issues of the two countries. Crisis events may lead to large fluctuations or even serious retrogression in relations, and have a profound impact on the direction of the Sino-U.S. relations and the international environment required for China's peaceful development. For this reason, crisis in Sino-U.S.

---

[152] Glenn Herald Snyder and Paul Diesing, *Conflict Among Nations: Bargaining, Decision-Making and System Structure in International Crises* (New Jersey: Princeton University Press, 1977), 4.

relations is in its own right a type of international crisis that China needs to focus on preventing.[153]

Since the end of the Cold War, cooperation and interdependence between China and the United States have continued to strengthen, but at the same time, the two countries have continued to see crises in the fields of human rights, security, international trade, energy and environment, etc. And the frequency of crisis events has accelerated significantly: on average once every 2-3 years.[154] The scope of these events have also broadened, for instance, from traditional security realms such as military and diplomacy to non-conventional security realms such as finance, environmental protection, climate, and public health. They intertwine with domestic crises, and mutually transform each other.[155]

Depending on whether the subjects of the crisis involves a third party or multiple parties, crises in Sino-U.S. relations are divided into bilateral crises and multilateral crises, albeit in bilateral crises there could be influence of other countries. Depending on their nature, crisis events in Sino-U.S. relations can be divided into four types: first, political and diplomatic events, such as the Taiwan Strait Crisis triggered by Taiwan leader Lee Teng-hui's visit to the United States in 1995; second, military events, such as crises caused by 1999 U.S. bombing of the Chinese embassy in Belgrade, and the 2001 China-U.S. Aircraft Collision Incident; third, economic events, such as the crisis sparked by then U.S. President Bill Clinton's linking the Most Favored Nation status to China's human rights situation during his first term in office; and fourth, crises caused by differences in cultural values and ideas, such as the long-standing human rights crisis between China and

[153] Yang Jiemian, *Broadening of International Crises and China-US Joint Responses* (Beijing: Current Affairs Press, 2010), 45.

[154] Department of Political Science at the University of Kansas, "Kansas Events Data System/Protocol for the Assessment of Nonviolent Direct Action (KEDS/PANDA) database," in *China and the World: Chinese Foreign Policy Faces the New Millennium*, ed. Samuel S. Kim (Boulder: Westview Press, 1998), 62.

[155] Yang Jiemian, *Broadening of International Crises and China-US Joint Responses* (Beijing: Current Affairs Press, 2010), 34-42.

the United States.[156] Traditional or narrowly defined international crisis events mainly refer to the first two types, namely political, diplomatic, and military events; while broadly-defined international crises include economic events and conflicts caused by differences in culture, values and ideas, involving more broad actors and contents, with globalized and diverse characteristics.

The crises in Sino-U.S. relations in this study fall into those under the traditional definition. That is, political, diplomatic, and military crises. Crisis events of this kind often involve differences in national sovereignty and territorial integrity, and are most likely to trigger tensions in relations. In addition, the subjects in the crisis do not involve third parties, but only bilateral. On this basis, the author has selected three crises in Sino-U.S. relations as the research cases of this book: the Taiwan Strait Crisis (1995-1996), the 2001 China-U.S. Aircraft Collision Incident, and the 2013 Sino-U.S. Maritime Rights and Interests Disputes (including China's establishment of the Air Defense Identification Zone on the East China Sea, and the stand-off between Chinese and U.S. warships on South China Sea).

The selection of these three cases is mainly due to the following considerations: First, the three are all conflicts involving China's sovereign independence and territorial integrity, which are related to China's core national interests; If the situations escalate, they tend to have a serious negative impact on Sino-U.S. relations; they are quintessential crises between the two countries since the end of the Cold War; Secondly, the U.S. media has paid much attention to these events, with much relevant coverage and participation in different degrees, fairly reprehensive of the role and function media coverage plays during international crisis events, which is the focus of this study; In addition, the three crisis events respectively occurred during the terms of three U.S. Presidents: Bill Clinton, George W. Bush, and Barack Obama, each with different backdrops of the time with regards to political environment, foreign policy, and the international situation. This is conducive for comparative studies to explore the interactive

---

[156] Qiu Meirong, "Crisis Management and Sino-US Relations," *Modern International Relations*, no. 3 (2005): 1-7.

relationship between the media's international news coverage and international crisis events.

In the following three chapters, the author will study in depth the relevant coverage in *The New York Times* on the three crises: the Taiwan Strait Crisis (1995-1996), the 2001 China-U.S. Aircraft Collision Incident, and the 2013 Sino-U.S. Maritime Rights and Interests Disputes (including China's establishment of the Air Defense Identification Zone on the East China Sea, and the stand-off between Chinese and U.S. warships on South China Sea). The study includes content layout, type of coverage, news frame, news sources, as well as reporting tendencies. Also discussed are the role of media coverage in crisis events and its impact on crisis events' processes.

CHAPTER 3

ANALYSIS OF *THE NEW YORK TIMES'* COVERAGE ON THE TAIWAN STRAIT CRISIS (1995-1996)

SECTION 1. OVERVIEW OF TAIWAN STRAIT CRISIS EVENTS (1995-1996)

Crisis Background

Since the end of the Cold War, the international landscape has undergone tremendous changes, and the strategic foundation of Sino-U.S. relations has been weakened with the disappearance of the Soviet threat. The negative impact of the Tiananmen political incident still exists in the United States, and Sino-U.S. relations remain in the recovery phase. There are serious differences between China and the United States on many issues such as human rights, trade, non-proliferation of nuclear weapons, ethnic group and religious issues, as well as intellectual property rights. In 1993, there was a series of events such as the Yinhe Incident, Washington's linking China's most-favored-nation treatment with human rights situations, and the resolution of the U.S. Congress to oppose Beijing's bid to host the 2008 Summer Olympics, events that severely weakened mutual trust. The U.S. policy toward China was in a vague and vacillating state, wandering back and forth under the influence of various factors such as geopolitics, economic interests, ideology, and values.

During the same period, relations between Beijing, Washington and Taipei were convoluted. In 1988, upon assuming office, Lee Teng-hui consistently tried to make breakthroughs in its external relations, especially with the United States. With a strong material foundation brought by economic progress, Taiwan authorities began to strengthen its lobbying activities in the United States. In April 1992, Lee Teng-hui planned and established the Taiwan Research Institute. In June of the same year, the Institute signed a three-year contract, worth 4.5 million U.S. dollars, with Cassidy, a government relations company in Washington. The company provided services for Taiwan-U.S. relations and guaranteed Lee Teng-hui a visit to the United States.[157] In 1994, owing to Taiwanese public relations activities, Lee Teng-hui's alma mater Cornell University invited Lee for a visit, which did not come through.

Thus, some pro-Taiwan political forces in the United States began to attack the Clinton administration on this incident, arguing that there was no need for Washington to continue conceding to China on Taiwan issues, and that the Clinton administration kowtowed to Beijing on U.S.-Taiwan relations and Lee's U.S. visit. On September 27, 1994, Washington announced the first adjustment of its Taiwan policy after the establishment of diplomatic relations with Beijing. The new change put dramatically more weight on arms sales to Taiwan and Taiwan-U.S. relations.[158] This policy shift indirectly encouraged Lee Teng-hui to make greater efforts to visit the U.S., inviting strong protest from Beijing.

On April 27, 1993, Wang Daohan, then President of the Association for Relations Across the Taiwan Straits, and Koo Chen-Fu, chairman of Taiwan's Straits Exchange Foundation, carried the "Wang-Koo Talks" in Singapore, making important contributions to the development of cross-strait relations. On January 31, 1995, then Chinese President Jiang Zemin issued a key speech entitled "Continue to Strive to Promote the Reunification of the Motherland." He put forward eight propositions for handling cross-strait relations and promoting reconciliation with

---

[157] Tao Wenzhao, *American Policy on China after the Cold War* (Chongqing: Chongqing Publishing Group, 2006), 83.

[158] Yang Jiemian, *Sino-US Relations in the Post-Cold War Period: Theory and Practice of Crisis Management* (Shanghai: Shanghai People's Publishing House, 2004), 134.

Taiwan. This was a major policy announcement by China on resolving the Taiwan issue. At the same time, the second "Wang-Koo Talks" were also under active preparations. However, just as cross-strait relations improved slightly, the Taiwan Strait Crisis occurred.

Event Review

The catalyst of the 1995-1996 Taiwan Strait Crisis came when Washington allowed Lee Teng-hui to visit the United States. In early 1995, Lee once again made a request to visit the U.S. and participate in the Cornell University alumni gathering as an alumnus of the university. Considering the nature of the unofficial relationship between Washington and Taipei and the serious consequences that might ensue, the U.S. State Department refused to issue a visa to Lee. The Taiwan authorities were not satisfied. Taipei worked through the Cassidy company to churn out various lobbying activities with the U.S. Congress.

In early March, the U.S. Senate and House of Representatives simultaneously proposed two resolutions of congressional intent with the same content, claiming that in view of Taiwan's achievements in economic development and political democratization, the U.S. President should agree to issue a visa to Lee, and welcome his visit in Lee's private capacity to the United States. On May 2, the House of Representatives passed a resolution approving Lee's visit by a vote of 396 to 0; on May 9, the Senate passed the same resolution by a vote of 97 to 1. Some pro-Taiwan lawmakers also pressured the President, claiming that if the executive branch ignored these two resolutions, they would resort to legislative means.

President Bill Clinton viewed the matter from the perspective of American cultural values rather than Sino-U.S. relations. He believed that Lee Teng-hui had the right to visit his alma mater on a private, non-political basis, and thus was inclined to issue him a visa. Meanwhile, some pro-Taiwan lawmakers were also actively lobbying Clinton. Under such circumstances, on May 17, Assistant to the President for National Security Affairs Anthony Lake, Secretary of State Warren Christopher, and Secretary of Defense William Perry decided at a breakfast meeting that the National Security Council draft a Memorandum of Action for Clinton, with two options either to allow or disallow Lee's visit. The next day, the White House Press Secretary revealed to the media that the matter of visa issuance was under consideration.[159] On the afternoon of May 19, the Memorandum of Action was submitted to Clinton and was quickly approved.

On May 22, National Security Advisor Anthony Lake and Under Secretary of State Peter Tarnoff informed Chinese Ambassador Li Daoyu that Washington had approved Lee's visit, emphasizing that the visit was private in nature and did not mean that U.S. foreign policy had changed, nor would it affect Sino-U.S. relations. Li Daoyu strongly protested on the spot. On May 23, the Chinese Ministry of Foreign Affairs issued a statement strongly protesting to the U.S. government. On May 24, the Foreign Affairs Committee of the Standing Committee of the Chinese People's Congress and the Foreign Affairs Committee of the Chinese People's Political Consultative Conference issued separate statements strongly protesting against the visit. On June 16, Chinese Ambassador to the U.S. Li Daoyu formally notified the U.S. government that he was summoned to go back to China to report on his duties due to the negative consequences caused by Washington's allowing Lee's visit.[160] In the summer of 1995, the capitals of China and the United States had no ambassadors from the other country for three months. This was an unprecedented situation since the time the two countries officially established diplomatic relations.

In order to deter the Taiwanese independence forces, in July and August 1995, the Chinese People's Liberation Army (PLA) conducted two missile exercises in the East China Sea north of the Taiwan Island. On January 31, 1996, the U.S. Congress issued a resolution requesting the President to condemn the "military intimidation" of Taiwan by the Chinese mainland, and asking the Clinton administration to report to Congress on these two exercises and how to defend Taiwan from missile attacks from mainland China, on the basis of the "Taiwan Relations Act". Clinton wrote to Congress stating that China's military action

---

[159] Robert L. Suettinger, *Beyond Tiananmen: The Politics of US-China Relations 1989-2000* (Washington, D.C: Brookings Institution Press, 2004).

[160] Qian Qichen, *Ten Notes on Diplomacy* (Beijing: World Affairs Press, 2003), 308.

was only to send political signals to Taiwan and the United States, and that it did not mean that the Chinese government wwould immediately take military actions against Taiwan, thus there was no need to report to Congress.[161]

In March 1996, Taiwan was on track to hold a direct election for its leader, the first time in history. In order to show the world the determination and strength to defend the territorial integrity of the motherland, China held several military exercises. On March 5, Xinhua News Agency was authorized to announce that the PLA would conduct missile launch trainings in the designated waters of the East China Sea and the South China Sea from March 8 to 15. From March 12th to 20th, the PLA conducted an air-and-sea live ammunition exercise along the coast of Fujian; from March 18th to 25th, it conducted a joint land-sea-air exercise in the Taiwan Strait.[162]

The United States believed that China's missile exercises were a challenge to Washington. When the U.S. tried to prevent the drills in vain, the Clinton administration dispatched two aircraft carrier battle groups, one centered on U.S.S *Nimitz*, another centered on U.S.S *Independence*, near the Taiwan Strait during the exercises of the PLA, to express concern about the cross-Strait situation and the American military resolve to defend Taiwan. The U.S. Congress also reacted strongly: On March 19, the House passed Resolution 148 by 369 to 14, criticizing the Clinton administration's ambiguous attitude towards the situation in the Taiwan Strait and urging the U.S. government to help defend Taiwan, "in the event of invasion, missile attack, or blockade by the People's Republic of China". On the 21st, the Senate passed the resolution by 97 to 0, requesting the Clinton administration to re-examine the defensive materials and services required to "enable Taiwan to maintain a sufficient self-defense capability", and consult with Congress on how to respond once the exercise became a real threat.[163]

---

[161] John W. Garver, *Face Off: China, the United States and Taiwan's Democratization* (Seattle and London: University of Washington Press, 1997), 97.

[162] Tao Wenzhao and He Xingqiang, *History of Sino-US Relations* (Beijing: China Social Sciences Press, 2009), 296.

[163] Bradley Graham, "U.S. Approves Arms Sales to Taiwan", *The Washington Post*, March 20, 1996, A-24.

During the Taiwan Strait Crisis, the Chinese military conducted a total of four exercises in the Taiwan Strait and waters near Taiwan in July, August, November in 1995, and March in 1996, showing a powerful naval and air strike and joint forces operational capabilities. On March 20, Xinhua News Agency announced that the PLA's air and sea live exercises in the East China Sea and the South China Sea had ended. On the 25th, Xinhua announced that the PLA's joint land-sea-air exercises in the Taiwan Strait had ended. A few days later, the U.S.S *Independence* aircraft carrier returned to Okinawa, and the *Nimitz* to Bremerton, Washington. The United States exerted pressure on Taiwan, prompting it to cancel the shooting exercise in the Matsu area originally scheduled for April and the live No.12 Han Kuang Exercise in May.[164] The situation in the Taiwan Strait gradually eased.

Decision-Making Process of Foreign Policy

The Taiwan issue has always been China's internal affair, involving China's territorial integrity and sovereign independence. Therefore, it has always been a core crisis between China and the United States and in the focus of China's international crisis prevention.[165] The formal establishment of diplomatic relations between China and the U.S. was only solidified after Washington made a commitment on the Taiwan issue and on the basis of the two countries' Three Joint Communiqués, causing the relations to improve and continuously progress. Since the end of the Cold War, in view of the changing circumstances, Washington has continuously adjusted its policies towards Beijing and Taipei, with a certain degree of synchronization between the two. With regards to its Taiwan policy, the U.S. recognizes "one China" to maintain Sino-U.S. relations and fundamental American interests. On the other hand, it supports Taiwan to a certain extent to counterbalance mainland China, showing an obvious double-sided strategy.

---

[164] Tao Wenzhao and He Xingqiang, *History of Sino-US Relations* (Beijing: China Social Sciences Press, 2009), 297.

[165] Yang Jiemian, *Broadening of International Crises and China-US Joint Responses* (Beijing: Current Affairs Press, 2010), 45, 48.

In 1995, the Clinton administration allowed Lee Teng-hui to visit the U.S., ending the policy of prohibiting visits by Taiwan officials, in effect for sixteen years since the establishment of diplomatic relations. This violated America's commitment to China on the Taiwan issue and severely damaged bilateral relations. The then U.S. Secretary of State Warren Christopher also admitted afterwards that although the U.S. government has always emphasized that Lee's visit was private, this action still had obvious political connotations and has led to the retrogression of Sino-U.S. relations.[166] Since then, the Taiwan question has turned more complicated, not only affecting the political and diplomatic areas in Sino-U.S. relations, but also becoming a serious military and security problem between the two countries. In the Taiwan Strait Crisis, China and the United States had their own goals and policies. And the decision-making processes of the two also showed different characteristics.

U.S. foreign policy: internal checks and balances, contradictions

Since assuming power, the Clinton administration had not made a complete and systematic presentation of its China policy. The outside world had only seen policy practices in a series of isolated incidents, from which a coherent China policy could not be understood.[167] During the various stages (lurking, outbreak, and resolution) of the Taiwan Strait Crisis between 1995 and 1996, the Congress and the executive branch often differed in views and wrestled with each other, leaving the decision-making of foreign policy in a state of inconsistency and confusion. On whether to issue a visa for Lee Teng-hui, considering the sensitivity and seriousness of the Taiwan issue in Sino-U.S. relations and the possible strong reaction from the Chinese government, the Clinton administration repeatedly emphasized the unofficial nature of U.S.-Taiwan relations, and argued that Lee's visit did not conform to the United States' policy toward Taiwan. During the review conference on the

---

[166] Warren Christopher, *In the Stream of History, Shaping Foreign Policy for a New Era* (California: Stanford University Press, 1998), 287.

[167] Tao Wenzhao, *American Policy on China after the Cold War* (Chongqing: Chongqing Publishing Group, 2006), 87-88

UN Treaty on the Non-Proliferation of Nuclear Weapons, U.S. Secretary of State Warren Christopher met with Chinese Foreign Minister Qian Qichen. Christopher made it clear that the United States would not issue a visa to Lee, and at most would consider extending his transit visa. However, pressure from Congress had increasingly mounted.[168]

Under the pressures from the Taiwan public relations offensive and Congress, Clinton finally signed the Memorandum of Action agreeing to Lee's U.S. visit. The State Department spokesperson stated at the press conference that President Clinton has decided to allow Lee Teng-hui's private visit to the United States as an outstanding alumnus, to participate in an alumni gathering at Cornell University. The Clinton administration's decision to break from its earlier stance directly showed its adjustment of Taiwan policy and the promotion of U.S.-Taiwan relations. Having decoupled the extension of China's Most Favored Nation status from China's human rights situation, the Clinton administration hoped to use the Taiwan issue to put pressure on Beijing.

However, the Clinton administration underestimated the importance of the Taiwan issue in Sino-U.S. relations and the firm determination of the Chinese government to safeguard sovereign independence and territorial integrity. With the solemn protests of the Chinese government and people, and the deterrence of PLA military exercises, the United States realized that the Taiwan issue may lead to direct confrontation between Beijing and Washington. On March 5, 1996, on the day Xinhua News Agency announced the launch of the missile exercise, the U.S. State Department urgently met with Chinese Ambassador Li Daoyu to express serious concerns about the matter, and protested to the Chinese government through the U.S. Embassy in Beijing. On the 6th, White House Press Secretary Mike McCurry called the drill "reckless", and that the President strongly felt that the U.S. must try its best to stop the increase in tension in the Taiwan Strait.[169]

U.S. Secretary of State Warren Christopher, Assistant Secretary of State Winston Lord, Director of the Central Intelligence Agency John

---

[168] Qian Qichen, *Ten Notes on Diplomacy* (Beijing: World Affairs Press, 2003), 305-306.

[169] Liu Liandi, *The Trajectory of Sino-US Relations: An Overview of Events from 1993 to 2000* (Beijing: Current Affairs Press, 2001), 102.

Deutch, Chairman of the Joint Chiefs of Staff John Shalikashvili, and others convened an emergency meeting in the office of Secretary of Defense William Perry at the Pentagon to discuss the situation across the Taiwan Strait. They concluded that Beijing's missile exercise was to deter Taiwan's election, which was only psychological and political warfare, and that the possibility of real military action was only between 5% and 10%. But they also believed that in addition to diplomatic statements and negotiations, the U.S. government must also take strong actions to prove that the U.S. security guarantee for Taiwan was still valid.[170]

At the same time, Washington made further institutional adjustments: First, the State Department established a special team to keep contact with the U.S. Embassy in China and follow the Strait situation twenty-four hours a day; Second, an emergency response mechanism for the Strait situation was jointly established by the Joint Chiefs of Staff, the Pacific Command and the Department of Defense, and was responsible for reporting emergency plans and options to the President. Third, the National Security Council held a series of heads of department meetings to coordinate policies, and was responsible for communicating in a timely manner with Mainland and Taiwan officials to ensure that all parties fully understand U.S. strategy, policies, and its priority for easing of tensions. In addition, the intelligence community established a twenty-four-hour monitoring mechanism, responsible for sending important intelligence directly to high-level decision-makers, and reporting daily situations and policy options.[171]

Facing the pressure from the Chinese government and people, after the PLA's drill, the Clinton administration reflected on its Taiwan policy from a strategic perspective. The administration recognized the core status of the Taiwan issue in Sino-U.S. relations, and decided to avoid confronting with China on Taiwan. The U.S. repeatedly reiterated that it would handle U.S.-China relations as well as U.S.-Taiwan relations in accordance with the principles of the Three Joint Communiqués,

---

[170] Nancy Bernkopf Tucker, ed., *China Confidential: American Diplomats and Sino-American Relations, 1945-1996* (New York: Columbia University Press, 2001), 485-486.
[171] Tao Wenzhao, *American Policy on China after the Cold War* (Chongqing: Chongqing Publishing Group, 2006), 90.

and warned Taiwan authorities not to act rashly. The U.S. government emphasized that in the future, visits by senior Taiwan officials to the United States must be unofficial, few in number and personal, and that they must be handled on a case-by-case basis.[172] The Taiwan Strait Crisis acted like a sedative, causing the U.S. administration and Congress to think more seriously and calmly about Sino-U.S. relations, adjust their Taiwan policy, and enhance the priority of preventing armed conflicts across the Strait in the U.S.' Asia-Pacific strategy.

On March 14, 1996, Assistant Secretary of State Winston Lord testified before the House Committee on International Relations that maintaining a fruitful relationship with China was vital to the United States, and that the United States would continue to maintain contact with China on issues of mutual interest, and not seek confrontation.[173] Since then, the Clinton administration had repeatedly released signals hoping to improve Sino-U.S. relations. On May 17 of that year, at a gathering of the Asia Society, the Council on Foreign Relations and the National Committee on U.S. - China Relations, U.S. Secretary of State Warren Christopher delivered a speech on behalf of the Clinton administration, expounding the U.S. policy on China, the first time since Clinton took office more than three years earlier.

During the 1995-1996 Taiwan Strait Crisis, President Clinton personally took charge of crisis management,[174] which meant that the United States had a critical turning point in its understanding of the importance and sensitivity of the Taiwan issue, and the United States' China policy became clearer. However, in the Taiwan Strait Crisis, the United States was concerned about the peace process of cross-Strait relations rather than the end result. The overall goal of the United States' China and Taiwan policy is to *manage* the crisis, not to *solve* the Taiwan issue.

---

[172] Shanghai Institute of International Studies, *Yearbook of International Situation 1996* (Shanghai: Shanghai Education Press, 1996), 64-65.

[173] Winston Lord, "The United States and the Security of Taiwan," US Department of State, accessed September 25, 2020, https://1997-2001.state.gov/current/debate/mar96_china_us_taiwan.html.

[174] Yang Jiemian, *Broadening of International Crises and China-US Joint Responses* (Beijing: Current Affairs Press, 2010), 150.

China's foreign policy: rational and disciplined; confronting without total conflict

The primary goal of the Chinese government in responding to the Strait crisis is to safeguard China's sovereign independence and territorial integrity. It firmly opposes the rise and development of forces in America who support Taiwan's independence. Beijing strongly urged the Clinton administration to handle Sino-U.S. relations and Taiwan issues on the basis of the principles of the Three Joint Communiqués and the One-China Policy. On the issue of Washington allowing Lee Teng-hui to visit the United States, Chinese leaders adopted the policy of "confronting without total conflict", remained principled and restrained, and immediately declared the end of the military exercises after the goals were achieved,[175] thus turning China's passive position into a proactive one, helping steer Sino-U.S. relations out from the crisis.

When Lee's visit was approved by Washington on May 22, 1995, the Chinese Ministry of Foreign Affairs filed a strong protest on the 23rd, accusing the U.S. of violating the fundamental principles of the Three Joint Communiqués, damaging China's sovereignty and creating a situation of "one China, one Taiwan" which undermined China's peaceful reunification. Beijing requested Washington to immediately rescind the wrong decision. In the next few days, Chinese Foreign Ministry spokesperson announced that the Chinese government would postpone and suspend a series of high-level bilateral military exchange activities, including delaying Chinese State Councilor and Defense Minister Chi Haotian's visit to the United States originally scheduled for June, terminating State Councilor Li Guixian and Air Force Commander Yu Zhenwu's visits to the U.S., postponing the China-U.S. expert-level meetings on the Missile Technology Control Regime as well as nuclear energy cooperation scheduled for June, and postponing the China visits of the Director of the U.S. Arms Control and Disarmament Agency and the Assistant Secretary of State for

---

[175] Yang Jiemian, *Sino-US Relations in the Post-Cold War Period: Theory and Practice of Crisis Management* (Shanghai: Shanghai People's Publishing House, 2004), 135.

Political-Military Affairs.[176] On June 16, Chinese ambassador Li Daoyu informed the Clinton administration that he was called back to China for work report, due to the bad consequences caused by Washington allowing Lee's visit. Thus, Sino-U.S. relations fell to the lowest point since the establishment of diplomatic relations in 1979. The relations were essentially reduced to the level of charge d'affaires.[177]

Upon the onset of the crisis, the Chinese government actively sought to resolve the issue through diplomatic matters such as negotiations. On August 1, the foreign ministers of China and the United States met in Brunei when they attended the Foreign Ministers' Meeting of the ASEAN Regional Forum, during which Christopher forwarded President Clinton's letter to President Jiang Zemin. In the letter, Clinton invited Jiang to visit the United States in the near future, emphasizing that the U.S. resisted and opposed Taiwan's efforts for independence and did not support "Two Chinas" or Taiwan's entry into the United Nations. This was the first time that a U.S. President has made such a written statement.[178] At the end of August, Under Secretary of State Peter Tarnoff visited China and held talks with Vice Foreign Minister Li Zhaoxing. Tarnoff said that the United States valued and respected China's position on the Taiwan issue. Since then, the Chinese government decided to gradually resume high-level exchanges with the U.S., and the tensed relations began easing. In late September, Beijing recognized Jim Sasser as the new U.S. ambassador to China. On October 24, on the sidelines of the United Nations commemoration of the 50th anniversary of victory of World War II, Jiang and Clinton had a two-hour formal meeting at the Lincoln Center in New York City. Ambassador Li Daoyu accompanied Jiang for the UN celebratory activities, and stayed in the United States after the summit between the two leaders.

---

[176] Tao Wenzhao, *American Policy on China after the Cold War* (Chongqing: Chongqing Publishing Group, 2006), 86-87

[177] Ni Shixiong, *A Thousand Miles Can't Separate a Friendship Made with One Promise: 30 Years of Sino-US Relations in the Eye of a Chinese Scholar* (Shanghai: Fudan University Press, 2009), 87.

[178] Zhong Zhicheng, *For a Better World: Jiang Zemin's Foreign Visits* (Beijing: World Affairs Press, 2006), 134.

Through meetings and dialogues, the U.S. generally accepted a framework of Sino-U.S. relations that can be termed as "12345": 1), upholding the One-China Policy; 2), reiterating two principles: Taiwan is an inseparable part of China and following the basic principles of the Three Joint Communiqués; 3), reiterating three promises: opposing "one China, one Taiwan, opposing Taiwan's independence, and opposing Taiwan's accession to the United Nations; 4), Establishing four rules for Taiwan leaders' future visits to the United States, namely: such visits should be private, unofficial, few, and handled on a case-by-case basis; and 5), the two sides intended to strengthen cooperation in five areas: major international and regional issues, military exchanges, economic and trade cooperation issues, seeking to resume and expand dialogue, and environmental issues.[179]

In March 1996, Taiwan held the so-called "presidential election", and the crisis between China and the United States and the two sides across the Strait rose again. The Chinese Government immediately stated its principles and announced missile exercises in the Taiwan Strait to demonstrate its determination to safeguard sovereign independence and territorial integrity. However, during the PLA' military exercises in the Taiwan Strait and the waters near Taiwan, the U.S. also dispatched its fleets consisting of two aircraft carriers, the *Independence* and the *Nimitz*, to the vicinity of the Taiwan Strait. In response, Shen Guofang, spokesperson of China's Ministry of Foreign Affairs, warned the U.S. not to send wrong signals to the Taiwan authorities on the Taiwan issue, and not to support the Taiwan authorities' independence and separatist attempts.

This Taiwan Strait event led the Clinton administration to finally determine to improve Sino-U.S. relations, after more than three years of hesitation and vacillation. From July 6 to 10, Assistant to the President for National Security Affairs Anthony Lake visited China, to which Beijing attached great importance. President Jiang Zemin, Premier Li Peng, Foreign Minister Qian Qichen and Defense Minister Chi Haotian met with Lake respectively. Lake's visit to China helped resume the

---

[179] Ni Shixiong, *A Thousand Miles Can't Separate a Friendship Made with One Promise: 30 Years of Sino-US Relations in the Eye of a Chinese Scholar* (Shanghai: Fudan University Press, 2009), 90.

high-level strategic dialogue between the two countries. Since then, mutual high-level visits have continued, and Sino-U.S. relations showed a momentum of continuous improvement, eventually leading to the visits of the two heads of state to each other's countries in 1997 and 1998.

SECTION 2. CONTENT ANALYSIS OF *THE NEW YORK TIMES* COVERAGE ON THE TAIWAN STRAIT CRISIS

Any international crisis is a process starting with the lurking of disagreements, to the incubation of crisis and the outbreak of conflicts. Then, the crisis spreads, and finally, ends in resolution. Its beginning and end may consist of a series of events or a series of policies being rolled out. Therefore, it is a very difficult task to clearly state the specific start and end dates of a crisis. The 1995-1996 Taiwan Strait Crisis was no exception. From its beginning to its ending, there was a continuously developing process. However, for research purposes, the author still defines a specific timeframe outlining the beginning and end: the beginning was when the resolution was passed by the U.S. House and Senate in May 1995 to allow Lee Teng-hui's visit to the United States, as well as President Clinton's signing a memorandum agreeing to issuing a visa to Lee; the end was when U.S. aircraft carriers the *Independence* and the *Nimitz* returned to their bases after the PLA concluded military exercises in the Taiwan Strait and the waters near Taiwan in March 1996, as well as when in April Taiwan announced to cancel the upcoming shooting exercises in the Matsu area and the live No.12 Han Kuang Exercise. Therefore, the object of study in this chapter is *The New York Times* coverage of the Taiwan Strait Crisis during the 12-month period from May 1995 to April 1996.

Volume and Lengths of Articles

Volume of articles

The author searched "China" and "Taiwan" in the "New York Times" subsection of the ProQuest database, for the *Times* articles from May 1995 to April 1996. A total of 124 relevant articles were obtained. In the same timeframe, using "China" as the search keyword, the results were 720 China-related articles in *The New York Times*. The author browsed through all 720 articles and screened out articles on the Taiwan Strait Crisis. These were then compared with the earlier 124 articles, and articles of readers' letters, corrections, and other articles of little relevance to the subject were excluded. Finally, the author determined that *The New York Times* had 115 articles on the Taiwan Strait Crisis between May 1995 and April 1996, accounting for 16% of the total number of China-related *Times* articles in the same period. That means about one in six *Times* China articles at the time was pertinent to the Taiwan Strait Crisis. (see fig. 3.1)

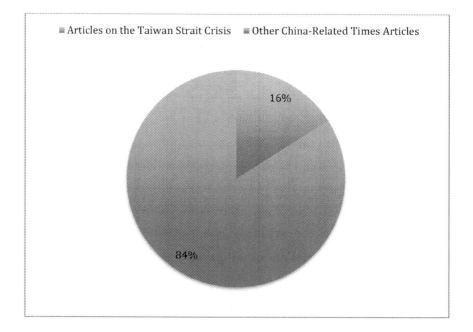

Figure 3.1 Portion of articles on Taiwan Strait Crisis (1995-1996) of all China-related articles in *The New York Times* in the same period.

Then, the numbers of articles on Taiwan Strait Crisis each month were counted, and the results are shown in the following table. (see table 3.1)

Month	May 1995	June 1995	July 1995	Aug. 1995	Sept. 1995	Oct. 1995	Nov. 1995	Dec. 1995	Jan. 1996	Feb. 1996	Mar. 1996	April 1996
Number of articles	8	5	8	15	4	3	3	2	8	15	43	1
Total	115											

Table 3.1 Monthly numbers of articles on Taiwan Strait Crisis (1995-1996) in *The New York Times*.

It can be clearly seen from the table that the number of articles in August 1995 and February and March of 1996 was relatively large, standing out from all other months. To understand this phenomenon, we need to compare and analyze it with the process of the Taiwan Strait Crisis.

The backdrop of the Taiwan Strait Crisis was two-fold: on one hand, Lee Teng-hui hoped to boost his campaign in the Taiwan leader's election in March 1996 and to win U.S. support; on the other hand, Sino-U.S. relations at that time were in a stage of being neither enemies nor friends—the two sides had disputes and conflicts in many areas such as human rights, trade, and prevention of nuclear proliferation. Out of considerations for its strategic interests in Asia and pressuring China through the Taiwan issue, the United States announced in May 1995 that it had agreed to let Lee visit the U.S., triggering the third Taiwan Strait crisis after the ones in 1954-1955 and 1958, all involving military forces.[180] It was in May that *The New York Times* began to pay attention to the crisis. When searching the ProQuest database, there were no reports or commentaries on the subject of "China" and "Taiwan" in *The New York Times* in March and April.

In June 1995, Lee Teng-hui successfully visited the U.S. to attend the Cornell University alumni gathering. He delivered a speech entitled "With the People Always in My Heart". The Chinese government strongly protested and called back its ambassador to the U.S. Li Daoyu that month. In July, China conducted the first missile launch training in

---

[180] Yang Jiemian, *Broadening of International Crises and China-US Joint Responses* (Beijing: Current Affairs Press, 2010), 129.

the East China Sea north of Taiwan. During this period, *The New York Times'* attention continued, with several relevant articles every month. In August, the number of articles on this crisis reached fifteen, almost twice the number in the previous month. This was one article of news report or commentary every two days. *The Times'* sudden and sharp increased attention was related to the intensification of conflicts and the escalation of the crisis. As the PLA conducted another live missile and artillery exercise over and in the waters of the East China Sea that month, tensions between the two countries ran higher. The Clinton administration began to realize the seriousness of the problem and used a variety of ways to express its position to China, including through the meeting between Secretary of State Warren Christopher and Chinese Foreign Minister Qian Qichen in Brunei, as well as Under Secretary of State Peter Tarnoff's visit to China, hoping to ease the confrontation.

After that, from September to the end of the year, *The New York Times'* attention to the crisis began to decline again, with the number of articles falling back to the level before the crisis escalated. During the period, the high-level dialogue and exchange of visits between China and the United States gradually resumed, and the tense relationship was eased and repaired—in September, the Chinese government recognized Jim Sasser as the new U.S. ambassador to China; in October, the heads of state of China and the United States took advantage of their participation of a UN commemorative event for holding a formal meeting in New York.

In February 1996, the number of articles in *The New York Times* on the Taiwan issue increased again: to 15 that month. In March, the number peaked with a total of 43 articles, six times the average number of other months, accounting for 37% of the total *The New York Times* articles during entire Taiwan Strait Crisis. That was on average 1.4 articles per day. In the same period, Taiwan was about to hold its first direct leader election, putting the Strait situation again in turbulence. In February, China purchased 72 SU-27 fighter jets from Russia, while Taiwan said that China had begun to deploy military forces in the waters near Taiwan Island. In March, the Taiwan Strait Crisis broke out in full swing. The PLA successively conducted missile launch training and live-fire land-sea-air exercises in South China Sea and East China Sea. And the U.S. deployed the *Independence* and *Nimitz* carriers in the waters near Taiwan. The situation in the Taiwan Strait was in high tension.

During the escalation and full-scale outbreak of the crisis, especially when major incidents or de facto military operations occurred, the attention of *The New York Times* rapidly heated up and even reached the highest point, with the number of relevant articles increasing significantly. When the crisis eased, the heat of reporting also dropped sharply.

Distribution of article lengths

By looking at the numbers of relevant articles during different stages of the crisis, we can measure how "heated" *The New York Times'* reporting varied during the crisis. Furthermore, the author looks at the *length* of the articles. Among the 115 reports, medium-and-long-length articles are the most: there are 74 articles of 500-1200 words, accounting for 64% of the total. In addition, there are 28 short articles of less than 200 words and 23 long reports of more than 1200 words. (see table 3.2)

Month Word count	May 1995	June 1995	July 1995	Aug. 1995	Sept. 1995	Oct. 1995	Nov. 1995	Dec. 1995	Jan. 1996	Feb. 1996	Mar. 1996	April 1996	Total
0-200	3	1	1	1	1	0	0	0	3	3	4	1	18
200-500	1	0	1	1	0	0	0	0	1	4	2	0	10
500-800	2	2	1	4	3	2	3	2	2	4	20	0	45
800-1200	2	2	3	8	0	0	0	0	1	2	11	0	29
1200-1500	0	0	1	1	0	1	0	0	1	2	5	0	11
1500-2000	0	0	1	0	0	0	0	0	0	0	0	0	1
2000+	0	0	0	0	0	0	0	0	0	0	1	0	1
Total	8	5	8	15	4	3	3	2	8	15	43	1	115

Table 3.2 Lengths of articles on the Taiwan Strait Crisis (1995-1996) in *The New York Times*.

March 1996 was when a barrage of events of the Taiwan Strait Crisis broke out, and it was also the period when *The New York Times* coverage was the most intense. In comparison, relevant *Times* articles are more scattered and less representative in other months. Therefore, in order to make the research more pertinent and doable, the author analyzes the content and framing of the 43 reports in the March of 1996, deciphering how *The New York Times* presented the crisis events. (see fig. 3.2)

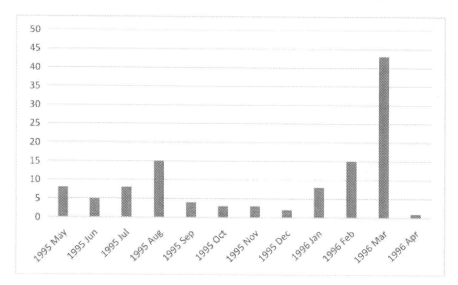

Figure 3.2 Monthly number of articles on Taiwan Strait Crisis (1995-1996) in *The New York Times.*

Content and Framing

Content analysis

In March 1996, Taiwan held its first direct leader election in history. In order to deter Taiwanese independence forces during the election campaign, Beijing held three military exercises in the waters off the Taiwan Island, including a missile launch training, a sea-to-air live-fire exercise, and a land-sea-air joint exercise. It was also the year of U.S. presidential election; how the Clinton administration would respond to Beijing's military exercises, what stance and attitude the U.S. would take towards Taiwan, the direction of Sino-U.S. relations, as well as America's China policy itself all were under the limelight of U.S. domestic political and media practitioners.

In this section, a total of 43 articles of news reports and commentaries on the Taiwan Strait Crisis in March 1996 in *The New York Times* are used as the sample for content analysis. In order to present the research process fully and clearly, and to ensure a scientific, accurate and rigorous analysis, the author classifies and presents in a detailed table the date, title, type, length, tendency, news sources and main content of each of the 43 articles based on the intensive reading of the articles. In view that the focus of this research is on the communication process of crisis events and the presentation of Sino-U.S. relations amid the bilateral crisis, the table lists "China-U.S. relations and foreign policy" separately. (see table 3.3)

Before proceeding to the analysis, it is necessary to provide definitive descriptions of each category in the table.

First, the "type" of articles points to the news genre. Combining the classification norms of news genres in China and Western countries, this book put types into six categories—short news articles, news stories, in-depth analyses, event feature stories, human-interest stories, and commentaries.[181] While the definitions and characteristics of short news articles, human-interest stories and commentaries are relatively clear, a brief description of the different characteristics of the other three categories is as follows: News stories complement short news articles; news stories are more detailed introductions to news events and their developments; in-depth analysis articles provide background materials, commentaries and opinions surrounding news events, aiming to reveal the causes of events and analyze event directions; event feature stories start from looking at a certain aspect and a small detail, and from there vividly and profoundly depict the whole event.

Secondly, with regard to reporting tendency, which is the position and attitude of news coverage, this study distinguishes between the positive, the neutral, and the negative. There are three main countries and regions involved in the Taiwan Strait Crisis coverage, namely the United States, China, and Taiwan. Here we only look at the newspaper's reporting tendency towards China. Among the articles, those which directly or indirectly praise, support, or affirm the Chinese government's foreign policies, positions, behaviors, reactions, etc., are positive

---

[181] Journalism Theory Research Office at Department of Journalism of Fudan University, *Introduction to Journalism* (Fuzhou: Fujian People's Publishing House, 1985), 77-79.

tendencies; those which only objectively report on events themselves and do not ostensibly incorporate personal attitudes and opinions, have their tendency defined as neutral; while articles that involve direct or indirect opposition, criticism, and satire with regards to the Chinese government's foreign policy, positions, behaviors, and reactions are defined as having a negative tendency.

Third, the news sources refer to the sources for the various materials, opinions, and comments in an article. Sources include direct or indirect references to official organs, social organizations, media, and individuals. News sources are the first link in news production, and play a key role in reporters bringing their job to completion—"Without news sources there is no news."[182] The credibility of sources determines the quality of reports. And the selection and use of sources can to a certain extent reflect the attitude and position of the reporter. Therefore, the author lists each source cited in the articles, and notes whether the source is named or anonymous, and whether it is a direct or indirect citation.

Fourth, the "main content" in the table shows an extracted and summarized version of an article's topic, angle, and key information. The author tries to be accurate and objective in the extraction process, but it is still difficult to avoid certain subjectivity. However, this item is mainly used as a cue and reference for content and framing analysis in the research, so it has little effect on the validity of research results. "China-U.S. Relations and Foreign Policy" refers to the statements and evaluations of China-U.S. relations, the foreign policies of the two countries, and the diplomatic positions and decisions of China and the United States amidst the Taiwan Strait Crisis. It is also the most crucial material for analysis in this research. Therefore, the author did not make any modifications, but simply sorted out the relevant sentences in the original text.

Finally, "Words of sentiment" are key words in articles that reflect the writer's attitude and sentiment towards China. They are mainly words that show certain tendencies on the position, decision-making, behaviors, etc., of the Chinese government amid crisis events (such as the PLA's military exercises near Taiwan Island).

---

[182] Jerry Palmer, *Spinning into Control: News Values and Source Strategies* (London: Leicester University Press, 2000), 4.

Report date and quantity analysis. During the 31 days in March 1996, *The New York Times* published a total of 43 articles (including commentaries) on the Taiwan Strait Crisis. With the exception of the 7 days of the 2nd, 3rd, 6th, 11th, 28th, 30th, and 31st when no relevant article was seen, the remaining 23 days had at least one article per day. The largest daily number—6—appeared on the 24th, which was the first day after the Taiwan leader election. In addition, the numbers of articles on the 10th and 12th were also relatively large, with 4 articles per day. (see fig. 3.3)

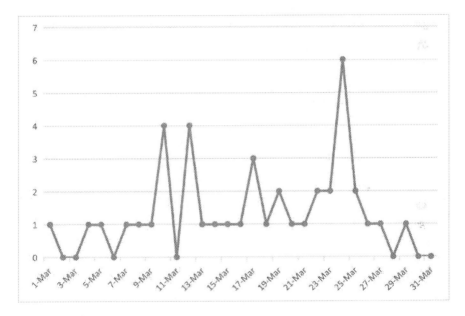

Figure 3.3 Daily number of articles on Taiwan Strait Crisis in *The New York Times* in March 1996.

In March 1996, the major events in the process of the Taiwan Strait Crisis were the three military exercises of the PLA in waters near Taiwan, and the deployment of America's two aircraft carriers to the Strait, as well as Taiwan's first direct leader election in history. During this period, the intensity of coverage by *The New York Times* was basically consistent with the onset and progress of the crisis. On March 10th, the four articles of *The Times* all revolved around China's new round of joint naval and air military exercises; the four articles on March 12 focused on the U.S. dispatch of aircraft carriers to the Taiwan Strait and the move's impact; and on March 24, *The Times* had four articles on the election of Taiwan's leader, and the other two were commentaries on U.S. foreign policy.

Article type and length analysis. *The New York Times* covered the Taiwan Strait Crisis in March 1996 in various forms, using all six genres, with medium-and-long-length news stories and event feature stories as the mainstay, and short news articles and human-interest stories as the minority. Among the 43 articles, there were 13 news stories, accounting for 30% of the total number in the month, and 11 event feature stories, accounting for 25.6%. In contrast, there were only 4 short news articles, and only 1 human-interest story. In addition, there were 8 commentaries and 6 in-depth analysis articles, which accounted for 18.6% and 14% respectively. (see table 3.4)

Length (word count)	Short news article	News story	In-depth analysis	Event feature story	Human-interest story	Commentary
0-200	4	0	0	0	0	0
200-500	0	1	1	0	0	0
500-800	0	7	1	3	1	8
800-1200	0	4	2	5	0	0
1200+	0	1	2	3	0	0
Total number of articles	4	13	6	11	1	8

Figure 3.4 Types and lengths of articles on Taiwan Strait Crisis in *The New York Times* in March 1996.

With regard to its coverage on the Taiwan Strait Crisis, *The New York Times* rarely used time-sensitive but short-length and concise news articles. It mainly covered the onset and development of an event through long-length news stories, such as the March 10th story "War Games off Taiwan to Expand, Beijing Says", March 16th article, "China Says Maneuvers Will Last Through Taiwan's Elections", and the March 26th article "Tensions Seen as Receding as China Ends War Games". Another crucial news type *The Times* used was event feature stories from various angles (e.g., mainland, Taiwan, public and private sectors of the U.S., politics and economy). These stories include "Chinese Missile Testing Fails to Disrupt Life on Taiwan" on March 9th, "Slogan for Many Chinese: Make Money, Not War" on March 15th, and "Off Taiwan, U.S. Sailors Are Unworried" on March 19th. In addition, in-depth analysis articles focusing on event causes and development trends, as well as commentaries expressing different views, positions, and attitudes were common types used by *The Times*. In view of the characteristics of such article types, *The New York Times* was keen on using comprehensive materials, in-depth analysis, and diversified perspectives in its coverage on the Taiwan Strait Crisis.

Analysis on news sources. News sources, as the name suggests, mean the original sources of news and information, including information release and data disclosure by governments, enterprises, public entities, social organizations and other sectors, as well as interviews with relevant authorities, parties involved in news events, and eye-witnesses.[183] The selection and presentation of news sources can to some extent reflect the reporter's certain preferences and attitudes. Therefore, the author analyzes statistically the sources of 43 reports on the Taiwan Strait Crisis in *The New York Times* in March 1996, and distinguishes whether the source is named or anonymous, and whether it is a direct or indirect citation. Specifically, sources with the identity of the interviewee and real name are regarded as anonymous; quotes that use quotation marks are regarded as direct citations; those that do not use quotation marks are regarded as indirect citations.

The purpose of statistically analyzing the news sources is to understand the *Times'* source preferences when covering the Taiwan Strait Crisis. That is, which types of departments, institutions, or individuals are selected as news sources, and frequency of occurrence of these sources in different articles. In view of such a purpose, and for the ease of sorting and calculations, the author uses the following statistical method:

The same source that appears multiple times in a same article is counted as only once. The same source that appears in different articles

---

[183] Liu Xiaoying, *International News Communication* (Beijing: China Radio and Television Press, 2013), 67-68.

is counted according to the number of articles that contain such source. And if the same source appears multiple times in a same article involves both direct and indirect quotations, only direct quotations are counted. The resultant numbers are as follows: (see table 3.5)

Citation method / Source type	Direct citation		Indirect citation		Official statement or report from other media	Sum	Percentage
	Named	Anonymous	Named	Anonymous			
Chinese government and officials	11	-	2	1	4	18	12%
American government and officials	9	4	1	5	3	22	15%
Taiwan government and officials	21	1	2	-	1	25	17%
Other governments and officials	2	5	3	3	-	13	9%
Chinese media	-	-	-	-	11	11	7%
American media	-	-	-	-	3	3	2%
Other media	-	-	-	-	3	3	2%
Chinese experts or scholars	1	1	-	-	-	2	1.4%
American experts or scholars	6	-	-	-	-	6	4%
Taiwan experts or scholars	3	-	-	-	-	3	2%
American enterprises or organizations	-	-	-	-	2	2	1.4%
Members of Chinese enterprises or organizations	6	-	-	-	-	6	4%

Members of American enterprises or organizations	2	-	-	-	-	2	1.4%
Members of Taiwan enterprises or organizations	7	-	-	-	-	7	5%
American military members	6	-	-	-	-	6	4%
Chinese individuals	8	-	-	-	-	8	5.4%
Taiwan individuals	11	-	-	-	-	11	7.4%
Sum	93	11	8	9	27	148	100%

Table 3.5 News sources in Taiwan Strait Crisis coverage
of *The New York Times* in March 1996.

The table above shows sources used most by *The New York Times* in its coverage on the Taiwan Strait Crisis were not from China or the United States, but rather from Taiwan: cited 46 times, or 31% of the total. Sources from China (including mainland China and Hong Kong) came just second in number: quoted 45 times, or 30% of the total. Sources from the United States were cited 39 times, or 26%. News sources from other countries and regions led to 16 citations. On the surface, the number of citations from Chinese sources is similar to that of Taiwan and greater than that of the United States. However, if sources from Taiwan, the United States and other countries and regions are added together, voices from China are in fact weakened to some extent.

The types of news sources are complex and diverse, including ones from governments, experts and scholars, the media, enterprises, and private individuals. As far as the volumes of citations are concerned, *The New York Times* paid high attention to authoritative information from the government, experts, scholars, and other media organizations, who were cited 112 times, accounting for more than 75%. These include information from active U.S. Navy troops of the fleet comprising the U.S.S *Independence.* In contrast, voices from enterprises, social organizations, and private individuals expressing concerns, feelings and attitudes are relatively weak, with only 36 citations.

In terms of the type of citations, named, direct quotations have the greatest number —93 times, or 63%, far exceeding other types. The second-largest number of types are citations from government statements and official reports from China, the United States, and Taiwan, as well as content quoted from other media reports; together these types appeared 27 times, accounting for 18%. It can be seen that *The New York Times* valued truthfulness, accuracy, and credibility of its sources in its Taiwan Strait Crisis coverage, as most of the sources were traceable and verifiable.

Among all the sources cited, Taiwanese officials appeared the most, with a total of 25 times, or 17% of the total. Chinese mainland government and officials were cited 18 times, or 12%, less than Taiwan and the United States. It is worth noting that *The New York Times* cited the official sources of mainland China and Taiwan mainly using named and direct quotes, while about half of the citations from the U.S. government and officials appeared in the report anonymously. And the proportion of other government and official sources cited anonymously is higher than 60%.

As for sources from reports of the media in various countries, *The New York Times* cited Chinese media reports the most frequently, mainly those from the Xinhua News Agency, and also from other mainstream media organizations such as China Central Television (CCTV), *People's Daily*, *PLA Daily*, and *China Daily*. However, when quoted, the government background of the Chinese media is often emphasized: the word "official" is added in front of Xinhua News Agency; "the Communist Party newspaper" is put in front of *People's Daily*; CCTV is labeled as "China's state television"; *China Daily* is noted to be "semi-official"; *PLA Daily* is introduced as "the official newspaper of China's military"; and The "Wen Wei Po" is called "a Communist Party-controlled newspaper in Hong Kong". This style of citation seems to imply doubts about the authenticity, objectivity, and fairness of Chinese media reports.

Among the 43 reports, only two are commentaries by independent writers. Ahead of the texts, the newspaper gives a brief introduction to the writer's identity. One article is titled "Taiwan Belongs to No One", written by Taiwan's Democratic Progressive Party presidential candidate Peng Ming-min, who defended his firm pro-independence stance. The other article, "Clinton's Gunboat Diplomacy", was written by James Shinn, senior fellow at the Council on Foreign Relations. It is the only article among the 43 which has a positive view towards China. Shin expressed strong dissatisfaction and criticism of U.S. policy towards China. He argued that the Clinton administration had treated China too harshly and with unfair standards.

In his book *Deciding What's News*, Herbert J. Gans argues that in the eyes of journalists the use of news source is not direct but potential. News sources hope to use the interviewing opportunity to promote their own claims and interests, but their applicability can only be screened and determined by journalists and editors.[184] Therefore, there is a process of wrestling between news sources and journalists, while the journalists possess the initiating and deciding power able to determine which sources can get more opportunities to express their opinions and defend their interests.

Report tendency analysis. As mentioned earlier, the tendency of *The New York Times'* coverage on the Taiwan Strait Crisis in this section of the study has only mainland China as its concern. That is, we only look at the newspaper's direct or indirect attitude towards in its coverage regarding Chinese government's foreign affairs position, decision-making and behavior in the crisis. The tendencies of some reports are fairly clear and explicit, especially in commentaries and in-depth analysis articles, which often directly criticize and bash the Chinese government's statements, decision-making, and military exercises, while some articles indirectly reflect the writers' attitude and tendencies when the articles attack the American policy towards China or through reporting on Taiwan's reactions and the repercussions it underwent. Based on such definition is the tendency analysis of the 43 reports as shown below. (see fig. 3.4)

---

[184] Herbert J Gans, *Deciding What's News: A Study of CBS Evening News, NBC Nightly News, Newsweek, and Time* (United Kingdom: Vintage Books, 1980)

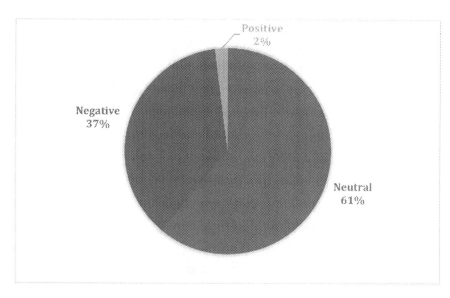

Negative

Positive

Neutral

Figure 3.4 Tendencies of *The New York Times* coverage
on Taiwan Strait Crisis in March 1996.

Among all the 43 articles in *The New York Times* during March 1996
covering the Taiwan Strait Crisis, articles with a neutral tendency have
the largest number of 26, or more than 60%. The number of articles
with negative tendencies is 16, while the number of articles with positive
tendency is just 1, which is a commentary. When articles are grouped
according to their types, there are more with a neutral tendency than
with a negative tendency among short news articles, news stories, and
event feature stories, showing that these types of news stress authenticity
and objectivity. In in-depth analysis articles and commentaries, however,
more pieces are seen with a negative tendency. (see table 3.6)

Type \ Tendency	Short news article	News story	In-depth analysis	Event feature story	Human-interest story	Commentary	Sum
Negative	1	5	4	2	-	4	16
Neutral	3	8	2	9	1	3	26
Positive	-	-	-	-	-	1	1
Sum	43						

Table 3.6 Tendencies of articles on Taiwan Strait
Crisis in *The New York Times* in March 1996

In fact, many Chinese scholars' studies on American media in the 1990s mentioned the prejudices and negative tendencies of the American media's China reporting as involving "hostilities" and "demonization",[185] especially when it came to coverage involving major national interests of the United States. Some scholars have pointed to the following reasons: the American media's modus operandi driven by commercial interests and the belief in the news value that "bad news is good news"; the long-standing differences in political systems, ideologies, and values of China and the United States; national interest concerns fearing the potential threat of China's economic development and the rise of China's international status; and finally: domestic political factors in the United States.[186]

Within such a media environment, the fact that *The New York Times* could still maintain a mostly neutral position and tone when covering the Taiwan Strait speaks much about it being a world-class newspaper and a "newspaper of record", with its seriousness, objectivity and fairness. Although there are also commentaries and analysis articles criticizing and accusing China's foreign policy stance and decision-making, and only one commentary is positive towards China, much is also seen in its reporting that expressed dissatisfaction with the Clinton

---

[185] Quintessential works include: Li Xiguang, Liu Kang. *Behind the Demonization of China* (Beijing: China Social Sciences Press, 1996); Fan Shiming, "Why US Media is Hostile to China," *International Political Studies*, no. 3 (1997): 45-50; Zhou Xinhua, "The Current Negative Influences of US News Media on International Relations," *Modern International Relations*, no. 12 (1999): 35-37.

[186] Fan Shiming, "Why US Media is Hostile to China," *International Political Studies*, no. 3 (1997): 45-50.

administration's China policy and crisis decision-making. However, during the crisis in March 1996, apart from the United States sending two aircraft carrier fleets to the Taiwan Strait, there was no serious and direct intense conflict between China and the United States. The major concern of U.S. officials and media was whether the military exercises aimed at Taiwan's presidential election would evolve into armed attacks on Taiwan. This may be one of the reasons why most of the articles in *The Times* could maintain a neutral attitude.

The analysis above on the tendency of *The New York Times* coverage on the Taiwan Strait Crisis is drawn from a general look at the articles. In fact, in addition to the attitudes expressed directly or indirectly in the content of the articles, the angles and emotional vocabulary used in the articles can also reflect certain tendencies. For example, of the 11 event feature stories, 7 of them were written from the angle of Taiwan, which include the impact of The PLA's exercises on Taiwan's economy and people's daily lives,[187] as well as Taiwanese people's views on the drills and their responses,[188] the views of Taiwanese businessmen in mainland China on the cross-strait situation,[189] and the reactions and expectations of various social spheres in Taiwan after Lee Teng-hui was elected president.[190] On the other hand, there are only two event feature stories from the vantage point of the Chinese mainland. One is about China's official announcement (e.g., geographical area for missile exercises) and the reactions from the United States, Taiwan, and Japan;[191] the other

---

[187] Edward A. Gargan, "Chinese Missile Testing Fails to Disrupt Life on Taiwan," *The New York Times*, March 3, 1996, A3; Edward A. Gargan, "Off China, Isle Waits Nervously," *The New York Times*, March 19, 1996, A3; Edward A. Gargan, "Long-Term Forecast for Taiwan Remains Upbeat," *The New York Times*, March 23, 1996, A35.

[188] Edward A. Gargan, "In Taiwan, Few Admit To Worries About China," *The New York Times*, March 17, 1996, A4.

[189] Seth Faison, "Executives from Taiwan Worry, but Stay in China," *The New York Times*, March 20, 1996, A1.

[190] Patrick E. Tyler, "Taiwan's Leader Wins Its Election and a Mandate," *The New York Times*, March 24, 1996, A1; Patrick E. Tyler, "In Taiwan, a Mandate, but for What?," *The New York Times*, March 29, 1996, A10.

[191] Patrick E. Tyler, "Beijing Steps Up Military Pressure on Taiwan Leader," *The New York Times*, March 7, 1996, A1.

is about ordinary Chinese people's views on the missile exercises and the cross-Strait relations.[192]. This can be explained by the reporting tendencies of *The New York Times*' reporters and editorial principles, and also possibly by China's strict management of foreign journalists in China at the time, which led to various restrictions on journalistic work. Patrick E. Tyler, *The Times* correspondent in Beijing at the time, wrote in a report that Chinese people often dared not boldly express their ideas to foreign reporters, especially the reporter who was followed by four agents of the National Security Agency.[193] For whichever reasons, the vantage point imbalance essentially led to a bias of the newspaper towards China.

In addition, when *The New York Times* reported on the Chinese government's positions, decision-making, behaviors, and statements during the Taiwan Strait Crisis, especially missile tests and military exercises in the waters near Taiwan, some emotionally-charged words appeared repeatedly. This is also a kind of euphemistic expression of the reporter's attitudes and tendencies, which make hints to the readers regarding the nature of the events, government decisions and behaviors. For example, many articles used "threaten", "intimidate", "cow", "frighten", "bludgeon", "blockade", "bully", "assault" and "invade" to characterize the PLA's missile tests and drills during the waters of Taiwan, and used words like "interruption", "roadblock", "sabotage", and "curb" when conveying the exercises' goal with regards to Taiwan's upcoming presidential election. Words like "intransigent", "stubborn", "reckless", "aggressive", "belligerent", "saber-rattling" and "out of control" were used to depict the Chinese government's behaviors in the course of the crisis, caused a "backfire", becoming "distasteful" to the people of Taiwan who turned "dismissive" towards the mainland. In dozens of articles, most of the vocabulary used to introduce and describe the Chinese government's foreign policy stance, decision-making, and behaviors are derogatory. Only one commentary argues that China's economic development is "vibrant", that the Chinese government shows

---

[192] Patrick E. Tyler, "Slogan for Many Chinese: Make Money, Not War," *The New York Times*, March 15, 1996, A3.
[193] Patrick E. Tyler, "Slogan for Many Chinese: Make Money, Not War," *The New York Times*, March 15, 1996, A3.

a "cautious" attitude is in the Taiwan Strait Crisis, that it was the U.S. government that mistakenly regarded China as an "adversary" and an "enemy", and that Clinton's decision-making on China was not "statesmanlike".[194]

From the above analysis, it can be concluded that *The New York Times* was generally neutral on the Chinese government's foreign policy stance, decision-making, and behaviors in the Taiwan Strait Crisis. However, the newspaper's choices of news sources and reporting angles have weakened the Chinese voice to a certain extent. The use of descriptive, emotionally-charged vocabulary also artfully expressed certain negative tendencies.

Framing

Framing was first introduced into the field of social sciences by Erving Goffman. He argued that the frame is the rule by which people organize fragments of real life into their own experience and knowledge. But what is the frame like for news reports? Tuchman argues that the media frame is the principle for news content selection, something that editors and reporters cannot go without and persist in using in news production, and the set of code that deliberately emphasizes, interprets and presents news.[195] According to the framing theory, news reports are the production process of selecting and framing certain societal facts which are then subjectively reorganized.[196]

Thus, in news reporting on international crises, the media will, based on a certain frame, introduce the onset and progress of the incidents and the positions and behaviors of the main actors in crisis, and predict the direction of the crisis with the background information it collects. Unsurprisingly, *The New York Times'* frames on the Taiwan Strait Crisis also include the construction of the background of the crisis,

---

[194] James Shinn, "Clinton's Gunboat Diplomacy," *The New York Times,* March 24, 1996, A15.

[195] Gaye Tuchman and Barbara W. Tuchman, *Making News: A Study in the Construction of Reality* (United Kingdom: Free Press, 1978)

[196] Liu Xiaoying, *International Journalism: Ontology, Methods and Functions* (Beijing: China Radio and Television Press, 2010), 266.

the progress of the situation, the foreign policy decisions by China and the U.S., and their potential implications. Specifically, when it comes to the presentation and construction of the state of Sino-U.S. relations in the course of the crisis, and of U.S. policy towards China, the frames of relevant articles in *The Times* mainly include the following aspects:

First of all, regarding the cause and background of the Taiwan Strait Crisis: the direct cause is Lee Teng-hui's visit to the United States, against the background that the Sino-U.S. relations are fraught with divisions in various areas. Some articles have pointed out that the direct cause of the Taiwan Strait Crisis and the increased tension between China and the United States was when in 1995 the Clinton administration allowed Lee to visit the States to participate in an alumni gathering at Cornell University, which the Chinese government since criticized consistently.[197] In addition, China's piracy problem, human rights situation, and the manufacture and sale of weapons of mass destruction were also the reasons for the rapid deterioration of Sino-U.S. relations.[198]

Second, regarding the U.S. official attitude and responses to China's missile tests and military exercises: The White House, the Pentagon and Congress all condemned China's missile tests and military exercises, and Congress urged the Clinton administration to clearly express its position to protect Taiwan. Some articles mentioned that the White House and the Pentagon repeatedly condemned China for testing missiles near the island of Taiwan.[199] Secretary of State Warren Christopher called China's military exercises "reckless" and "irresponsible".[200] Other articles expressed dissatisfaction with the Clinton administration's attitude towards China upon the crisis, arguing that it should more directly and clearly express its concerns about the Strait situation, and

---

[197] Barbara Crossette, "U.N. Mission to Haiti is Reprieved," *The New York Times*, March 1, 1996, A8; Reuters, "China Announces Tests of Missiles near Taiwan," *The New York Times*, March 5, 1996, A10; Edward A. Gargan, "In Taiwan, Few Admit To Worries About China," *The New York Times*, March 17, 1996, A4.

[198] Elaine Sciolino, "White House Snubs China Over Military Maneuvers," *The New York Times*, March 23, 1996, A5.

[199] Patrick E. Tyler, "War Games Off Taiwan To Expand, Beijing Says," *The New York Times*, March 10, 1996, A12.

[200] Patrick E. Tyler, "China Warns U.S. to Stay Out of Taiwan Feud," *The New York Times*, March 12, 1996, A6.

immediately stop Beijing's blockade and aggression against Taiwan, so as to prevent the missile tests from developing into a more serious crisis.[201] Some Republican members in Congress believed that the government should straightforwardly admits its stance to defend Taiwan, with a pro-resolution passed in the House by 369 to 14 votes, which stated that the U.S. military should defend Taiwan from Chinese aggression, missile attacks or blockade.[202] The House Republican Policy Committee also issued a statement specifically opposing the Clinton administration's ambiguous position on whether it should defend Taiwan.[203]

Third, the explanation for the U.S. deployment of aircraft carrier fleets to the waters near Taiwan: to ensure the freedom of international navigation, and to emphasize to the Chinese mainland the U.S. stance to defend Taiwan from the threat of force. Some articles stated that President Clinton should immediately send a part of the Seventh Fleet to the Taiwan Strait to fulfill the United States' commitment to ensure freedom of international navigation;[204] saying even if China warns the U.S. warships to stay away from the Taiwan Strait, the United States still should insist on its claim of free passage on international waterways because freedom of navigation on international waters is to the United States what territorial integrity is to China, both of which are core interests that cannot be challenged.[205] Other articles stated that the U.S. dispatch of the aircraft carriers was to dampen China's threat to Taiwan and to show the U.S.'s determination to defend Taiwan,[206] and that it was to enforce U.S. legislation and commitments that cross-

---

[201] "The Bludgeoning of Taiwan," *The New York Times*, March 8, 1996, A30.

[202] Steven Erlanger, "Ambiguity' On Taiwan," *The New York Times,* March 12, 1996, A1; Steven Erlanger, "Christopher to Meet His Chinese Counterpart," *The New York Times*, March 20, 1996, A6.

[203] Patrick E. Tyler, "Beijing Steps Up Military Pressure on Taiwan Leader," *The New York Times,* March 7, 1996, A1.

[204] "The Bludgeoning of Taiwan," *The New York Times*, March 8, 1996, A30.

[205] Patrick E. Tyler, "TENSION IN TAIWAN: THE POLITICS; War Games Play Well for Taiwan's Leader," *The New York Times,* March 22, 1996, A1; William Safire, "New Mandate of Heaven," *The New York Times*, March 25, 1996, A15.

[206] Philip Shenon, "Gunboat Diplomacy, '96 Model," *The New York Times*, March 17, 1996, D1; Nicholas D. Kristof, "Off Taiwan, U.S. Sailors Are Unworried," *The New York Times*, March 19, 1996, A3.

Strait relations cannot be resolved by force as well as to emphasize Washington's position that the differences between China and Taiwan can only be resolved through peaceful means.[207]

Fourth, the evaluation of the Clinton administration's China policy: one that lacked clear goals, swinging between engagement and containment, therefore one that needed to be adjusted urgently. Some articles in *The Times* stated that although the Clinton administration has made a lot of efforts to improve Sino-U.S. relations, the onset and continuation of the Taiwan Strait Crisis showed that there still were problems with America's China policy.[208] They stated that Washington should adopt a more rational and stable foreign policy based on the public's expectations of policy outcomes, protect Asian allies from China's threats, encourage China to realize its ambitions in economic development, and present a path for the Chinese mainland and Taiwan to resolve issues through political dialogue.[209] Some other articles associated the Taiwan Strait Crisis with China's sale of weapons of mass destruction to Pakistan, stating that President Clinton should impose economic sanctions on China. However, U.S. officials countered that they would look at Sino-U.S. relations from a comprehensive perspective and prevent certain individual issues from affecting America's China policy.[210]

From the above analysis, we can conclude that the framing of China-U.S. relations and U.S. policy toward China in *The New York Times* articles on Taiwan Strait Crisis was mainly constructed with analyses of the causes of crisis, the attitude and response of the U.S. government,

---

[207] A. M. Rosenthal, "On My Mind: Indicting China's Terrorism," *The New York Times*, March 12, 1996, A21; Patrick E. Tyler, "China Warns to Keep Away From Taiwan Strait," *The New York Times*, March 18, 1996, A3.

[208] Patrick E. Tyler, "China Sends Taiwan A Dangerous Signal," *The New York Times,* March 10, 1996, D2; A. M. Rosenthal, "On My Mind: Indicting China's Terrorism," *The New York Times*, March 12, 1996, A21.

[209] "China's Military Power," *The New York Times,* March 17, 1996, D14; Thomas L. Friedman, "Bending the Mountains," *The New York Times,* March 17, 1996, D15; Thomas L. Friedman, "Help Wanted: Deal Makers," *The New York Times*, March 24, 1996, A15.

[210] Steven Erlanger, "Christopher to Meet His Chinese Counterpart," *The New York Times*, March 20, 1996, A6.

and the problems and ways of adjustment for U.S. policy toward China. This frame can be summarized as:

There were a series of conflicts between China and the United States on areas including intellectual property rights, human rights, and arms sales; When the Clinton administration allowed Lee Teng-hui to visit the United States, the conflicts were further intensified, causing the relations to severely deteriorate; The White House's dispatch of the aircraft carriers to the Taiwan Strait was a correct act, which showed the determination of the United States to defend Taiwan from the threat of Chinese military force and maintain the freedom of international navigation; The Clinton administration's attitude towards China was weak, and its China policy lacked clear goals, vacillating between engagement and containment, and was therefore unable to solve the series of problems in Sino-U.S. relations; The Clinton administration should make rational and comprehensive adjustments to its China policy based on the public's expectations of policy outcomes, guide China and Taiwan to resolve differences through peaceful dialogue, and guide China to better integrate into the international system.

CHAPTER 4

ANALYSIS OF *THE NEW YORK TIMES* COVERAGE ON CHINA-U.S. AIRCRAFT COLLISION INCIDENT OF 2001

SECTION 1. OVERVIEW OF CHINA-U.S. AIRCRAFT COLLISION INCIDENT OF 2001

Background of the Crisis

In every year of a U.S. presidential election, the American China policy will become a political football, used by candidates as a tool and bargaining chip to attack competitors and win the favor of voters. In 2000, the Bush campaign began to constantly attack the Clinton administration's statement that China was a strategic partner. The former instead argued that China and the U.S. are strategic competitors. On January 20, 2001, George W. Bush was formally sworn in as the 54th U.S. President. Upon assuming office, Bush called the leaders of more than 20 countries, but he deliberately ignored China and did not call Chinese President Jiang Zemin.[211] Globally, Bush began to adjust U.S. foreign policies, publicly stating that the Clinton administration's China policy was too weak, and should be tougher.

---

[211] Tao Wenzhao and He Xingqiang, *History of Sino-US Relations* (Beijing: China Social Sciences Press, 2009), 338-339.

In diplomacy, the status of strategic competitors means a certain degree of antagonism. Therefore, if this formulation were to be finally written into the Bush Administration's China policy, it would have a very negative impact on Sino-U.S. relations. In order to show its high priority to Sino-U.S. relations and promote the relationship's healthy and stable development, on March 19, the Chinese government sent Vice Premier Qian Qichen to the United States to communicate and enhance mutual understanding and trust. The visit achieved positive results. Since then, the United States no longer insisted on the term "strategic competitor", saying that China was not a strategic partner, nor was it an irreconcilable enemy, that China and the United States had common interests in many areas where cooperation could be carried out, and that it is was in the interest of the United States to develop friendly relations with China.[212] However, just as the tension between China and the United States eased, a sudden collision happened between the military planes of the two countries, and their relationship was put to the test again.

Since the founding of the People's Republic of China, the United States has never stopped its reconnaissance flights over the coast of China. In May 2000, the two countries reached a consensus to avoid dangerous military operations over the sea. That is, when military aircraft of the two countries meet in international airspace, the two sides should properly abide by the current international laws and customs, and give due consideration to the safety of navigation of both parties, in order to prevent dangerous approaches and avoid collision. However, despite this consensus, there are still profound differences between the two countries.[213]

As the United States' strategic adjustments in the 21st century elevated the Taiwan issue to a crucial status involving its national interests, in order to contain China's influence in Asia, Washington urgently needed to understand the growth of China's military power and the

---

[212] Wu Jianmin, *Cases of Foreign Affairs* (Beijing: China Renmin University Press, 2007), 324.

[213] Zhang Tuosheng, Michael D Swaine, and Danielle Cohen, *Managing Sino-American Crises: Case Studies and Analysis* (United States: Carnegie Endowment for International Peace, 2006)

adjustment of its military strategy in recent years. The reconnaissance collecting military intelligence in sensitive coastal areas of China came to be regarded by the Pentagon as one of the most effective means. Since the latter half of 2000, the reconnaissance activities of U.S. spy planes became more frequent and were getting increasingly closer to China's territorial waters. The Chinese government had repeatedly confronted the U.S. on this matter, demanding it to stop such activities. However, Washington turned a deaf ear to China and repeatedly sent reconnaissance aircraft to continue its activities.[214] China believed that such frequent reconnaissance flights over China were a serious threat to China's national security, while the U.S. was still only emphasizing technical issues, saying that Chinese surveillance aircraft were often too close to the U.S. aircraft, affecting flight safety. Such close sparring finally led to a collision incident. The collision seemed accidental, but it had deep roots which made the event inevitable.

Event Review

On the morning of April 1, 2001, a U.S. Navy EP-3 reconnaissance plane was spotted operating over the southeastern waters of China's Hainan Island. China immediately ordered two J-8 fighter jets to take off and track the U.S. spy plane. At 9:07 a.m., 104 kilometers southeast of Hainan Island, when the Chinese plane was flying normally, the U.S. plane suddenly turned to the Chinese jet, in violation of regulations. The EP-3's nose and left wing collided with the J-8, causing the Chinese plane to crash. The pilot Wang Wei parachuted but went missing. After that, the damaged U.S. plane, with twenty-four people on board, entered into China's sovereign airspace without permission, and landed at Lingshui Airport on Hainan Island at 9:33 a.m. After the incident, China's Ministry of Foreign Affairs spokesperson Zhu Bangzao made an address stating that the responsibility for this incident rested solely with the United States, and that China lodged solemn representations and protests with the United States on this issue.

---

[214] Tang Jiaxuan, *Strong Rain, Gentle Winds* (Beijing: World Knowledge Press, 2009), 267, 273.

At 3 p.m. that day, six hours after the collision incident, the U.S. Pacific Command took the lead and published a brief statement on its official website announcing the incident, stating that the Chinese government should respect the integrity of the aircraft, the health and safety of the crew, and facilitate the immediate return of the aircraft and crew to the United States.[215] In the statement, there was no mention of the Chinese plane's damage and crash in the collision and the missing Chinese pilot.

Regarding the course of the incident, the U.S. Navy's declassified investigative report recorded this: The Chinese pilot flew close to the U.S. aircraft three times. The first time the two planes were about 10 feet apart, the Chinese pilot paid a military salute to the U.S. aircraft and left immediately; in the second approach, the two planes were at the same altitude and only 5 feet apart. The Chinese pilot made a forward gesture to the crew of the U.S. plane and then left again; when the Chinese pilot flew to EP-3 for the last time, due to the high speed, it missed the opportunity to approach the U.S. plane. When Wang tried to raise its nose to reduce the speed, the vertical tail of the Chinese plane collided with the fuselage of the EP-3 and its No. 1 propeller. The Chinese J-8 was broken into two halves while the EP-3 was severely damaged.[216]

On the night of the incident, Minister of Foreign Affairs Zhou Wenzhong, as ordered by the central government, urgently summoned the U.S. Ambassador to China Joseph Prueher. Zhou pointed out that the Chinese military aircraft's tracking and monitoring of U.S. military reconnaissance aircraft along the coast of China was a legitimate flight activity, which was in line with international practice. Zhou emphasized that the responsibility for the incident rested entirely on the U.S. side. Prueher said he could not agree with China's statement on the responsibility for the incident, and requested to meet with the American

---

[215] US Pacific Command, http://www.pacom.mil/imagery/archive/0103photos/index4.shtml.

[216] Zhang Zhaozhong, "What Actually had Happened on the Day of the Sino-American Plane Collision over the South China Sea," Sina Military, http://mil.news.sina.com.cn/china/2016-04-02/doc-ifxqxcnr5208661.shtml.

crew as soon as possible and inspect the aircraft.[217] The United States argued that China should release the personnel as soon as possible and return the plane to the U.S. Washington even requested that Chinese personnel be prohibited from boarding the U.S. plane for inspection.

After the incident, President Bush did not communicate directly with President Jiang through the Sino-U.S. heads of state hotline, nor did he send a special envoy to respond to the crisis. Instead, he frequently presented a tough posture in front of the media and insisted on communicating with China at the working level.[218] On April 2 and 3, Bush delivered two speeches in a row, stating that the United States had already given China time to do what he calls the right thing, and that it was time that China return the plane and the crew. At the same time, the U.S. Navy sent three destroyers to cruise near Hainan Island in the name of monitoring the development of the situation and linger in the South China Sea region.[219]

The U.S. simply expressed "regret" over the incident and its willingness to assist China in the search and rescue of the missing pilot. China insisted that the U.S. should apologize, but the U.S. Secretary of State Colin Powell refused. As Bush kept asking for the return of the U.S. crew, the handling of the matter came to a stalemate. On April 4, before his trip to Latin America, Jiang Zemin instructed the Ministry of Foreign Affairs that the solution to the problem should be "apology-release", and once again publicly reiterated the position of asking the U.S. to apologize. At 5:30 p.m. that day, Foreign Minister Tang Jiaxuan summoned Prueher, and emphasized that the essence of the incident was not a purely technical dispute, but a serious political and diplomatic issue between China and the United States. China's attitude towards the actions of the United States is "Firstly, opposed; secondly, not afraid."

Having perceived such important signals from the Chinese government, the U.S. attitude changed and became pragmatic. The

[217] Xiong Zhiyong et al, *Lecture Notes on Sino-US Relations* (Beijing: World Knowledge Press, 2015), 294.

[218] Robert Sutter, "Grading Bush's China Policy," *Pac Net Newsletter*, no. 10, March 8, 2002.

[219] Tang Jiaxuan, *Strong Rain, Gentle Winds* (Beijing: World Knowledge Press, 2009), 270.

two sides communicated many times on the wording of an "apology" and the release of the plane crew. At 5:30 pm on April 11th, on behalf of the U.S. government, Prueher presented to Chinese Foreign Minister Tang Jiaxuan a letter of apology from the U.S. to China for the U.S. reconnaissance plane crashing into and destroying a Chinese military plane. This is the sixth draft that the U.S. had to revise at the request of China. The letter stated that "Both President Bush and Secretary of State Powell have expressed their sincere regret over your missing pilot and aircraft. Please convey to the Chinese people and to the family of pilot Wang Wei that we are very sorry for their loss."[220] After accepting the letter, Tang Jiaxuan informed Prueher that, given that the U.S. government has apologized to the Chinese people, out of humanitarian considerations, the Chinese government decided to allow the U.S. crew to leave China after completing the necessary procedures. At 7:30 a.m. on April 12, twenty-four American crew members returned home from the Haikou Meilan Airport on a commercial aircraft chartered by the United States.

After that, China and the United States continued to negotiate on how to deal with the EP-3 plane. The Chinese government publicly announced its position that due to the nature of the U.S. plane—a reconnaissance aircraft—China would not allow it to fly back to the United States. On May 24, the spokesperson of the Chinese Ministry of Foreign Affairs announced that China had accepted the U.S. proposal to allow the U.S. to disassemble the EP-3 and transport it back to the U.S. on a chartered aircraft. On June 7, Pentagon officials stated that the U.S. planned to disassemble the EP-3 into four parts and lease an Antonov-124 commercial long-range heavy transport aircraft from a Russian airline to complete the return. On June 13, the United States began the disassembly and transshipment of the EP-3; on July 3, the components of EP-3 were transported out of China by two transport planes and arrived in Hawaii at 12:09 am EDT on July 4th.[221] At this point, the collision incident finally came to an end.

---

[220] Tang Jiaxuan, *Strong Rain, Gentle Winds* (Beijing: World Knowledge Press, 2009), 279-281.
[221] Wu Jianmin, *Cases of Foreign Affairs* (Beijing: China Renmin University Press, 2007), 331-332.

On July 5, Jiang spoke with Bush on an appointed phone call. Bush said that the relationship between the United States and China was of vital importance, that the two countries could work together on many international issues, and that he believed that the two countries could find a wide range of areas of cooperation. In early July, China decided to resume the routine visits of U.S. naval ships to Hong Kong. At the end of July, U.S. Secretary of State Powell visited Beijing after attending the Foreign Ministers' Meeting of the ASEAN Regional Forum in Hanoi, thus becoming the highest-level official visiting China since Bush took office. From that point, Sino-U.S. relations gradually recovered.

Decision-Making in Foreign Affairs

From the sudden onset of the plane collision to the conclusion of its handling, China and the United States differed in goals of decision-making, management methods, and handling procedures of the crisis. Yet although there were differences, both showed a certain degree of restraint. The entire process of the crisis can be roughly divided into two stages: from April 1st to April 12th was the first stage, beginning with the collision and ending with the release of the U.S. crew members. During this stage, the two sides fought over the issue of accident liability. The second stage was from April 12th to July, ending with the U.S. reconnaissance plane returning to the U.S. At this phase, China and the United States disputed over the return method of the spy plane. Judging from the final result, the crisis was handled and resolved relatively peacefully. Throughout the course of the incident, there were significant differences in the goals, performance, and internal mechanisms in decision-making by the two governments.

First stage: from collision to release of U.S. crew

Regarding the cause of the incident, China believed that the sudden turn of the U.S. reconnaissance plane was the direct cause of the collision, and that the U.S. side must bear full responsibility. Beijing argued that although on the surface it looked like a serious emergency case, the root cause was in the long-term flight reconnaissance on China's coastal areas by the U.S. military; after the incident, the damaged U.S. plane illegally entered China without permission and landed at Hainan Lingshui Airport; this was a serious violation of China's sovereignty and territory. The U.S., for its part, insisted that its aircraft was performing a routine reconnaissance mission over the high seas and that it was a normal flight. Washington argued that the collision was caused by the Chinese aircraft being too close to the U.S. aircraft so that it lost control, and that the U.S. military plane had to make an emergency landing at Hainan Airport when it was severely damaged—it issued 15 distress signals in advance, therefore this had not constituted an infringement of China's sovereignty and territory.

The policymakers of the two countries reacted differently to the incident: the Chinese government decided to separate the crew from the plane, and immediately summoned the staff of the U.S. Embassy in China. Chinese ambassador to the U.S. Yang Jiechi and other diplomats initiated meetings with U.S. officials twice, while President Jiang Zemin made several statements during state visits to foreign countries to express China's position. As for the U.S., after the collision, President George W. Bush convened an emergency meeting in the White House to discuss strategies and also made two speeches. He believed that the U.S. was not at fault and demanded that China return the crew and the plane. It was only after the staff of the U.S. Embassy in China visited the detained flight crew that Bush expressed regret at the disappearance of China's pilot Wang Wei after the collision. Bush also asked U.S. officials not to make irresponsible remarks on this matter.

In the early stage of the crisis, both China and the United States made clear the common goal of their decision-making—that is—to strive to safeguard bilateral relations and prevent Sino-U.S. relations from being harmed. Therefore, the two sides began to communicate and negotiate gradually. However, due to differences in national interests and values, the two countries also differed in their specific goals. The Chinese people have had a humiliating history of being a semi-colony and thus have a strong sense of collective consciousness and national honor. Similar incidents can easily arouse a sense of national victimhood and nationalist sentiments in China. Therefore, asking the U.S. to apologize became the core issue at this stage. In the U.S. political culture, freedom, democracy, and human rights are extremely important values. As a result, the U.S. was more concerned about the safety and return of the twenty-four crew members onboard, and only expressed "regret" to the Chinese side on the disappearance of pilot Wang Wei.

In terms of decision-making mechanism, China's process was specifically: The Party at the core, decision-making at the high level, enforcement by the Ministry of Foreign Affairs, and cooperation by other departments. The decision-making mechanism of the United States is controlled by the President, led by the State Department, coordinated by Congress, participated in by the military, and through cooperation of other departments. [222] Because of such differences, the channels through which China and the United States released information also showed different characteristics. China's official voice mainly came from the Ministry of Foreign Affairs and the country's main leaders, with a unified voice to the outside world and the internal debates and reconciliations of various departments hidden. In the United States, it was the military that first revealed the news, not the White House and the State Department. In the course of negotiations between the two sides, there were different voices from the U.S. government: the military kept making tough remarks; Congress linked the incident to human rights issues and applied pressure through proposals.

Second stage: handling the return of the U.S. reconnaissance plane

Regarding the issue of the return of the U.S. EP-3 reconnaissance aircraft, the main point of divergence between China and the United States lay in whether China could board and inspect the aircraft and how to return it. The U.S. insisted that the military aircraft was property of the U.S. government and enjoyed sovereign immunity, so China could not board or inspect it. Washington requested that the aircraft fly back to the United States, in order to end the whole crisis. China argued that

[222] Chu Yingchun, "On the Similarities and Differences of Sino-US Decision-Making in Foreign Affairs: Taking the Airplane Collision Incident as an Example," *China's Extracurricular Education (Theories),* no. 2 (2007): 15-16.

according to the relevant provisions of international aviation law, foreign military aircraft landing on the territory of another country without consent and approval cannot enjoy sovereign immunity privileges; the unauthorized landing of U.S. military aircraft at a Chinese airport had seriously violated China's sovereignty, and to allow it to flying away by itself would further damage China's sovereignty and dignity, which China would by no means allow.

During the negotiating process, on the Chinese side, the foreign affairs department mainly handled the incident and engaged in talks. A delegation was sent, headed by Lu Shumin, Director-General of the Department of North American and Oceanian Affairs of the Ministry of Foreign Affairs and other officials of the Ministry of Foreign Affairs as negotiators, thus not highlighting military participation. The U.S. negotiation team, on the other hand, was led by the military. It was headed by the Acting Defense Undersecretary for Policy Peter Verga, with main team members from the Department of Defense and the U.S. Pacific Command. The U.S. State Department only sent two officials to the delegation.[223]

Throughout the negotiation process, China always adhered to the same principles and policy goals, namely: the U.S. government should apologize to the Chinese people and the U.S. military aircraft must be dismantled before being shipped back to the United States. On the other hand, the United States went back and forth in its attitude and policies. After China received a letter of apology and released the crew, the U.S. attitude changed again. Bush issued a statement stating that it was not in line with the relationship both sides had hoped to be when China decided to not let the crew return until after eleven days after the collision.[224] The United States threatened that delaying the return of the U.S. plane would affect Sino-U.S. relations, and repeatedly asked for the plane to be fixed and fly away. Meanwhile, Washington also linked the incident with other issues in Sino-U.S. relations. The Chinese side instead emphasized that given the nature of the U.S. plane, how it

---

[223] Tang Jiaxuan, *Strong Rain, Gentle Winds* (Beijing: World Knowledge Press, 2009), 284.

[224] Ding Xiaowen, "Safeguarding National Interests in Crisis—A Study on China's Handling of Sino-US Diplomatic Crises" (PhD diss., Peking University, 2005), 158.

would be returned was not only a technical issue, but also a political and diplomatic issue of symbolic significance.

Throughout the crisis handling process, China followed the principles of being reasonable, productive, and restrained. China's handling methods were flexible and boldly principled. After much deliberation, the U.S. had to make substantial concessions, proposing a plan to dismantle the aircraft before taking it away. The collision incident was thus finally resolved.

SECTION 2 CONTENT ANALYSIS OF *THE NEW YORK TIMES* COVERAGE ON THE CHINA-U.S. PLANE COLLISION INCIDENT OF 2001

Although the U.S. media is not controlled by the government, it is difficult to avoid the influence of national interests and ideology when reporting international news. From April to July 2001, the collision of Chinese and U.S. military planes over the South China Sea triggered a crisis in the two countries' political, diplomatic, and military relations. During the crisis, the U.S. media carried out high-density coverage from various angles, but were also full of voices including requests for the government to recall the U.S. ambassador to China, terminating military exchanges, opposing China's hosting of the 2008 Olympic Games and its accession to the WTO, and aligning the incident with the extension of China's most-favored-nation status and Washington's arms sales to Taiwan.[225] "The U.S. media cooperated with the government in creating a favorable public opinion environment through various forms such as editorials, column articles, interviews, commentaries, and opinion polls. When the government's stance was tough, the media denied the reality in every possible way and helped shirk the U.S.'s responsibility; when the White House accused China, the media rallied to follow up."[226]

The biased tendencies in American media coverage directly

---

[225] Yang Jiemian, *Broadening of International Crises and China-US Joint Responses* (Beijing: Current Affairs Press, 2010), 115.

[226] China Institute of Contemporary International Relations, *Introduction to International Crisis Management* (Beijing: Current Affairs Press, 2003), 261-202.

contributed to the misunderstanding and misjudgment of the American public on the incident, and to a large extent damaged an adequate and rational public opinion atmosphere needed to resolve the crisis; Congress quickly passed a series of anti-China motions; and the government's crisis decision-making process was also affected. This phenomenon has attracted the attention of many Chinese scholars. They studied the U.S. media coverage during the crisis from the perspectives of crisis management and international communication, and discussed the impact of media coverage on government crisis management and decision-making processes during Sino-U.S. relations crises. The research in this section analyzes the content and frames of relevant articles (including commentaries and column articles) on the collision incident in *The New York Times*, and discusses how the newspaper's presented Washington's foreign affairs decision-making and the status quo and direction of the Sino-U.S. relations during the crisis.

Volume and Lengths of Articles

Volume of articles

In the "New York Times" subsection in the ProQuest database, the author searched "China" for *The Times* articles from April to July 2001, a timeframe marking the beginning and end of the Plane Collision Incident. A total of 309 articles were found involving "China". When classified according to the subject, 94 articles were found on the China-U.S. aircraft accident, accounting for 30% of the total number of China-related articles in *The New York Times* in the same period. In other words, between April and July 2001, about one out of every 3.3 China-related articles in *The Times* was about the South China Sea collision incident. (see fig. 4.1)

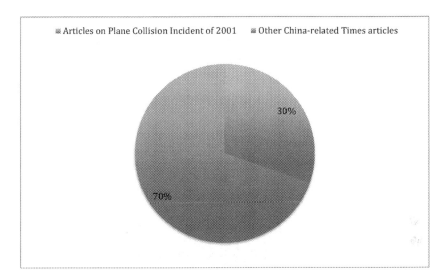

Figure 4.1 Number of articles on China-U.S. Plane Collision Incident of 2001 vs. other China-related articles in *The New York Times* between April and July 2001.

Next, the author counted the number of articles by month on the collision incident within this time frame. It turned out that April had 88 articles, the largest monthly number; that was on average about 3 articles per day. The later months saw a decline in articles about the incident: 5 in May and 1 in June. And beginning July, *The New York Times* stopped paying attention to the incident, publishing zero articles. (see table 4.1)

Month	April	May	June	July
Number of articles	88	5	1	0
Sum	94			

Table 4.1 Monthly number of articles on China-U.S. Plane Collision Incident of 2001 in *The New York Times*.

As for April, the month with the largest number of articles, the days with 2 or more articles per day only lasted from April 2 to 16, for a total of 15 days. Therefore, judging from the distribution of the volume of articles, it can be seen that the sudden outset of the incident was the period that *The New York Times* paid the most attention to. Since April 12 the twenty-four crew members of the U.S. reconnaissance planes were released from China to go back to the United States, the volume of articles began decreasing. The high sensitivity, large-scale coverage, and in-depth mining of crisis events are due to the nature of the media who favors bad news.[227] After the Chinese government released the crew and the crisis suspended, the number of relevant articles in *The New York Times* went down dramatically, reflecting the media'

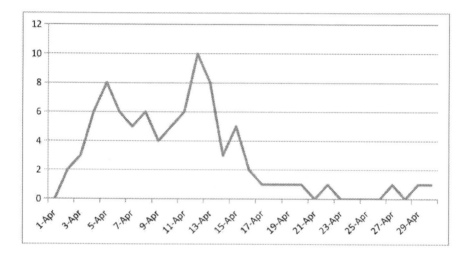

s characteristic of loving the new and detesting the old. (See fig. 4.2)

Figure 4.2 Daily number of articles (April, 2001) on the China-U.S. Plane Collision Incident in *The New York Times*.

Article lengths

Statistical analysis on the volume of relevant articles can reveal how the intensity of *The Times* coverage changed during the different stages of the onset, development, and handling of the Sino-U.S. Plane Collision

---

[227] Hu Baijing, *Crisis Communication Management* (Beijing: Renmin University Press, 2014), 135.

Incident. Next, the author looks at the length of relevant articles during the crisis. Among the 94 articles on the Plane Collision Incident in *The New York Times* from April to July 2001, most were medium and long articles: there were a total of 59 articles of 500-1200 words, accounting for 63%; there were a total of 26 long articles of more than 1200 words; and the number of short articles under 500 words is the fewest: only 9 articles. (see table 4.2)

Month / Word count	April	May	June	July	Sum
0-200	0	0	0	0	0
200-500	7	2	0	0	9
500-800	30	2	0	0	32
800-1200	26	1	0	0	27
1200+	25	0	1	0	26
Sum	88	5	1	0	94

Table 4.2 Length of articles on the China-U.S. Plane Collision Incident of 2001 in *The New York Times.*

Although the crisis in Sino-U.S. relations caused by the Plane Collision Incident lasted from April all the way through July 2001, the most tense phase of the relationship and the fiercest confrontation between the two sides occurred at the sudden outbreak of the crisis— from April 1 to 13—beginning with the collision until the return of the twenty-four crew members to the United States. This period also saw the most concentrated numbers of *Times* articles: from April 2 to April 13 (due to time difference and the time it took from the newspaper's editing to its publication, the dates in this analysis are one day after the event date), there were 70 articles, an average of 6 per day. In this period of time, the number of China-related articles by *The New York Times* was 85, which means that the aircraft collision incident accounted for 82% of them, and it often occurred that all China-related articles by *The New York Times* issued on the same day were reports on the situation of the Plane Collision Incident. In terms of the distribution of the number of articles, after the crew arrived at the Whidbey Island Naval Base in the United States, *The New York Times* paid close attention to the incident until April 16. In order to make the research more pertinent and maneuverable, and to consider the completeness of the analysis, the author will conduct a content analysis of 80 articles on the China-U.S. Plane Collision Incident in *The New York Times* from April 2 to 16, 2001, as well as a frame analysis, and interpretation of the way *The New York Times* presented the crisis.

Content and Frames

Article content

The Sino-U.S. aircraft collision incident over the South China Sea was the most serious military crisis between China and the United States since U.S. military planes attacked the Chinese Embassy in Belgrade in May 1999 ("the bombing incident"). The extent of the U.S. media's attention to this matter is shown by the fact that *The New York Times* had published 80 prevalent articles within 15 days of the incident. Many Chinese scholars believed that the U.S. media had many prejudices when dealing with news, reports and commentaries related to China when looking at relevant coverage from the beginning and end of the crisis; though most U.S. journalists did not intentionally produce unfairness, they did engage in the demonization of China in actuality, even if not on purpose.[228]

This section uses 80 reports and commentaries in *The New York Times* on the Sino-U.S. Plane Collision Incident from April 2 to 16, 2001 as the content analysis. In order to present the research process fully and clearly, and to ensure a scientific, accurate and rigorous analysis, the author classifies and presents in a detailed table form the date, title, type, length, tendency, news source, angle and other aspects of each of the 80 articles based on the intensive reading of the articles. It should be noted that when analyzing the content of *The Times* articles on the Taiwan Strait Crisis, the "main content" category in the table is replaced

---

[228] Li Xiguang and Zhao Xinshu, *The Power of The Media* (Guangzhou: Nanfang Daily Press, 2002), 66-73.

by "angle" in the analysis of the collision crisis. Because the Taiwan Strait Crisis lasted for a long time, the events and subjects involved were more complicated, and the content the media paid attention to was more diverse; in contrast, the content that the media focused on with regards to the collision incident was relatively unitary and concentrated, so analyzing the "angle" of the coverage is more reasonable and efficacious. (see table 4.3)

Dates and volume. During the 15 days from April 2 to 16, 2001, *The New York Times* published a total of 80 reports (including commentaries) on the Plane Collision Incident and the resultant crisis in Sino-U.S. relations, averaging 5.3 articles per day. (see fig. 4.2 for the distribution of the numbers). There were two days when less than 3 articles were published: April 2, the second day after the collision and April 16, four days after the U.S. crew arrived at the U.S. Naval base (after that relevant *Times* coverage reduced dramatically). The largest number of articles was seen on April 12, with a total of 10 published; in addition, April 5 and April 13 saw relatively big numbers, with each day having 8 articles.

Looking at the crisis management processes of China and the United States after the collision: President Bush stated in two consecutive public speeches on April 2 and 3 that the United States had given China time to do what he called the right thing, and demanded the return of the U.S. crew and the plane in its entirety as soon as possible. This posture aroused strong dissatisfaction on the part of China. From April 4th to 6th, after President Jiang gave the instruction to resolve the issue by way of "apology-release", Foreign Minister Tang Jiaxuan clearly stated China's position to U.S. ambassador to China Joseph Prueher, demanding the U.S. take full responsibility for the incident and that if the U.S. wants China to release the crew, the U.S. must first apologize.[229] Thus, Beijing and Washington launched a bout of fierce confrontation. The volume of articles in *The New York Times* on this also peaked in these three days, releasing 20 articles (commentaries included), of which 8 were about China's request for an apology from the United States, and how the United States reacted.

On April 12, the day when twenty-four U.S. crew members left

---

[229] Tang Jiaxuan, "Recalling the 'Aircraft Collision Incident' over the South China Sea in 2001 (Part 1)," *Party Literature*, no. 5 (2009): 15-23.

Haikou Meilan Airport on a commercial aircraft chartered by the United States, the volume of relevant articles in *The New York Times* peaked. On the 12th and 13th there were 18 articles, 7 of which focused on the crew, while 6 articles analyzed or evaluated the Bush administration's performance in this crisis of relations between the two countries.

Based on the above analysis of the dates and volume distribution of the relevant articles of *The New York Times*, it can be seen that during the period from the collision to the release of the U.S. crew, *The New York Times* paid the most attention to the detention, release and return of the crew, as well as the positions and postures of the Chinese and American governments and the public confrontation between the two sides in diplomacy.

Types and lengths. The sample studied in this section are 80 reports and commentaries of *The New York Times* on the Sino-U.S. Plane Collision Incident and the resultant Sino-U.S. relations crisis from April 2 to 16, 2001. The types of articles are concentrated in four kinds: news story, in-depth analysis, event feature story and commentary. In addition, there are 5 short news articles and 1 personal interview. What needs special explanation here is that in this section of the study, presidential speeches and diplomatic letters published in full text in *The New York Times* are also classified as "short news articles".

Of the 80 articles, the number of medium-to-long length news stories is the largest. There is also a considerable number of medium-to-long length in-depth analysis articles, event feature stories, and commentaries. The number of short news articles is relatively small, and there is only one personal interview. There are 30 news stories, accounting 37.5%; There 15 in-depth analysis articles, and 15 commentaries, each accounting for 18.75%; There are 14 even feature stories, accounting for 17.5%. (see table 4.4)

Length (Word count)	Short news article	News story	In-depth analysis	Event feature story	Personal interview	Commentary
0-200	0	0	0	0	0	0
200-500	4	2	0	0	0	0
500-800	1	6	2	7	1	12

800-1200	0	9	5	6	0	2
1200+	0	13	8	1	0	1
Total number of articles	5	30	15	14	1	15

Table 4.4 Types and lengths of *The New York Times* articles from April 2 to 16, 2001 on the China-U.S. Plane Collision Incident.

At the stage beginning with the collision and ending with the release of the U.S. crew, *The New York Times* mainly used news stories to produce in-depth coverage of the core events, key turning points, and crucial clues that led to each escalation point or easing of the crisis: long-length stories that are detailed and with various perspectives, with seldom use of short news articles that were more time-sensitive. For example, after the collision, the article "China's Shadowing Had Annoyed U.S." analyzed and introduced the incident on April 2; While articles including "Bush Is Demanding a 'Prompt' Return of Plane and Crew" on April 3, "Beijing Steps up Its War of Words Over Air Collision" on April 5, and "Bush and Jiang Exchange Drafts Of a Letter Stating U.S. Regrets" on April 7, reported on the progress of the incident, as well as the attitudes and positions of the two countries. Regarding the causes of the collision, the impact of the crisis on Sino-U.S. relations, and the performance of the Bush administration responding to the crisis, articles of in-depth analysis and commentaries were utilized. These include the in-depth analysis articles of "U.S. Plane in China After It Collides with Chinese Jet" on April 2 and "Now for Bush, a Novelty: Having to Face Novelty" on April 5, the April 12 commentary "Ending the Spy Plane Deadlock", and the April 13 commentary "One Nation, 3 Lessons".

Sources. The author has mentioned in Chapter 3 that the selection and presentation of news sources can to a certain extent reflect the reporter's preferences and attitudes. The author statistically analyzed the sources of 80 articles on the Sino-U.S. Plane Collision Incident in *The New York Times* from April 2 to April 16, 2001. Sources are categorized into whether the source is named or anonymous, and whether it is a direct or indirect citation. In doing this *The Times'* preference of sources in the coverage of this crisis can be understood—that is, what types of departments, organizations, or individuals were chosen as sources and how they were cited and how often they appeared in different articles. Regarding the methodology of sorting news sources, the author has explained in detail in the previous chapter, but will emphasize here the counting method of the same source that appears multiple times in the same article:

The same source that appears multiple times in the same article is counted only once. The same source that appears in different articles is counted according to the number of articles that contain such source. And if the same source appears multiple times in a same article involves both direct and indirect quotations, only direct quotations are counted. The resultant numbers are as follows. (see table 4.5)

Type of citation	Direct citation		Indirect citation		Official statements or reports from other media	Sum	Percentage
Type of source	Named	Anonymous	Named	Anonymous			
Chinese government and officials	10	2	5	5	5	27	6.3%
American government and officials	68	53	4	42	29	196	46%
Other countries' governments and officials	-	1	-	-	1	2	0.5%
Chinese media	-	2	-	1	23	26	6%
American media	3	-	-	-	6	9	2.1%
Other countries' media	-	-	-	-	4	4	1%
Chinese experts or scholars	4	5	-	5	-	14	3.3%
American experts or scholars	36	2	10	8	-	56	13.1%
Other countries' experts or scholars	1	-	-	1	-	2	0.5%

Members of Chinese private organizations or enterprises	-	-	-	2	-	2	0.5%
Members of American private organizations or enterprises	9	1	-	3	-	13	3%
Members of international organizations	5	-	1	1	-	7	1.6%
Members of American military (including the EP-3 crew)	14	3	1	1	-	19	4.5%
Members of Chinese military	-	-	-	1	-	1	0.2%
Ordinary Chinese citizens	20	12	-	1	-	33	7.7%
Ordinary American citizens	14	-	-	-	-	14	3.3%
Ordinary citizens of other countries	-	1	-	-	-	1	0.2%
Other sources	-	-	-	1	-	1	0.2%
Sum	184	82	21	72	68	427	100%

Table 4.5 Sources of *The New York Times* coverage (April 2 to 16, 2001) on the China-U.S. Plane Collision Incident.

The table shows that that the types of sources cited in *The New York Times* on the Sino-U.S. Plane Collision Incident were rich and diverse, including not only governments, militaries, experts, scholars, enterprises, ordinary people, and media organizations from China, the United States, and other countries, but also experts and members from international organizations and institutions. Regarding the classification of sources, the following special circumstances need to be explained: First, the author regards government officials who have left their posts as "experts or scholars", while researchers working in government departments, members of think tanks, and experts are classified as "governments and officials".

Secondly, in view of the official nature of the Chinese and American ministries of defense, navies, and air forces, they are collectively classified as "governments and officials", too. Third, the official statements, documents, leaders' speeches, letters, recordings and other materials from the Chinese and American governments and militaries that are published or partially quoted in *The Times* articles, as well as information and news content cited from other media, because they are not the original reporting of *The New York Times*, in order to clearly distinguish them from other sources, are separately listed as "Official statements or reports from other media" in the table. However, reporters or editors of other media organizations interviewed by *The New York Times* are not specially classified.

In terms of the number of citations, in the articles on the Sino-U.S. Plane Collision Incident, *The New York Times'* original sources accounted for an absolute majority of 84%, with second-hand sources accounting for only 16%. Among all types of sources, *The New York Times* cited a total of 307 times from United States sources, accounting for nearly 72% of the total. The most cited are authoritative information from the U.S. government, military, and senior officials—196 times, accounting for 46%, much higher than all other types of sources. When going through each of the articles in this sample, the author did find that in the process of covering the collision incident, *The New York Times*, regardless of its subjective intent, was in many times replaying the voices of the U.S. government and military, thus in reality acting as their microphone. The second most cited source type (13.1%) is "American experts and scholars", mainly on their analysis of the background, cause and process of the crisis, evaluation and analysis on the performance of the Bush administration in response to the crisis, as well as the analysis of the possible impact on and direction of Sino-U.S. relations.

The collision incident triggered an international political crisis between China and the United States. The positions, attitudes, evidence and materials available to the governments of the two countries and their respective decision-making processes are all crucial to promoting the easing and resolution of the crisis. However, compared with information sourced from the U.S. government and military, sources from the Chinese government and officials only accounted for 6.3%, which is even lower than from the ordinary Chinese people. The citation rate of Chinese experts or scholars is only 3.3%, which is a quarter of that of American experts or scholars. *The New York Times* also paid some attention to the attitudes of the Chinese public, especially their voices on the Internet, which mainly reflected their protests and nationalist sentiments. However, in terms of citations of other media coverage, *The New York Times* cited more Chinese media reports (6%) than other American organizations (2.1%).

Whether in covering the Taiwan Strait Crisis in March 1996 or the Sino-U.S. Plane Collision Incident in 2001, besides China and the U.S., *The New York Times* also used sources from governments, experts, media, and ordinary people in other countries, as well as international organizations and institutions. Such citations were less frequent than those of China and the United States, but they still to some extent reflected the international public's stance and attitude towards these two Sino-U.S. crises.

In terms of how sources were cited, the most frequently used were named and anonymous direct citations: 184 and 82 times respectively, in combination comprising 62%. As for indirect citations, the number of anonymous citations is 3.4 times that of named ones. For sources from the Chinese government and officials, *The New York Times* used more named citations; while there were more sources from the U.S. government and officials being anonymous. This is closely related to the habit of Washington's core political circles in dealing with the media: at press briefings at the White House, one of the most repeated phrases by the spokesperson are probably "off the record"; many senior officials, do not speak with reporters without anonymity. Former U.S. Secretary of State Henry Kissinger is the most typical example; In a report on Kissinger's visit to a foreign country, the reporter, in order to vent his dissatisfaction, described Kissinger, without naming him, as a senior government official with curly hair, horny framed glasses, and a German accent.[230]

Among the 80 articles on the collision incident, there are 3 commentaries from independent writers, one editorial reprinted from *The Weekly Standard*, and a personal interview. The 3 independent contributors' commentaries were: "No Easy Way Forward With China"

---

[230] Lin Yan, "American Journalists and Anonymous Sources," *International Journalism*, no. 5 (2000): 39-43.

written by David Shambaugh, Director of the China Policy Program in the Elliott School of International Affairs at George Washington University, and a senior fellow at The Brookings Institution, analyzing the impact of the collision incident on Sino-U.S. relations; "The Dangers of Spy Planes" rethinking U.S. reconnaissance behaviors since the end of the Cold War, written by James Bamford, author of the book *Body of Secrets: Anatomy of the Ultra-Secret National Security Agency*; and "China Policy, Without Regrets" written by The Brookings Institution researcher Bates Gill, advising on how the U.S. government should adjust its China policy after the crash. The one personal interview was with Nicholas R. Lardy, expert on China issues and the interim director of Foreign Policy Studies at The Brookings Institution; Lardy analyzed the possible impact of the bilateral crisis on American companies in China.

Similar to the citations of *The New York Times*' articles on the Taiwan Strait Crisis in March 1996, *The Times* preferred elites for covering the collision incident. That is, sources of government officials, military leaders, experts/scholars, and the news media. It seems that the closer the source is to the government politically, the more credible it is for the media.[231] The interactive relationship between reporters and sources plays an important role in the agenda-setting process of media. Weaver even argues that it is not reporters who are setting news agendas, but it is sources wanting to structure information and deliver to the public who play a fundamental agenda-setting role.[232] Therefore, when analyzing the selection and use of sources, it is not just enough to look at how media constructs agenda issues, but also whose information the reports are passing on to the public. Only in this way can we analyze more clearly the power relations in the communicating of a certain agenda. In its coverage on Sino-U.S. crisis events, *The New York Times*, which has always regarded objectivity and fairness as its foundation, undoubtedly have chosen the side of favoring U.S. national interests, in its process of pursuing the truth and disseminating facts.

---

[231] Herbert J Gans, *Deciding What's News: A Study of CBS Evening News, NBC Nightly News, Newsweek, and Time* (United Kingdom: Vintage Books, 1980), 80.
[232] David Weaver and Swanzy Nimley Elliott, "Who Sets the Agenda for the Media? A Study of Local Agenda-Building," *Journalism Quarterly* 62, no. 1 (March 1985): 87–94.

Tendency. Analysis of the tendency of *The New York Times* coverage on the collision incident is a rather complicated task. This study has defined tendencies as the attitudes directly or indirectly reflected in the content of the coverage on the Chinese government's foreign affairs stance, decision-making, and behaviors in a crisis. When it comes to a specific report however, although some lines express negative sentiments towards the Chinese government, the article as a whole is neutral; some other reports, while appearing to be neutral, actually imply a negative attitude toward the Chinese government. Therefore, when analyzing each article in detail, not only a sharp eye is required, but also a holistic grasp and judgment. It is based on this principle that the author conducted the tendency analysis of the 80 *Times* articles (from April 2 to April 16, 2001) on the collision incident. Although subjectivity and limitations cannot be got entirely rid of in this independent work, the author tried her best to ensure that the results are objective and accurate. (see fig. 4.3)

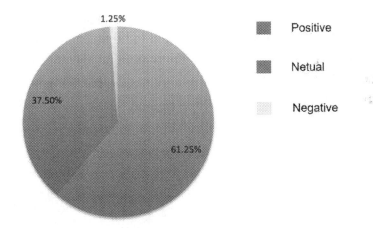

Figure 4.3 Tendencies of *The New York Times* articles (from April 2 to 16, 2001) covering the China-U.S. Plane Collision Incident.

Among the 80 articles, the number of those with a negative tendency (49) is the largest, accounting for more than 60%. The number of articles with a neutral attitude is 30, and there is only one in-depth analysis article with a positive tendency. In terms of the types of articles, for event feature stories, there is an equal number of articles with negative and neutral attitudes; the one and only personal interview has a neutral tone; while for all other types, there are more articles with negative attitudes than neutral tendencies. (see table 4.6)

Tendency \ Type	Short news article	News story	In-depth analysis	Event feature story	Personal interview	Commentary	Sum
Negative	4	18	9	7	0	11	49
Neutral	1	12	5	7	1	4	30
Positive	0	0	1	0	0	0	1
Sum	5	30	15	14	1	15	80

Table 4.6 Tendencies of *The New York Times* articles (April 2 to 16, 2001) on the China-U.S. Plane Collision Incident.

In contrast, *The New York Times* reported on the Taiwan Strait Crisis in March 2001 with the most neutral articles. The reason may be the great differences in the nature and extent of bilateral crises caused by the two different events. During the Taiwan Strait Crisis in March 1996, the main difference between China and the United States was that the United States believed that it had an obligation to protect Taiwan from the threat of force from mainland China, and that China accused the United States of gross interference in China's internal affairs. Except for the two aircraft carriers sent by the U.S. to the Taiwan Strait, there was no direct, serious, and intense conflict between the two countries. But the collision incident was a serious collision between a Chinese fighter jet and a U.S. reconnaissance plane, leading to the disappearance of Chinese pilot Wang Wei. Then, the U.S. reconnaissance plane made an emergency landing at Lingshui Airport on China's Hainan Island without permission, and the crew was detained by the Chinese. The two countries then engaged in multiple rounds of fierce talks regarding who should be responsible for the incident, the release of the crew, and the return of the plane. For the United States, this crisis was no longer about the so-called "Asian ally" of the United States, but its more sensitive and core national security interests: including the safety of the twenty-four detained crew members, the military secrets the crew might not have time to destroy, and whether the plane could return.

Based on the special nature and severity of the collision crisis, it is not difficult to understand why national interests became a direct factor influencing the tendency of relevant *Times* articles. In fact, the articles often express the official U.S. views. Moreover, amid an international crisis, because the government is the largest owner of information and can indirectly intervene in media reports, the press has to toe the State Department's line more than its strict principle of objectivity during normal times.[233]

The tendency embodied in *The Times* coverage on the collision incident is shown in two aspects. First, immediately after the incident, many articles hinted to the cause and responsibilities of the accidents by choosing certain sources and materials, thus expressing a negative attitude towards China; after about a week or so, coverage generally resumed rationality, and the number of articles with a neutral attitude began to increase, which were no longer constrained to the debate on the cause and responsibility of the incident but turned to discussing solutions, the U.S. foreign affairs decisions, and the potential impact of the crisis on Sino-U.S. relations; however, after the crew was released and returned to the U.S. base, the newspaper's coverage began to turn back to discussing the cause of the accident, continuing to insist that the responsibility lay with China. Thus, tendencies are sometimes not only reflected in separate articles, but can also be expressed through a series of related articles over a period of time. Secondly, *The New York Times* not only has expressed negative attitudes towards the Chinese government, military, media reports, etc.—For example, many reports criticized and were puzzled by the fact that China's foreign affairs decision-making process was not transparent and there were conflicts between the government and the military —it also has published many articles criticizing and satirizing the Bush administration's China policy and decision-making mechanism in foreign policy. Thus, its tendency is still restricted by its value on objectivity.

The tendency of news, whether direct, implicit, obvious, or obscure, always exists, and ultimately manifests itself through the selection of facts, articulation, news editing, and other ways. A fairly intuitive

---

[233] Jaap van Ginneken, *Understanding Global News: A Critical Introduction* (India: SAGE Publications, 1998), 28.

indicator of tendency is found in the emotionally-charged vocabulary used in a news article. When *The New York Times* covered the cause and responsibility of the incident, as well as the position, attitude, decision-making, behaviors, and statements of the Chinese government in the ensuing bilateral crisis, there were some recurring emotionally-charged vocabulary in some articles—a manifestation of media attitude and tendencies. It is a direct expression or hint to the audience regarding the nature of the incident, the responsible party, governmental decision-making mechanism, and the impact of the crisis.

For example, many articles in *The New York Times* believed that it was precisely because the Chinese pilot Wang Wei "harassed" the U.S. EP-3 reconnaissance plane, his "shadowing", and his "dangerous," "aggressive," and "reckless" flight maneuvers[234] that finally led to the collision. When China detained the plane and the crew, the *Times* articles reported that China's explanation of the situation was untimely and "uninformative", that it remained silent on when the crew would be released, rejected the request of U.S. diplomats to immediately meet the crew, and was "accusatory" and "caustic" towards the U.S. The reports also said that the Chinese government's attitude in the crisis was "obfuscated", its behaviors "unprofessional", and "uncooperative", which would inevitably "harm" the relationship between China and the United States.[235] In contrast, the White House, the U.S. Pacific Command, and U.S. diplomats in China were depicted as using a "moderate" tone, expressing Washington's objectives in a "clear" and "reasonable" way, while the new administration was "steady" as it faced the first international crisis upon coming into power; In contrast, the Chinese government's demand that the U.S. first apologize before the release of the crew is "offensive", "bootless", while attempting to "slander" the United States

---

[234] James Dao, "China's Shadowing Had Annoyed U.S.," *The New York Times*, April 2, 2001, A1; Steven Lee Myers and Christopher Drew, "Chinese Pilot Reveled in Risk, Pentagon Says," *The New York Times*, April 6, 2001, A1.

[235] David E. Sanger, "Bush Is Demanding a 'Prompt' Return of Plane and Crew," *The New York Times*, April 3, 2001, A1; "Delicate Passage With China," *The New York Times*, April 3, 2001, A18; David Shambaugh, "No Easy Way Forward With China," *The New York Times*, April 3, 2001, A19.

through "propaganda"—an "enormity"[236] which would only lead to the "escalating war of words"[237] between the two countries. Some scholars explained that it was due to China's "sense of victimization" rooted in Chinese history and its "bargaining, haggling culture" at work.[238] In the process of resolving the crisis, *The Times* read the "dictatorship" of the Chinese Communist Party and its "unwieldy" "bureaucracy" meant that every important decision needed to go through layers of authorization, and that the intervention of senior Chinese military officials served to not only "delay" the process of crisis resolution, but also severely "distort" the prospects of Sino-U.S. relations.[239]

In addition, an analysis into the different angles of articles also gave insight into the newspaper's pattern of tendencies. Among all the 80 *Times* articles from April 2 to 16, 2001 on the crisis, 9 articles explain and analyze the cause and responsibility of the collision: all with a negative attitude towards China. There are the 18 articles covering the attitudes and positions of the Chinese and American governments (or militaries) on the incident, of which 15 are negative towards China, while only 3 are neutral. Of the 11 articles that analyze and comment on the impact of the incident on Sino-U.S. relations, there are 7 with negative attitudes, 3 with neutral attitudes, and 1 with a positive attitude (this is also the positive one of all 80 articles). Most of the articles with a neutral tone are articles on reactions, whose angles and contents are mainly the evaluation of the Bush administration's response to the crisis by the American people, the attitudes of American companies in China towards the incident, interviews with crew members and their families, the attitudes of ordinary Chinese people, and relevant reports from Chinese media.

---

[236] "Managing the Spy Plane Incident," *The New York Times,* April 5, 2001, A20; William Safire, "The Politic of Apology," *The New York Times,* April 5, 2001, A21.

[237] Elisabeth Rosenthal, "Beijing Steps up Its War of Words Over Air Collision," *The New York Times*, April 5, 2001, A1.

[238] Butterfield Fox, "China's Demand for Apology Is Rooted in Tradition," *The New York Times*, April 7, 2001, A6.

[239] Elisabeth Rosenthal, "Many Voices for Beijing," *The New York Times,* April 10, 2001, A1.

Framing

Framing is a construction process in which news items are presented. Analyzing news frames in media coverage is a complex work. Regarding the Sino-U.S. relations crisis surrounding the collision incident, the kind of frames the U.S. media used to present and interpret the incident would inevitably affect the American public's understanding of the incident and Sino-U.S. relations, leading to convergence of public opinion in a specific direction. Eventually, this might have indirectly influenced the formulation and adjustments of the Bush administration's China policy.[240] When analyzing the frames of *The Times'* coverage from April 2 to 16, 2001 on the collision incident, from a news constructivist point of view, it can be concluded that the newspaper's frames include the cause and background of the incident, the process of crisis resolution, the positions and attitudes of China and the United States, the decision-making of the Chinese and American governments, the conditions of the U.S. crew and their families, the reactions of the Chinese and American people, the impact of the incident on Sino-U.S. relations, and the impact of the incident on the adjustment of America's policy toward China, etc. Regarding the development of the crisis and the presentation and construction of the U.S. policy toward China and the status of Sino-U.S. relations in the resolution process, the frames of relevant articles in *The New York Times* mainly include the following:

First of all, on the cause and background of the collision: Chinese pilot Wang Wei's dangerous and provocative maneuvers while following the U.S. reconnaissance plane was the direct cause of the incident.[241] Some articles reported that the "lumbering" EP-3 reconnaissance aircraft was in a "slow-moving" flight in international airspace 50 to 80 miles away from the coastline of Hainan Island at that time, and was far less maneuverable than the Chinese fighter. The collision occurred less than two years after the U.S. bombing of the Chinese Embassy in

---

[240] Chen Hanxi, "How the American Media 'Shaped' China's Image—Take the 'China-US Airplane Collision Incident' as an Example," *International Journalism*, no. 3 (2001): 5-12.

[241] James Dao, "China's Shadowing Had Annoyed U.S.," *The New York Times*, April 2, 2001, A1.

Yugoslavia in 1999; China, from the government to the public, was full of mistrust towards the United States, and therefore could not accept that the collision was an accident. At the time of the collision, Sino-U.S. relations were in a sensitive, transitioning stage—President Bush was about to make a decision on whether to sell sophisticated weapons and radar equipment to Taiwan; In addition, in the months preceding the collision, China fighters frequently trailed U.S. reconnaissance planes in the airspace around the South China Sea and made dangerous moves, which were repeatedly protested by the U.S.[242]

Secondly, regarding the U.S. government's position and attitude, which changed in different stages, towards the incident: immediately after the collision happened, the Bush administration took a hawkish attitude, demanded that China immediately release the crew and return the plane, and protested when Beijing did not immediately allow U.S. diplomats to meet with the crew. Washington also warned that if China continued to remain silent and delay the request of the U.S., it would seriously damage the already "fragile" relationship between the two countries.[243] Some articles said that if the location of the collision was as stated by the Pentagon, then Bush's tough attitude and strong protest were "right"[244] and had "strong legal standing"; other articles said it was "curious" that Bush did not directly communicate with Jiang through the heads-of-state hotline but chose to make a statement in the Rose Garden of the White House,[245] and that the U.S. position in the crisis was to some extent undermined by a similar action by the U.S. Department of Defense when in 1976 U.S. intelligence agents ignored Soviet protests and dismantled a Soviet Mig-25 fighter.[246]

---

[242] Rosenthal Elisabeth and David E. Sanger, "U.S. Plane in China After It Collides with Chinese Jet," *The New York Times,* April 2, 2001, A1; Christopher Drew, "Old Tactics May Pull the Rug From the U.S. Claim to Plane," *The New York Times,* April 4, 2001, A1.

[243] David E. Sanger, "Bush Is Demanding a 'Prompt' Return of Plane and Crew," *The New York Times,* April 3, 2001, A1.

[244] "Delicate Passage With China," *The New York Times*, April 3, 2001, A18.

[245] David E. Sanger, "Powell Sees No Need for Apology; Bush Again Urges Return of Crew," *The New York Times*, April 4, 2001, A1.

[246] Christopher Drew, "Old Tactics May Pull the Rug From the U.S. Claim to Plane," *The New York Times,* April 4, 2001, A1.

When the settlement of the incident came to a deadlock due to the issue of apology, Washington began to ease its attitude and proposed a solution to the problem to China. Bush asked government and military officials to be cautious in making comments on China,[247] and try not to let the confrontation become too militarized.[248] Some articles said that it was because of Bush' unnecessary provocation immediately after the collision that he missed the best time to ease the situation;[249] some officials believed that Bush's "harsh" remarks would "drive... into a corner" his Chinese counterpart,[250] and that if he could make a private call with Jiang, it might be of great help for a solution.[251] But a commentary argued that it was already "appropriate" for Bush and Powell, though lacking information, to have expressed publicly their "regret" to the crash of the Chinese pilot.[252] One article said that a more constructive solution was for both parties to work together on "fact-finding" and "sharing of information".[253] In addition, some articles compared the collision incident with a 1960 incident when a U.S. reconnaissance plane was shot down by the Soviet Union.[254] There are also many articles comparing the resolution of the crisis with U.S. arms sales to Taiwan, China's most-favored-nation trade status, China's entry into the World Trade Organization, Beijing's bid to host the Olympics, etc., which were linked together for interpretation and analysis— similar discussions were also facilitated by more and more

---

[247] David E. Sanger, "Powell Offers China Aides Outline for Standoff's End," *The New York Times*, April 5, 2001, A10; Jane Perlez and David E. Sanger, "Bush Aides Saying Some Hope Is Seen to End Standoff," *The New York Times,* April 6, 2001, A1.

[248] Jane Perlez, "Powell Is in Driver's Seat On Plane Crisis Strategy," *The New York Times,* April 7, 2001, A6.

[249] Lewis Anthony, "Molehill Into Mountain," *The New York Times*, April 7, 2001, A15.

[250] David E. Sanger, "Bush Team Is in Search Of Way Out Of Impasse," *The New York Times*, April 8, 2001, 1.10.

[251] Rick Gladstone, "Will Business Suffer in a China Stalemate?," *The New York Times*, April 8, 2001, 3.4.

[252] "China's Costly Rigidity," *The New York Times*, April 9, 2001, A16.

[253] "Managing the Spy Plane Incident," *The New York Times*, April 5, 2001, A20.

[254] Elisabeth Rosenthal, "Beijing Steps up Its War of Words Over Air Collision," *The New York Times*, April 5, 2001, A1.

members of Congress;[255] however, the Bush administration made it clear that it opposed impeding Beijing's Olympic bid as a means to pressure China to release the crew.[256]

Third, regarding the impact of the collision incident on the direction of Bush administration's China policy: In the process of resolving the deadlock in the bilateral relations caused by the incident, newly-sworn President Bush faced a dilemma because his party was split into two factions; one side wanted to "contain" China, while the other wanted to strengthen diplomatic ties with China and deepen economic cooperation.[257] This crisis revealed that the Bush administration did not pay enough attention to China, and its core team lacked high-level China experts, so when faced with China's "opaque" ways and processes of decision-making, the administration felt "repeatedly frustrated".[258] After China released the crew, the confrontation between the two countries eased greatly, but the Bush administration's China policy would have to face the following choices and adjustments:

1, when the U.S. should resume reconnaissance flights along the coast of China and whether these flights should be reduced. Regarding this issue, there are articles saying that the U.S. has categorically rejected China's request that these flights be stopped, and that reconnaissance

---

[255] Alison Mitchell, "Anti-China Coalition in Congress Is Emboldened," *The New York Times*, April 5, 2001, A1; Thomas Friedman, "Sorry About That," *The New York Times*, April 6, 2001, A21; Rick Gladstone, "Will Business Suffer in a China Stalemate?," *The New York Times*, April 8, 2001, 3.4.

[256] Jere Longman, "Standoff Unlikely To Affect Beijing's Bid," *The New York Times*, April 11, 2001, D1.

[257] David E. Sanger, "Powell Sees No Need for Apology; Bush Again Urges Return of Crew," *The New York Times*, April 4, 2001, A1; Richard L. Berke, "Now for Bush, A Novelty: Having to Face Novelty," *The New York Times*, April 5, 2001, A17.

[258] Elisabeth Rosenthal, "China's Bonus: Attention, and Respect," *The New York Times*, April 12, 2001, A13; Bates Gill, "China Policy, Without Regrets," *The New York Times*, April 12, 2001, A29; David E. Sanger, "How Bush Had to Calm Hawks In Devising a Response to China," *The New York Times*, April 13, 2001, A1.

flights to China would be reduced.[259] 2, whether Washington should continue the sale of weapons to Taiwan, and if yes, which weapons; arms sales to Taiwan may threaten the relationship between Bush and Jiang who had not met yet.[260] 3, whether the U.S. should take punitive measures against China in the field of trade and whether to extend China's most-favored-nation status; there were two different voices in Congress on this issue: some lawmakers proposed ending normal trade relations with China, while some Republicans who supported the Sino-U.S. trade relations hoped that the end of the confrontation could bring trade relations back on track.[261] 4, whether the U.S. should reduce or suspend military exchanges with China. To this there was no shortage of yea-sayers in Congress and the Pentagon, but there was also the view that after the crisis caused by the collision, the U.S. should instead strengthen its military ties with China so that it could better understand the Chinese People's Liberation Army.[262]

In addition, there was an in-depth analysis article on how the U.S. policy toward China should be adjusted after the collision incident, saying that bridges should be built in all possible areas, but red lines should be drawn also when necessary. It said that any extreme U.S. policy toward China is very "foolhardy".[263]

---

[259] David E. Sanger, "Delicate Diplomatic Dance Ends Bush's First Crisis," *The New York Times,* April 12, 2001, A1; Craig S. Smith, "China Releases U.S. Plane Crew 11 Days After Midair Collision," *The New York Times*, April 12, 2001, A1; "Ending the Spy Plane Deadlock," *The New York Times*, April 12, 2001, A28; Marc Lacey and Steven Lee Myers, "With Crew in U.S., Bush Sharpens Tone Toward China," *The New York Times*, April 13, 2001, A1.

[260] David E. Sanger, "Delicate Diplomatic Dance Ends Bush's First Crisis," *The New York Times,* April 12, 2001, A1; Craig S. Smith, "China Releases U.S. Plane Crew 11 Days After Midair Collision," *The New York Times*, April 12, 2001, A1; Joseph Kahn, "Taiwan Arms Sales and China's W.T.O. Application Will Test a Relationship," *The New York Times*, April 12, 2001, A12.

[261] Alison Mitchell, "Tempers Are Cooling, But A Cloud Remains," *The New York Times*, April 12, 2001, A14; "Ending the Spy Plane Deadlock," *The New York Times*, April 12, 2001, A28.

[262] Bates Gill, "China Policy, Without Regrets," *The New York Times*, April 12, 2001, A29.

[263] Thomas Friedman, "One Nation, 3 Lessons," *The New York Times,* April 13, 2001, A17.

Fourth, regarding the impact of the collision incident on Sino-U.S. relations: the incident occurred when Sino-U.S. relations were in a state of adjustment. After Bush took office, he regarded China as a strategic competitor of the United States and abandoned Clinton-era policy of seeing China as a strategic partner and military ties with Beijing.[264] Some articles said that since the Tiananmen incident, Sino-U.S. relations had experienced many serious blows, and that the continued conflicts between the two countries caused by the collision incident might shake the foundation of bilateral relations and undermine the willingness of China and the United States to build a fruitful relationship.[265] In the short term, the tension on the one hand might cause American investment in China to suspend; on the other hand, the U.S. Congress may obstruct China's efforts to join the WTO, its bidding for the Olympic Games, and cancel its most-favored-nation status.[266] Compared with *The New York Times*' coverage on the Taiwan Strait Crisis, there were more articles appearing more frequently analyzing and reflecting on Sino-U.S. relations in the later period of the collision crisis. Some articles said that the collision incident aroused in the United States a debate on U.S.-China relations, for which a crucial question was whether the rift caused by the crisis could be repaired.[267] There were also articles summarizing the lessons on Sino-U.S. relations for Washington brought about by the collision incident, the most important one being that the U.S. should further recognize the complexities of Sino-U.S. relations and understand deeply the relationship's innate instability: the relationship

---

[264] Rosenthal Elisabeth and David E. Sanger, "U.S. Plane in China After It Collides with Chinese Jet," *The New York Times,* April 2, 2001, A1.

[265] David Shambaugh, "No Easy Way Forward With China," *The New York Times*, April 3, 2001, A19; "In Statement Of President: 'It Is Time'," *The New York Times*, April 4, 2001, A11; Joseph Kahn, "Standoff Brings Calls to Boycott Chinese Goods," *The New York Times*, April 11, 2001, A1.

[266] Thomas Friedman, "Sorry About That," *The New York Times,* April 6, 2001, A21; Mark Landler, "Standoff Worries U.S. Companies in China," *The New York Times*, April 6, 2001, C3.

[267] Craig S. Smith, "China Releases U.S. Plane Crew 11 Days After Midair Collision," *The New York Times*, April 12, 2001, A1; Joseph Kahn, "Taiwan Arms Sales and China' W.T.O. Application Will Test a Relationship," *The New York Times*, April 12, 2001, A12.

could not be simply interpreted as a strategic partnership like the Clinton administration did, nor could it be erroneously defined as strategic competition as the Bush administration did, but that Washington should hold a big stick in one hand and a dictionary in the other, and get used to this status for a long period of time.[268]

Through the above analysis of the frames on how *The New York Times* presented China-U.S. relations and the U.S.'s China policy when covering the collision incident, it can be seen that although the proportion of articles (including commentaries) with negative tendencies reached 61%, there was no lack of voices of rational thinking and calm analysis on the adjustment of the U.S.'s China policy and how to view Sino-U.S. relations. The framing of the *Times* emphasized three aspects: First, the foreign affairs decision-making process in China's bureaucratic political system was complicated and opaque; the participation of China's military has amplified this feature; the United States should strengthen military exchanges and establish a more effective communication mechanism with China; second, the confrontation between the two countries caused by the Plane Collision Incident and the resolution process exposed the lack of Chinese experts among the senior officials of Bush's team; third, the U.S. government should form a clear understanding of the complexities and instability of Sino-U.S. relations, and that it could not simply treat China as either strategic partner or strategic competitor. In short, despite the special nature of the collision incident, involving the safety of the twenty-four crew members and the national security interests of the United States, the construction of news frames in *The New York Times* was still based on facts. With the exception of a small number of commentaries with ideological lenses and vivid remnants of cold war thinking, most articles have a certain degree of objectivity and rationality in the presentation, interpretation, analysis, and commentary of facts.

---

[268] Bates Gill, "China Policy, Without Regrets," *The New York Times*, April 12, 2001, A29; Thomas Friedman, "One Nation, 3 Lessons," *The New York Times*, April 13, 2001, A17.

CHAPTER 5

ANALYSIS OF *THE NEW YORK TIMES* COVERAGE ON THE SINO-U.S. MARITIME RIGHTS DISPUTE IN 2013

SECTION 1. OVERVIEW OF THE SINO-U.S. MARITIME RIGHTS DISPUTE IN 2013

Crisis Background

In 2009, in response to the profound changes in the international political and economic landscape, as soon as the Obama administration took office, it launched an important foreign strategy of Pivot to Asia, shifting U.S. strategic focus to the Asia-Pacific region and proposed strengthening military alliances to maintain the United States dominance in the Asia-Pacific region and share the rapid economic growth in the region. Although different names were used, such as the notion of returning to Asia or strategic eastward movement,[269] from the beginning of its formulation, in addition to the well-known core objectives, the strategy has always harbored the hidden intention of being vigilant toward China's rapid rise and counterbalancing Beijing's influence. Island ownership and maritime rights disputes between

---

[269] Ni Feng, "The Foreign Policy Trends of the Obama Administration in the Second Term," *New Vision*, no. 2 (2013): 125-128.

China and neighboring countries, as well as issues involving the Diaoyu Islands and South China Sea, have become an important starting point for American intervention in East Asian and Southeast Asian affairs.

In the same year, there were frequent frictions between China and the United States in South China Sea and the exclusive economic zone of the Yellow Sea. During the reconnaissance and counter-reconnaissance activities between U.S. warships and Chinese ships, there were a number of face-offs. The most famous one was the *Impeccable* Incident.[270] In March 2009, the U.S. surveillance ship *Impeccable* encountered "interference" by Chinese fishing boats while sailing 120 kilometers away from China's Hainan Island. The incident was hyped up by the U.S. media. In his testimony at the Senate Foreign Relations Committee hearing, Deputy Assistant Secretary Scot Marciel, of the Bureau of East Asian & Pacific Affairs at the U.S. Department, said China used unsafe ways (interfering with navigation) to affirm its maritime rights, which interfered with the U.S.'s international freedom of navigation.[271]

In 2010, both the Diaoyu Islands and South China Sea issues continued to heat up. In July, U.S. Secretary of State Hillary Clinton declared at the ASEAN Foreign Ministers' Meeting: "The United States, like every nation, has a national interest in freedom of navigation, open access to Asia's maritime commons, and respect for international law in the South China Sea." This speech is generally considered a turning point of Washington's' South China Sea policy, which marked the U.S.'s transition from observation to formal intervention and side-taking on the South China Sea issue. On September 23 and October 28, Clinton made two statements declaring that the Security Treaty Between the United States and Japan also cover the Diaoyu Islands, transforming the Diaoyu Islands issue from a Sino-Japanese territorial dispute into an agenda of competition in the power games between China and the

---

[270] Fu Ying and Wu Shicun, "Sovereign Rights Dispute or Geopolitical Dispute? How Tensions in the South China Sea Evolve Step by Step," *People's Daily (Overseas Edition),* May 13, 2016, 10.

[271] Scot Marciel, "Maritime Issues and Sovereignty Disputes in East Asia," U.S. Department of State, accessed September 25, 2020, https://2009-2017.state.gov/p/eap/rls/rm/2009/07/126076.htm.

United States in the East China Sea, further exacerbating tensions in the area.[272]

In 2012, when the Obama administration entered the second term, the U.S. policy toward China remained ambiguous and continued to swing between engagement and containment. Although there were more and more dialogue mechanisms to enhance strategic mutual trust, bilateral relations did not advance but, rather, regressed. The increasing strategic distrust became the most serious issue facing the two countries. As an American scholar said, what China considered to be defensive was defined by the United States as aggression; while regional stability in the eyes of the United States became containment in China's eyes.[273] The game between China and the United States in areas like maritime disputes and cyber security reached new heights. The Diaoyu Islands and South China Sea issues increasingly became the focus of the game between the two sides in the Asia-Pacific region, and they were also the toughest issues in the new U.S. administration's China policy.[274]

Entering 2013, the United States paid more attention to counterbalancing China's maritime power. It not only strengthened the presence of the U.S. Navy in the South China Sea and strengthened the surveillance of China's military operations in the South China Sea, but also consistently and actively intervened in maritime territorial disputes pertaining to China, while favoring allies like Japan, the Philippines and other disputing parties. Washington used many measures such as politics, military, diplomacy, and public opinion to pressure China, and increased the cost of China's operations in the East China Sea and the

---

[272] Shu Biquan, "Inhibitory Understanding: An Analysis of the Path of China and the US in Dealing with the Diaoyu Islands Dispute," *International Relations Research*, no. 6 (2013): 70-82.

[273] Li Shenming and Zhang Yuyan, ed., *Global Politics and Security Report (2014)* (Beijing: Social Sciences Literature Press, 2014), 37.

[274] Wang Guanghou and Tian Lijia, "On the Characteristics of the Obama Administration's South China Sea Policy," *Southeast Asian Studies*, no. 1 (2015): 58-65; Ni Feng, "The Foreign Policy Trends of the Obama Administration in the Second Term," *New Vision*, no. 2 (2013): 125-128.

South China Sea, eventually causing the continuous escalation of the maritime game with Beijing.[275]

With many island disputes in the East China Sea and the South China Sea, and China's maritime rights and interests facing severe challenges, in order to strengthen the defense space and maintain sea and air security, on November 23, 2013, the Chinese government announced the establishment of an air defense identification zone in the East China Sea and issued the rules for aircraft identification and the map of the zone. Although prior to this, more than twenty countries in the world had established their own air defense identification zones, U.S. Secretary of State John Kerry and Pentagon still criticized and even opposed Beijing's move. Before all public arguments on the zone subsided, a face-off between the two countries' warships occurred in the South China Sea the following month.

Event Review

On November 23, 2013, China announced the establishment of the East China Sea Air Defense Identification Zone, according to the National Defense Law of the People's Republic of China (March 14, 1997), the Civil Aviation Law of the People's Republic of China (October 30, 1995), and the Basic Rules of Aviation of the People's Republic of China (July 27, 2001).[276] On the same day, the Ministry of National Defense of China issued an announcement on the rules for aircraft identification in the East China Sea Air Defense Identification Zone in accordance with the Chinese government's statement on the establishment of the Zone.

After China's announcement, the U.S. immediately criticized and even moved to oppose it. U.S. Secretary of State John Kerry, who was in Geneva for nuclear negotiations with Iran, issued a statement, saying, "The United States is deeply concerned about China's announcement

---

[275] Fu Ying and Wu Shicun, "Sovereign Rights Dispute or Geopolitical Dispute? How Tensions in the South China Sea Evolve Step by Step," *People's Daily (Overseas Edition)*, May 13, 2016, 10.

[276] "Statement by the Government of the People's Republic of China on Establishing the East China Sea Air Defense Identification Zone," Xinhua News Agency, November 23, 2013.

that they've established an "East China Sea Air Defense Identification Zone." This unilateral action constitutes an attempt to change the status quo in the East China Sea. Escalatory action will only increase tensions in the region and create risks of an incident."[277] Kerry said that the United States had also established air defense identification zones, but foreign aircraft that do not intend to enter U.S. airspace need not declare to the United States; he called on China to exercise caution and restraint and refrain from threatening aircraft that do not identify themselves or comply with orders.[278] U.S. Secretary of Defense Chuck Hagel also stated in a statement, "The United States is deeply concerned by the People's Republic of China announcement today that it is establishing an air defense identification zone in the East China Sea. We view this development as a destabilizing attempt to alter the status quo in the region. This unilateral action increases the risk of misunderstanding and miscalculations."[279] Hagel also stated that China's announcement would not affect U.S. military operations in the East China Sea. He said the U.S. was in close consultation with allies and partners including Japan, saying that the U.S. would honor its commitments to them and reiterating that the U.S.-Japan Mutual Defense Treaty applies to the Diaoyu Islands.

On November 24, China's Assistant Minister of Foreign Affairs Zheng Zeguang made solemn representations to the U.S. Ambassador to China Gary Locke, demanding that the U.S. immediately correct its mistakes and stop making irresponsible remarks to China. The Foreign Affairs Office of the Chinese Ministry of National Defense

---

[277] John Kerry, "Statement on the East China Sea Air Defense Identification Zone," U.S. Department of State, accessed August 25, 2020, https://2009-2017. state.gov/secretary/remarks/2013/11/218013.htm.

[278] John Kerry, "Statement on the East China Sea Air Defense Identification Zone," U.S. Department of State, accessed August 25, 2020, https://2009-2017. state.gov/secretary/remarks/2013/11/218013.htm.

[279] Chuck Hagel, "Statement by Secretary of Defense Chuck Hagel on the East China Sea Air Defense Identification Zone," U.S. Department of Defense, accessed August 25, 2020, https://archive.defense.gov/releases/release. aspx?releaseid=16392#:~:text=November%2023%2C%202013-,Statement%20 by%20Secretary%20of%20Defense%20Chuck%20Hagel%20on%20the%20 East,in%20the%20East%20China%20Sea.

also lodged solemn representations with the Defense Attache Office of the U.S. Embassy in Beijing on the U.S. remarks.[280] On November 25, the spokesperson of the Chinese Ministry of National Defense Yang Yujun emphasized in response to reporters that the Diaoyu Islands and its affiliated islands are China's inherent territory, that China will firmly defend the territorial sovereignty of the Diaoyu Islands. Yang said the United States should not take sides on the sovereignty of the Diaoyu Islands, make inappropriate remarks, or release false signals that may encourage Japan's risk-taking moves. Yang urged the United States to truly respect China's national security and stop making irresponsible remarks about China's establishment of an air defense identification zone in the East China Sea. White House Deputy Press Secretary Josh Earnest also reaffirmed the U.S. position on the 25th, saying that the U.S. believed that China's announcement was unnecessarily inflammatory, and that territorial disputes in the East China Sea should be resolved through diplomatic channels.[281]

From 11am to 1:22p.m. on November 26, Beijing time (evening on November 25, Washington time), without having notified China in advance, two U.S. B-52 long-range bombers from the base in Guam flew back and forth in the north-south direction on the eastern edge of the East China Sea Air Defense Identification Zone, about 200 kilometers east of the Diaoyu Islands. There were no weapons on the two planes, and no other fighters were escorting them. Speaking of this maneuver, the U.S. Department of Defense stated that when they fly into this airspace, they will not notify their flight plan, nor will they self-report their transponder, identification, radio frequency or identification.[282] The U.S. military said the operation was an order from the Pentagon and a long-planned exercise, saying the purpose was to show that the U.S. military would not make the slightest change in the military

[280] Wu Xinbo, ed., *China-US Relations Strategy Report 2013* (Beijing: Current Affairs Press, 2014), 296.

[281] "Press Gaggle by Principal Deputy Press Secretary Josh Earnest — Los Angeles, CA," Office of the Press Secretary of the White House, accessed August 25, 2020, https://obamawhitehouse.archives.gov/the-press-office/2013/11/26/press-gaggle-principal-deputy-press-secretary-josh-earnest-los-angeles-c.

[282] Wang Peng, Miao Xinping, and Zhang Qin, *A Brief Look into Air Defense Identification Zones* (Beijing: Military Science Press, 2014), 121.

deployment and the way operations are performed in the region in order to comply with the new requirements of the Chinese Ministry of Defense. On November 27th, Geng Yansheng, spokesperson of the Ministry of National Defense of China, said in response to reporters' questions on this matter that the Chinese military had monitored the U.S. aircraft the whole process, and identified them in a timely manner, including the type of the aircraft. Geng said China will identify any aircraft activities in the East China Sea Air Defense Identification Zone, and that China has the ability to effectively manage and control the relevant airspace.

Just as the public opinion struggle between China and the United States over China's designation of the East China Sea Air Defense Identification Zone was going on, and the media of the two countries were still reporting it on full swing, another incident involving a face-off between Chinese and U.S. warships occurred in the South China Sea. It happened on December 5, but it was not reported by American media until December 13. Regarding the incident, China and the United States held their own opinions: the United States called the Chinese warships aggressive, and that it was the U.S. ship that voluntarily retreated to avoid collision; China, on the other hand, criticized the U.S. for being the guilty party who sought to accuse the other first. Beijing said that China's naval fleet very early issued wireless warnings on safe navigation, but the U.S. ship still insisted on approaching the Chinese aircraft carrier formation, posing a threat to the normal navigation of the Chinese Navy. Based on the relevant coverage of the Chinese and American media on the incident and the official statements of the two countries, a rough sketch of the process of the face-off is drawn as follows:

On December 5, the U.S. Navy's Ticonderoga-class guided-missile cruiser U.S.S Cowpens was monitoring the Chinese Navy's aircraft carrier Liaoning in the South China Sea (the Liaoning had earlier set off from Qingdao Port in northern China and entered the South China Sea for training). The Cowpens broke into the "internal defense zone" of the Chinese aircraft carrier fleet. Previously, the China Maritime Safety Administration had publicly issued a ban on navigation on its website, stating that "from 18:00 on December 3, 2013 to 18:00 on

January 3, 2014, military activities in the relevant waters of the South China Sea will be conducted. The area will be prohibited for entrance", and announced the coordinate points of the waters pertaining to the military activities. Upon the Cowpens' arrival, a Chinese amphibious ship went to verify the situation and blew its whistle to warn the Cowpens to stop advancing and leave the training area. When the U.S. ship turned a deaf ear and continued sailing forward, the Chinese ship ventured head-on towards the Cowpens and stopped in front of it, forcing the captain of the Cowpens to order the ship to stop fully and make an emergency evasion.

The incident was only exposed by the media on December 13. Western media took the opportunity to expound on the danger of the incident and the what they said the tough attitude of the Chinese military, and called this near-collision incident the most serious maritime incident in the South China Sea since 2009 when five Chinese ships "harassed" the U.S. marine surveillance ship *Impeccable.*

The U.S. claimed that the Cowpens was legally sailing in the international waters of the South China Sea, while the Chinese ship's actions were fairly dangerous and aggressive. Washington said it was the emergency maneuvering of the American ship that prevented the collision. The U.S. Pacific Fleet stated that close-distance navigation by navies of various countries is not uncommon, which is why it is important that navies of nations comply with the international standards of maritime traffic rules.[283] U.S. State Department officials stated that the U.S. had protested to China through diplomatic and military channels.

On December 18, the Press Affairs Bureau of the Ministry of National Defense of China confirmed the incident, stating that it was a normally patrolling Chinese naval ship and an American warship that had met in the South China Sea. Beijing said the Chinese warship properly handled the situation in strict accordance with the operational procedures, and that the defense departments of China and the U.S. had also notified each other the relevant situation through normal working channels and conducted effective communication. On December 19, the Pentagon

---

[283] "Inside Story of the Near Collision of Warships of China and the US," *Global Times*, accessed August 27, 2020, http://world.huanqiu.com/depth_report/2013-12/4664817.html.

also issued a statement stating that the Chinese and American militaries should work hard to establish bilateral mechanisms to alleviate such problems and avoid misjudgments or accidents.[284]

After the Chinese and American officials each confirmed the incident and clarified the details, both countries' media attention also quickly cooled down. Later, senior U.S. officials occasionally made remarks on China's East China Sea Air Defense Identification Zone and South China Sea issues. For example, Secretary of State John Kerry, during his visit to the Philippines on December 17, warned China not to establish a similar air defense identification zone in the South China Sea as the one in the East China Sea. As a powerful maritime power with powerful naval power, the United States has always used the preservation of freedom of navigation as its legal justification to maintain and expand maritime rights and interests, and will continue to use this reason to intervene in China's East and South China Sea affairs in the future.

SECTION 2. CONTENT ANALYSIS OF *THE NEW YORK TIMES'* COVERAGE ON CHINA'S ESTABLISHMENT OF THE EAST CHINA SEA AIR DEFENSE IDENTIFICATION ZONE AND THE FACE-OFF BETWEEN CHINESE AND U.S. WARSHIPS IN THE SOUTH CHINA SEA

After the Chinese government announced the establishment of the East China Sea Air Defense Identification Zone, the public opinion dispute between China and the United States and the immediately ensuing face-off between Chinese and U.S. warships that occurred in the South China Sea were regarded by both countries as sensitive incidents of core national interests. The Chinese side considered them to be related to China's strategic security and maritime rights and interests, while the U.S. regarded them as a threat to U.S. Pacific maritime rights and freedom of navigation in the East China Sea and South China Sea. The two incidents' outbreak at the end of 2013 led to further deepening of strategic mutual distrust between China and the

---

[284] Wu Xinbo, ed., *China-US Relations Strategy Report 2013* (Beijing: Current Affairs Press, 2014), 310-312.

United States, as well as tensed bilateral relations. Therefore, the author believes that the two events can be defined as international crisis events, throwing China and the United States into another crisis in political and military ties. The two crisis incidents have similar backgrounds and properties, and American media often linked the two incidents in their coverage, believing that the cause of face-off between Chinese and American warships in the South China Sea was Beijing expressing its dissatisfaction with Washington's accusations and provocation against China's newly established Air Defense Identification Zone in the East China Sea. In view of the above reasons, and to make this analysis more clearly and concisely, the author hereinafter refers to the two crisis events in tandem, as the 2013 Sino-U.S. Maritime Rights Dispute.

The roles played by the media in these two crisis events are worthy of attention. On the one hand, the media reported news facts as soon as they happened, playing the roles of information release, transmission, and communication during the crisis; on the other hand, the media, through its interplay with the government's agenda as well as the shaping of public opinion during different periods of crisis communication, played a unique role of agenda-setting. Moreover, the face-off between Chinese and U.S. warships in the South China Sea attracted widespread attention from the international community only after the media first exposed it—one could argue that the media "discovered" the crisis.

This section of the study analyzes the content and frames of *The New York Times'* coverage on the 2013 Sino-U.S. Maritime Rights Dispute (including commentaries and column articles, etc.), and discusses how *The Times* portrayed Beijing and Washington's foreign affairs decision-making, the status and direction of Sino-U.S. relations. The timeframe of the sample starts from November 23, 2013 when the Chinese government announced the establishment of the East China Sea Air Defense Identification Zone and ends with December 20, 2013, when both China and the United States made official explanations on the face-off between the two countries' naval vessels in the South China Sea. The reason for choosing December 20 as the end of the sample timeframe is that since that time, the attention to the two incidents in the U.S. media plummeted: on December 31 the number of articles on this subject in *The New York Times* was zero.

Volume of Articles

The author searched "China" in the "New York Times" section in the ProQuest database to search the newspaper's articles from November 23 to December 20, 2013, and obtained a total of 88 China-related articles in this time period. Due to duplications in the classifications of the search results, the author read the 88 articles one by one, and eventually screened out 15 articles on China's establishment of the East China Sea Air Defense Identification Zone, and 3 articles on the face-off between Chinese and U.S. warships in the South China Sea (whose content also involves the East China Sea Air Defense Identification Zone). That is, a total of 18 articles used for the research sample. What needs to be explained here is that the actual number of articles on China's establishment of the East China Sea Air Defense Identification Zone is 16, but one article in the database, titled "Airlines Urged By U.S. to Give Notice to China" does not contain the original text: only a summary is provided. This makes it impossible for a detailed content and frame analysis of this article. Therefore, it was not included in the research sample. Nevertheless, it is included in the total number of articles on the topic of 2013 Sino-U.S. Maritime Rights Dispute. Thus, it can be seen that a total of 19 articles on this topic accounted for 21.6% of the total number of China-related articles in *The New York Times* during the period. In other words, among all China-related articles in *The New York Times* from November 23 to December 20, one out of 4.6 articles is about the 2013 Sino-U.S. Maritime Rights Dispute. (see fig. 5.1)

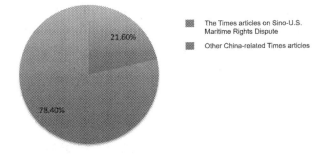

Figure 5.1 Number of *The New York Times* articles on Sino-U.S. Maritime Rights Dispute compared with that of other China-related *Times* articles in the same period.

Content and Frames

Content

This section uses as research sample the 18 reports and commentaries in *The New York Times* from November 23 to December 20, 2013, on China's establishment of the East China Sea Air Defense Identification Zone and the face-off between Chinese and U.S. warships in the South China Sea, for analysis. In order to clearly present the research process in its entirety, and to ensure that the analysis is scientific, accurate, and rigorous, the author has carefully read each of the 18 articles, and on this basis, classified the articles according to the categories of date, title, type, length, tendency, source, angle, etc. Emotionally-charged words which showed certain bias in the articles when portraying the Chinese government's position, decisions, and behaviors in the crisis, as well as content related to Sino-U.S. relations and U.S.'s China policy are summarized and presented in detail in a table. (see table 5.1)

Dates and volume. From November 23 to December 20, 2013, *The New York Times* published a total of 19 reports and commentaries on China's establishment of an air defense identification zone in the East China Sea and the face-off between Chinese and U.S. warships in the South China Sea. Among them, articles on China's establishment of the East China Sea Air Defense Identification Zone all appeared in the 14 days from November 24 to December 7, with at least 1 relevant article every day; the 3 reports on the face-off between Chinese and U.S. warships in the South China Sea respectively appeared on December 15, 18, and 20. (see fig. 5.2)

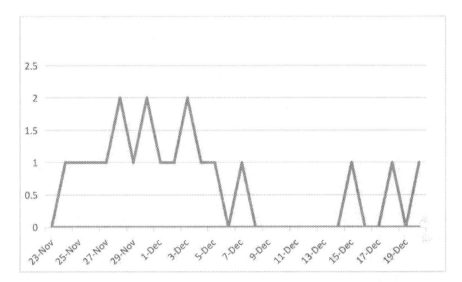

Figure 5.2 Number of articles on the 2013 Sino-U.S.
Maritime Rights Dispute in *The New York Times*.

Compared with the number of articles on the Taiwan Strait Crisis in March 1996 and the Plane Collision Incident in April 2001 in Chapters 3 and 4, the volume of *The New York Times*'s coverage appears much smaller on China's establishment of an air defense identification zone in the East China Sea and the face-off between Chinese and U.S. warships in the South China Sea. The reason may to a certain extent have to do with the differences in the nature and extent of the different crisis events. During the Taiwan Strait Crisis in March 1996, the Chinese People's Liberation Army conducted large-scale joint land, sea, and air exercises in the Taiwan Strait and the waters near Taiwan. The U.S. worried that the situation in the Taiwan Strait might spiral out of control and therefore sent two aircraft carrier formations to the waters near Taiwan. Armed conflicts were on the verge of breaking out, the intensity of the crisis was high, and the United States was deeply involved, leading to high attention paid by *The New York Times*. The April 2001 Plane Collision Incident was a direct conflict between the Chinese and American armed forces. It involved the military secrets yet to be destroyed on the U.S. reconnaissance plane and the safety of twenty-four U.S. crew members. *The New York Times*, thus, published more than 80 articles on the issue in just over ten days from when the incident occurred to the crew's return to the States. In contrast, although China's announcement of the East China Sea Air Defense Identification Zone was considered by the United States to be threatening to its dominance in the Pacific, the degree of crisis was relatively low. While the confrontation between Chinese and U.S. warships in the South China Sea had ended by the time the incident was exposed by the media, post the crisis. Therefore, *The New York Times* paid relatively low attention to the two incidents, with the volume of article relatively small.

Article types and lengths. From November 23 to December 20, 2013, *The New York Times* articles on the Sino-U.S. Maritime Rights Dispute were in four types: short news articles, in-depth analysis, and commentaries. Medium-and-long-length news stories and articles are the two major types, with only 1 short news article and 1 commentary. Among all the 18 articles, there are 10 short news articles, accounting for 55.6%; 6 in-depth analysis articles, accounting for 33.3%. (see table 5.2)

Length (Word count)	Short news article	News story	In-depth analysis	commentary
0–200	0	0	0	0
200–500	1	0	0	0
500–800	0	5	0	1
800–1200	0	4	4	0
1200+	0	1	2	0
Sum (number of articles)	1	10	6	1

Table 5.2 Types and lengths of *The New York Times* articles on 2013 Sino-U.S. Maritime Rights Dispute.

When reporting on the details and latest developments of China's establishment of an air defense identification zone in the East China Sea and the face-off between Chinese and American warships in the South China Sea, *The New York Times* mainly used long length news stories such as the "China Claims Air Rights Over Disputed Islands" on November 24, "U.S. Sends Two B-52 Bombers Into Air Zone Claimed by China" on November 27, and "American and Chinese Navy Ships Nearly

Collided in South China Sea" on December 15. When in discussing the impact of the incident on Sino-U.S. relations and U.S. adjustments in its China policy, *The Times* mainly used in-depth analysis articles, such as "Chinese Claim Forces Obama to Flesh Out His Asia Strategy" on November 28, and "Biden Faces a Delicate Two-Step in Asia" on December 3.

Sources. The author has classified the news sources—named and anonymous, direct and indirect—in 18 relevant articles in *The New York Times* between November 23 and December 20, 2013 on China's establishment of the East China Sea Air Defense Identification Zone and the face-off between Chinese and U.S. warships in the South China Sea, and on this basis analyzes *The New York Times'* preference for news sources in covering this topic: that is, which types of departments, institutions or individuals were selected as sources, the ways the sources were cited and the frequency of the citations. Regarding the counting method of the sources, including the calculation rule for a same source that appears multiple times in a same article, the author has explained in detail in the first two chapters, and will not repeat here. The statistics are as follows. (see table 5.3)

	Direct citation		Indirect citation		Official statements or reports from other media	Sum	Percentage
	Named	Anonymous	Named	Anonymous			
Chinese government and officials	11	–	1	1	7	20	16.3%
American government and officials	15	7	1	6	13	42	34.1%
Japanese government and officials	5	1	1	4	4	15	12.2%
South Korean government and officials	2	–	2	–	–	4	3.3%
Other governments and officials	1	–	–	–	–	1	0.8%
Chinese media	–	–	–	–	9	9	7.3%
American media	–	–	–	–	2	2	1.6%
Japanese media	–	–	–	–	1	1	0.8%

	Direct citation		Indirect citation		Official statements or reports from other media	Sum	Percentage
	Named	Anonymous	Named	Anonymous			
South Korean media	–	–	–	–	1	1	0.8%
Other countries' media	–	–	–	–	1	1	0.8%
Chinese experts and scholars	4	–	1	3	–	8	6.5%
American experts and scholars	8	1	1	6	–	16	13%
Other countries' experts and scholars, including those whose citizenship is not identified	1	–	–	1	–	2	1.6%
Members of international organizations and institutions	1	–	–	–	–	1	0.8%
Sum	48	9	7	21	38	123	100%

Table 5.3 News sources of *The New York Times* coverage
on the 2013 Sino-Us Maritime Rights Dispute.

In the above table, the "official statements or reports from other media" are singled out because they are not sources procured by *The New York Times* itself. In terms of citation volumes, second-hand sources accounts for 31%. In addition, the table shows in *The New York Times* coverage on China's designation of the East China Sea Air Defense Identification Zone and the face-off between Chinese and U.S. warships in the South China Sea, sources from the United States (including officials, media and experts) were cited the most frequently—a total of 60 times, accounting for 48.7%. In other words, nearly half of the sources cited were from the United States. Specifically, sources of the U.S. government, the military and their officials accounted for 34.1%; it shows that in reporting international crises, *The New York Times*, though enjoying the title "newspaper of record", inevitably showed an ostensible bias: it achieves its purpose of protecting national interests through influencing international and domestic public opinion, by presenting more official U.S. information. On the other hand, news sources from China were cited 37 times, accounting for 30.1%; News sources from Japan were cited 16 times, sources from South Korea 5 times, and sources from other countries 3 times. On the issue of China's establishment of the East China Sea Air Defense Identification Zone, the United States, Japan, and South Korea all opposed and constantly criticized and protested against China; the combined number of citations from sources from these three countries were 81, accounting for as high as 66% of the total. It can be seen that although China is the most important country involved in the two crises in the coverage of *The New York Times,* the voices from China were weak. *The New York Times* has not done a fair and just job in source citations.

In terms of source types, there are three main categories: governments, experts/scholars, and the media. Compared with the types of sources cited in its coverage of the 1996 Taiwan Strait Crisis and the 2001 Plane Collision Incident, the types of sources cited in *The Times* articles on the 2013 Sino-U.S. Maritime Dispute appear to be relatively unitary, with almost no voices from enterprises, social organizations, and the general public. The citations were significantly concentrated on official voices and appeared elitist.

In terms of the way sources were cited, named, direct citations appear the most often, with a total of 48 times. This is then followed by official sources from China, the United States, Japan, and South Korea, and content quoted from other media; such citations appear a total of 38 times. It is worth noting that in *The New York Times'* coverage on the 2013 Sino-U.S. Maritime Rights Dispute, sources from the Chinese government and military officials were cited mostly named, and directly; while nearly half of the sources from the United States and Japanese government and military officials were cited anonymously.

As for content cited from other media organizations, the ones from the United States, Japan, and South Korea appeared only once or twice. In contrast, the number of citations from Chinese media sources appeared as many as 9 times, almost all from mainstream media like the Xinhua News Agency, China Central Television, the PLA Daily, and the Global Times

(English version). However, when quoting the content of these media, *The New York Times* still emphasized their official nature and government backgrounds; for example, by adding the word "state-run" in front of "Xinhua News Agency", or calling it "the state news agency"; while the English version of the Global Times was described as one that "often strikes a nationalist tone". In this way *The Times* hinted that the content of these Chinese media are inherently ideological and their attitude biased, thus indirectly weakening their objectivity, impartiality and credibility.

Tendency. In the process of reading and sorting out *The New York Times* articles on China's establishment of the East China Sea Air Defense Identification Zone and the face-off between Chinese and U.S. warships in the South China Sea, the author finds that *The New York Times* was subtle and indirect about its attitudes and tendencies towards the responsibilities, positions, decisions, statements, and behaviors, etc. of the Chinese government in the crisis. The attitudes and tendencies were expressed not outright but indirectly by citing facts and sources. Therefore, it needs to be pointed out that while some articles are classified as neutral because they do not directly express attitudes and tendencies in their content, they actually imply tendencies in subtle ways. The tendencies of 18 articles published by *The New York Times* from November 23 to December 20, 2013 on the China-U.S. Maritime Rights Dispute are as follows. (see Figure 5.3)

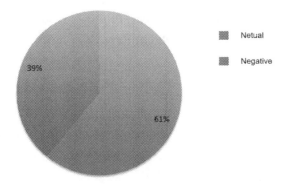

Figure 5.3 Tendencies of *Times* articles on 2013
Sino-U.S. Maritime Rights Dispute.

Of all the 18 articles in *The New York Times* from November 23 to December 20, 2013, on China's establishment of the East China Sea Air Defense Identification Zone and the face-off between Chinese and U.S. warships in the South China Sea, there were many neutral articles, totaling 11 and accounting for 61%; the remaining articles have a negative attitude, numbering 7 articles and accounting for 39%. There was no article with a positive attitude towards China. (see table 5.4)

Type \ Tendency	Short news article	News story	In-depth analysis	Commentary	Sum
Negative	0	3	3	1	7
Neutral	1	7	3	0	11
Positive	0	0	0	0	0
Sum	18				

Table 5.4 Tendencies of articles on the 2013 Sino-U.S. Maritime Rights Dispute by *The New York Times*.

In terms of article types, short news articles, which focus on timeliness and objectivity, as well as news stories, which focus on facts and strive for sufficiency, completeness and details—most of them are neutral in tendency. In-depth analysis articles, which aim at exploring the causes, background, and impact of the events are evenly divided by articles with a neutral tone and ones with a negative tone. In addition, the only commentary in the sample, the editorial "China's Coercive Play" published on November 26, has a clear negative attitude towards China.

As the author mentioned in the previous two chapters, there is often a certain relationship between the reporting angle and tendency. For example, articles, when reporting from the angle of introducing event details and progress, tend to be neutral to China; while articles written from the angle of analyzing the nature of the incident, its impact on Sino-U.S. relations, and adjustments of Washington's China policy, tend to display a negative tone towards China. It is worth noting that on the Taiwan Strait Crisis and the Plane Collision Incident, although many articles show an ostensibly negative attitude towards China, *The New York Times* has also published many articles which criticized the Clinton and Bush administrations' diplomacy and vacillating China policies in the crises. However, in the newspaper's coverage on China's air defense identification zone and the face-off of Chinese and American warships in the South China Sea, there were few articles expressing dissatisfaction and criticism against the Obama administration's decision-making and China policy. Even when involving the status and direction of Sino-U.S. relations, as well as Washington's Asian policy and China policy, the newspaper conducted analysis in a mostly gentle, calm and objective manner. The only dissatisfaction expressed in the coverage was against the Obama administration's unwillingness to show a clear gesture of containing China in handling Sino-U.S. relations.[285] This essentially suggests that during the crisis the Sino-U.S. Maritime Rights Dispute in 2013, *The New York Times* and the U.S. government took the same position, believing that China's actions threatened U.S. dominance in the Pacific region and Washington's relations with Japan, South Korea, the Philippines, and other allies.

Furthermore, when covering China's East China Sea Air Defense Identification Zone and the face-off between Chinese and U.S. warships in the South China Sea, *The New York Times* repeatedly used some emotionally-charged vocabulary in response to the Chinese government's decisions, actions, positions, and statements—also a clear expression of attitudes and tendencies of the reporters. For example, when evaluating the nature of the Chinese government's announcement of the establishment of the East China Sea Air Defense Identification Zone, many articles stated that this move "threatens to escalate" the existing territorial water dispute between China and Japan, called China's behavior "unilateral", "provocative", "coercive", "aggressive" and even "illegitimate"; some articles called China's move and the possibility of China establishing air defense identification zones in more areas in the future "disturbing", saying that such was to use "intimidation" to advance the claim of disputed territories. On the near collision of Chinese and U.S. warships in the South China Sea, some articles called the Chinese warship's tactic for force-stopping the Cowpens "particularly aggressive" and a "dangerously" "irresponsible" behavior.

Based on the above analysis, we can conclude that in *The New York*

---

[285] Mark Landler, "Chinese Claim Forces Obama to Flesh Out His Asia Strategy," *The New York Times*, November 28, 2013, A14.

Times' coverage on the China-U.S. Maritime Rights Dispute in 2013 (China's establishment of the East China Sea Air Defense Identification Zone and the face-off between Chinese and American warships in the South China Sea), although the newspaper on the surface retained a neutral tone when covering the decisions, positions, and statements of the Chinese government and the military, through the selection of facts, source citations, reporting angles, and the use of emotionally-charged vocabulary, it still to a certain extent subtly and implicitly expressed its negative tendency towards China.

Framing

In the process of international crisis coverage, the media uses specific frames to present and construct crisis events. On the one hand, the media introduces and explains the causes, background and details of the crisis events, and on the other hand, it analyzes, evaluates and predicts the attitudes, positions, decisions, and behaviors, etc. of the parties in crisis. Since the focus of this research is on the media's presentation of Sino-U.S. relations and the U.S. policy towards China when covering bilateral crisis events, this section will mainly discuss the newspaper's presentation and construction of such aspects as: the status of China-U.S. relations, the crisis' impact on the Sino-U.S. relations, the adjustments of U.S.'s China policy, etc., in analyzing the frames in *The New York Times* coverage of the 2013 Sino-U.S. Maritime Rights Dispute. The frames are specifically as follows:

First, with regard to the cause and nature of China's establishment of the East China Sea Air Defense Identification Zone and the face-off between Chinese and U.S. warships in the South China Sea: China's announcement of the Zone is a means to put pressure on Japan in response to the island disputes. Beijing intends to control the airspace above these islands with the purpose to claim sovereignty.[286] One article stated that China was trying to sabotage Japan's de-facto control of the

---

[286] Chris Buckley, "China Claims Air Rights Over Disputed Islands," *The New York Times*, November 24, 2013, A12.

disputed islands by setting up the air defense identification zone;[287] thereby breaking the shackles of the First Island Chain, expanding China's access to the western Pacific, and ensuring the long-term smoothness of the waterway.[288] The face-off between Chinese and American warships in the South China Sea was one of the manifestations of the escalation of the confrontation between China and the United States in the high seas of the Pacific, with one article linking the Chinese warship's force stopping the Cowpens and the Obama administration's accusation of China's designation of the East China Sea Air Defense Identification Zone.[289] Another article linked the face-off of the naval ships in the South China Sea with the 2001 Plane Collision Incident and the 2009 U.S.S *Impeccable* incident, saying that the three incidents were all caused by China's reckless provocations, while the U.S. military aircraft and warships at the time were all conducting legal navigations on the high seas or international airspace.[290]

Second, regarding the Obama administration's stance and attitude in the dispute over maritime rights and interests between China and the United States: On the territorial issue of disputed islands in the South China Sea and East China Sea, Washington has chosen to stand on the side of its allies such as Japan and the Philippines. Many high-level American officials including Vice President Joe Biden, Secretary of State John Kerry, and Defense Secretary Chuck Hagel stated on different occasions that China's announcement of the East China Sea Air Defense Identification Zone was a unilateral act provoking the status quo in the Pacific region, and that the United States would not change its military operation plans in the region.[291] One article said

---

[287] Martin Fackler, "Japan Rejects China's Claim to Air Rights Over Islands," *The New York Times,* November 25, 2013, A4.

[288] Jane Perlez, "Chinese Leader's Rise Came With New Attention to Dispute With Japan," *The New York Times*, December 3, 2013, A6.

[289] Jane Perlez, "American and Chinese Navy Ships Nearly Collided in South China Sea," *The New York Times*, December 15, 2013, A21.

[290] Thom Shanker, "Hagel Criticizes Chinese Navy, Citing Near Miss," *The New York Times*, December 20, 2013, A4.

[291] "China's Coercive Play," *The New York Times*, November 26, 2013, A24; Thom Shanker, "U.S. Sends Two B-52 Bombers Into Air Zone Claimed by China," *The New York Times*, November 27, 2013, A1.

that China's move had aggravated tensions in the Pacific region and increased the risk of conflicts due to miscalculations.[292] In order to show its position, the United States sent two B-52 bombers into the East China Sea Air Defense Identification Zone, and the U.S. State Department also issued a statement urging China to exercise caution and restraint.[293] Some articles mentioned that the United States would maintain communication with its Asian allies and fulfill its obligation to protect Japan under the framework of the U.S.-Japan Security Treaty.[294] When reporting the face-off between Chinese and American warships in the South China Sea, the incident was linked with the East China Sea Air Defense Identification Zone, saying the U.S. urged China not to take similar unilateral actions, especially not to establish an air defense identification zone in the South China Sea.[295]

Third, regarding the impact of the Sino-U.S. Maritime Rights Dispute on the direction of the Obama administration's policy toward China: China's establishment of the East China Sea Air Defense Identification Zone forced Obama to further clarify the U.S. government's Asian policy and China policy. Some articles said that in the power game with China in the Pacific region, the United States should deploy more military forces in this area, strengthen the defense capabilities of allies, and once again emphasize Obama's Pivot to Asia strategy to China.[296] Another article reported that Obama repeatedly emphasized that the United States would not adopt a strategy to contain China, but he must prove to the U.S. Congress and Asia-Pacific allies that he would invest

[292] Mark Landler, "Biden Backs Ally Japan But Avoids Roiling China," *The New York Times*, November 25, 2013, A4.

[293] Jane Perlez and Martin Fackler, "China Patrols Air Zone Over Disputed Island," *The New York Times,* November 29, 2013, A16.

[294] Choe Sang-Hun, "After China, South Korea to Expand Its Own Air Defense Zone," *The New York Times*, December 9, 2013, A4; Martin Fackler, "Japan Rejects China's Claim to Air Rights Over Islands," *The New York Times*, November 25, 2013, A4.

[295] Keith Bradsher, "Bolstering Military Ties, U.S. Gives Philippines Aid," *The New York Times*, December, 18, 2013, A8.

[296] Mark Landler, "Chinese Claim Forces Obama to Flesh Out His Asia Strategy," *The New York Times,* November 28, 2013, A14.

more energy in the Asia-Pacific region in military, diplomatic, and economic fields.[297]

Fourth, regarding the impact of the Sino-U.S. Maritime Rights Disputes on Sino-U.S. relations: the frame of the newspaper is that China's establishment of the East China Sea Air Defense Identification Zone seriously hindered Presidents Barack Obama and Xi Jinping's joint efforts to establish a new type of relationship between major powers.[298] One article said that during Obama's presidency, Sino-U.S. relations fluctuated repeatedly, and a series of issues including arms sales to Taiwan caused China to cut off military exchanges with the United States.[299] Another article mentioned that the United States welcomed President Xi's proposal for building a new type of major power relations, but that its foundation lay in the sincerity and trust between the two countries, and that the face-off of warships in the South China Sea further showed that the two countries should conduct long-term, continuous military dialogue to ease regional tensions.[300]

---

[297] David E. Sanger, "In the East China Sea, a Far Bigger Test of Power Looms," *The New York Times*, December 2, 2013, A3.

[298] "China's Coercive Play," *The New York Times*, November 26, 2013, A24.

[299] David E. Sanger, "In the East China Sea, a Far Bigger Test of Power Looms," *The New York Times*, December 2, 2013, A3.

[300] Mark Landler, "Biden Urges Restraint by China in Airspace Dispute," *The New York Times*, December 5, 2013, A4.

CHAPTER 6

MEDIA PRESENTATIONS OF THE CRISES IN SINO-U.S. RELATIONS AND U.S. DECISION-MAKING ON CHINA

On November 9, 2016, Donald Trump defeated Hillary Clinton to be elected the 45th President of the United States. According to the pattern of Washington electoral politics, a new president from another party often adjusts the foreign policy of the predecessor. On the one hand, this is to demonstrate the new administration's resolve and position to correct what they see as the wrongs done previously. On the other hand, it is done to fulfil campaign promises. Trump is no exception. During his campaign, he criticized Obama's foreign policy, saying that it made the United States weak that it had lost its leadership and he would work hard to "Make America Great Again".[301]

During the presidential election, a tough China policy is often used as a good card to win over voters. Therefore, in the adjustments and making of the new president's foreign policy, China policy naturally becomes an important part. Even before he was formally sworn in, Trump made some fierce remarks on China, and even tried to take the "red line" that cannot be touched in Sino-U.S. relations—the Taiwan issue and the One-China Principle—as a bargaining chip, and tried to isolate China using the triangular relationship between China,

---

[301] Lin Hongyu, "Where will Sino-US Relations Go in the Trump Era," *People's Forum*, no. 1 (2017): 108-110.

the United States and Russia.[302] Regarding the direction of Sino-U.S. relations during the Trump administration, some scholars predicted that the new government would make major adjustments to its China policy, especially in the early days of Trump's tenure, likely to show a tough attitude towards China, leading to increased tension in Sino-U.S. relations in the short term.

Severe challenges or even crises that future Sino-U.S. relations may face are mainly in the following aspects:

First, the Taiwan issue. Since the end of the Cold War, there have been at least two Taiwan Strait Crises between China and the United States. In addition to the crisis that was triggered by Washington allowing Lee Teng-hui to visit the U.S. from 1995 to 1996 (analyzed in Chapter 3), there was also the 2007-2008 crisis caused by Chen Shui-bian's attempts for a referendum on joining the United Nations.[303] Trump tried to elevate U.S.-Taiwan relations, using the Taiwan issue as a bargaining chip to pressure China, forcing China to make concessions on economic, trade, and security issues, etc. It is foreseeable that Taiwan will once again become the core issue that will trigger a crisis between the two powers.

Second, the South China Sea issue. Trump may continue to regard the Asia-Pacific region as the center of U.S. global strategy and increase the deployment of military forces in the region. Therefore, the U.S. government will definitely continue to use freedom of navigation on the high seas as an excuse to strengthen its cruising in the South China Sea, which is actually reconnaissance, and interfere in China's territorial disputes with third countries in the East China Sea and South China Sea. During Trump's tenure, as China continues to strengthen its military presence in the South China Sea, the power game between Beijing and Washington in the Western Pacific will continue. The South China Sea will not be calm for the foreseeable future. Greater crises are lurking.

Third, economic and trade issues. Businessman-turned-President Trump is undoubtedly trad-and-profit oriented. He criticizes Obama's

---

[302] Qian Wenrong, "The US Election, Trump's Policy Trend, and Sino-US Relations," *Peace and Development*, no. 1 (2017): 1-16.

[303] Yang Jiemian, *Broadening of International Crises and China-US Joint Responses* (Beijing: Current Affairs Press, 2010), 132.

globalization and free trade policies, talks about trade protectionism, and even threatened to levy a 45 percent tariff on Chinese goods. Therefore, in the future, China-U.S. economic and trade relations may show tension around issues like RMB exchange rate, trade imbalance, and market-access.[304] The possibility of a low-intensity trade war between the two countries needs to be cautiously prevented.

Fourth, the North Korean nuclear issue. According to U.S. media reports, after Trump entered the White House, the top issue to be addressed on his Asian strategic agenda was on North Korea. If Pyongyang unilaterally continued to carry out nuclear weapons tests, the possibility that Trump will take preemptive military strikes cannot be ruled out.[305] In addition, Trump said that China should take responsibility for the North Korean nuclear issue, leveraging issues of Taiwan and the One-China Principle to up the ante. If the United States carries out a military strike against North Korea, or simply drags China into the quagmire of the North Korean nuclear issue, it will be a threat to China's integrity of sovereignty and territorial security.

Professor Yan Xuetong once proposed the "false friend" theory of Sino-U.S. relations, arguing that pretending to be friends with each other is the cause of the ups and downs of Sino-U.S. relations.[306] After Trump took office, China and the United States might continue to maintain the relationship of "fake friends". Although the two sides will still cooperate in various fields, there will be no lack of competition and friction, and the possibility of political and military crises still exists. Once a crisis event occurs between the two countries, the U.S. media will inevitably chase and dig it, and certain patterns will inevitably manifest themselves in the process of reporting the crises. In the first three chapters, the author has analyzed the relevant articles of *The New York Times* on the Taiwan Strait Crisis in 1996, the Plane Collision

---

[304] Lin Hongyu, "Where will Sino-US Relations Go in the Trump Era," *People's Forum*, no. 1 (2017): 108-110.

[305] Brian Padden, "Former US Envoy: Don't Expect Strategic Patience on N. Korea From Trump," VOA News, accessed September 4, 2020, https://www.voanews.com/east-asia-pacific/former-us-envoy-dont-expect-strategic-patience-n-korea-trump.

[306] Yan Xuetong, "An Analysis of the Instabilities of Sino-US Relations," *World Politics and Economy*, no. 12 (2010): 4-30.

Incident in 2001, and the Sino-U.S. Maritime Rights Dispute in 2013, and deducted the characteristics in the newspaper's coverage on these three crises. Building on that, this chapter will discuss the characteristics and patterns of U.S. media, *The New York Times* included, during Sino-U.S. relations crises, and try to study the roles and functions of the media in the U.S. decision-making process on China affairs. The goal is to provide some insight for China's international communication practice in the future.

SECTION 1. CHARACTERISTICS AND PATTERNS OF U.S. MEDIA COVERAGE ON CRISES OF SINO-U.S. RELATIONS

Crisis is a special state of state-to-state relations. In a crisis, long-term, latent or hidden contradictions in international relations manifest themselves in the forms of frictions, conflicts, or confrontations in a short period of time. International crises often receive high attention from the media, and they are the most newsworthy items in international news. When covering international crises, in addition to introducing the details, background and latest developments of crisis events, the media will also analyze the background, nature, and responsible parties of the crisis, and discuss or evaluate the relationship between the countries involved and their respective foreign policies. Because the media plays the roles of transmitting information and agenda-setting in the process of international crises, it will inevitably, to a certain degree, influence domestic and even international public opinions. From this perspective, a series of news coverage conducted by a country's media during a crisis involving its own country and another country can also be regarded as a process of competing for the power of discourse; excellent coverage capabilities and skills may change the tendencies of international public opinions, and even eventually influence the process of crisis resolution and management.

The relationship between China and the United States is currently the most important major power bilateral relationship, and the most prominent feature of the relationship is that it is unstable. When two countries are in conflict or confrontation due to competition, it is important to understand and grasp the characteristics and patterns of American media in their crisis coverage; it offers significant implications for China's foreign policy adjustments, international crisis management, and formulation communication strategy, etc. In this book, the author has selected three post-Cold War Sino-U.S. relations crises: the Taiwan Strait Crisis in 1996, the Plane Collision Incident in 2001 and the 2013 Sino-U.S. Maritime Rights Dispute; they respectively occurred during the tenures of three U.S. presidents—Bill Clinton, George W. Bush and Barack Obama. *The New York Times* coverage on these three crises is used as the research sample. Content and frame analyses are conducted, upon which the characteristics and patterns are deducted regarding *The New York Times'* Sino-U.S. crisis coverage. In view of the representativeness and influence of *The New York Times* in the United States and even the world, the author believes that the newspaper can reflect to a certain extent the general characteristics and patterns of American news media in crisis coverage.

Media Attention is Positively Correlated with the Nature and Intensity of the Crisis

The degree of media attention to crisis events (measured by the volume of coverage) is closely related to the nature of the crisis itself (i.e. whether it is related to the country's core interests) and its intensity (whether there is a direct conflict, and whether there is a risk of accidental clash or even war). The three Sino-U.S. relations crises studied in this book, if sorted by their nature and intensity, then the order from high to low should be: the Plane Collision Incident in 2001, the Taiwan Strait Crisis in 1996, and the Sino-U.S. Maritime Rights Dispute in 2013; the specific reasons the author has given in the previous analyses. *The New York Times* also appeared to follow the same order in the number of articles on the three crises: in 2001, from the plane collision to the American crew return, in just 15 days, there were 80 relevant *Times* articles; in March 1996, in 31 days there were 43 articles on the Taiwan Strait Crisis, while there were only 19 articles on the Sino-U.S. Maritime Rights Dispute between November 23 and December 20, 2013.

Specifically, during each crisis, the peak of the number of articles in *The New York Times* basically coincided with the key events in the crisis process. This characteristic was especially obvious in the newspaper's coverage of the 1996 Taiwan Strait Crisis and the 2001 Plane Collision Incident. In the 1996 Taiwan Strait Crisis, the days with the largest number of articles are March 10, 12, and 24, which coincided with the three major events in the Taiwan Strait Crisis that month, namely: the Chinese People's Liberation Army's new round of joint naval and air military exercises in Taiwan waters, the U.S. dispatch of the aircraft carrier fleet to the Taiwan Strait, and Taiwan's first direct leader election in history. In the Plane Collision Incident in 2001, the two peaks in the number of articles appeared between April 4 to 6, and from April 12 to 13, which also corresponded to two key events in the crisis resolution process: when foreign Minister Tang Jiaxuan clearly stated China's position to the U.S. Ambassador to China Joseph Prueher, under the instructions of President Jiang Zemin's "apology-release" solution, as well as when the twenty-four U.S. crew members left Haikou Meilan Airport by plane and returned to the U.S. naval base.

If we compare the distribution of article volume with that of reporting angles in the coverage of *The New York Times* during these crises, we can also find that during the process of Sino-U.S. relations crises, the media often pays the most attention to the positions and decisions of the Chinese and U.S. governments, the two sides' direct wrestling on diplomatic fronts, the fate of individuals involved in the crisis, and the future direction of the relationship between the two countries. In addition, in terms of the overall distribution of article genres, *The New York Times* tends to use long-length news stories and event feature stories to present international crises, in-depth analysis articles to scrutinize the issues, and supplements with editorials, column commentaries and other articles to express attitudes and convey opinions.

The Media has Clear Tendencies when Covering International Crises

The New York Times' coverage of the three crises as a whole—the 1996 Taiwan Strait Crisis, the 2001 Plane Collision Incident, and the 2013 Sino-U.S. Maritime Rights Dispute—directly or indirectly expressed negative tendencies towards China. Direct expression, as the name suggests, is that the content of the coverage contains words and sentences that directly bash, criticize or satirize the Chinese government or related parties; It is more commonly seen in the two genres of in-depth analysis and commentary. Besides direct expressions of its tendencies, *The New York Times* report also indirectly expresses attitudes towards China in a variety of ways, such as in the preference in source choices, ways of citation, vivid emotionally-charged vocabulary, the screening of news facts, the selection of reporting angles, and the editing and processing of news content, etc. These methods have been reflected in the coverage process of all three crises.

First, regarding preference in source choices and ways of citation: When *The New York Times* covers crises in Sino-U.S. relations, the number of citations from U.S. sources (including the U.S. government, military, media, experts, scholars, and the public) is often larger than that of the sources from China. In the newspaper's coverage on the Plane Collision Incident in 2001, the number of citations from U.S. sources accounted for nearly 72% of the total, and news from U.S. officials alone accounted for 46%. In contrast, the citation rate of all sources from China was only 24%. In coverage of Sino-U.S. Maritime Rights Dispute in 2013, the proportion of citations from U.S. sources was 48.7% of the total, which was also higher than that of sources from China, which accounted for 30%. In the 1996 Taiwan Strait Crisis, although on the surface it appears that sources from mainland China were cited more frequently than sources from the United States, there is another crucial party—China's Taiwan; Therefore, if citations from sources from the United States and Taiwan are added up, the combined proportion will reach 57%; with the proportion of sources from China being 30%, China's voice actually was still weakened.

Contents from mainstream Chinese media—Xinhua News Agency,

People's Daily, China Central Television, *PLA Daily*, etc.—were often cited when *The New York Times* covers crises in Sino-U.S. relations. But whenever the source was mentioned, the official nature and government background of these media organizations were repeatedly emphasized; the purpose being to question the objectivity and impartiality of the mainstream Chinese media and shake the audience's trust in Chinese media. On the other hand, in the relevant coverage of the 1996 Taiwan Strait Crisis and the 2001 Plane Collision Incident, there were interviews with ordinary people in China and the United States, and most of them appeared in the form of direct quotes; However, in these reports, the voices of the Chinese people often showed strong nationalist sentiments, and were not calm and rational.

Second, when covering the crises in Sino-U.S. relations, *The New York Times* frequently used some emotionally-charged words when analyzing and evaluating the Chinese government's foreign affairs stance, decisions, statements, and behaviors, etc.; This is also a clear display of the newspaper's attitude and tendency. For example, *The New York Times* used "aggressive", "reckless", "dangerously", "intimidation", and other derogatory words many times when covering the 1996 Taiwan Strait Crisis, the 2001 Plane Collision Incident, and the 2013 Sino-U.S. Maritime Rights Dispute, to describe the performance of the Chinese government in the course of the crises; this is also a way to suggest who should be the party responsible for the crisis.

Media Coverage on International Crises Follows Specific News Frames

While agenda-setting means the media can arrange "what to report", news frames are when the media decides on "how to report". A news event will be approached from a completely different angle due to a different news frame, which in turn will produce completely different communication effects. The media reconstructs events through the news frames and the audience understands and thinks about the events based on such construction. American scholar Todd Gitlin argues that the mechanisms of news frame includes selection, emphasis and exclusion; William Gamson also argues that news frames deliberately emphasize or ignore certain facts, and that the definition of the frame is on one hand about picking and choosing, the other on construction.[307] In the process of presenting the crises in Sino-U.S. relations, *The New York Times* followed specific news frames, emphasizing certain facts while ignoring some others, just as explained by the definition of the aforementioned news frames.

First, when analyzing the causes and backgrounds of crises in Sino-U.S. relations, *The New York Times* often uses fact selection and editing—ignoring some facts and emphasizing some details—cleverly assigning responsibility for the incident to China. For example, the direct cause of the 1996 Taiwan Strait Crisis should have been Lee Teng-hui's visit to the United States and Taiwan's direct presidential election; Both incidents were blatant provocations against the One-China Principle and the integrity of China's sovereignty. However, *The New York Times* attributed causes of the deterioration of Sino-U.S. relations to China's piracy problems, human rights situation, and other unrelated issues such as the manufacture and sale of weapons of mass destruction, etc. When analyzing the reasons for the Plane Collision Incident in 2001, *The New York Times* deliberately ignored the fact that the U.S. EP-3 military reconnaissance plane was conducting reconnaissance in sensitive areas along the coast of China before the collision occurred. The newspaper instead emphasized that the U.S. plane was at the time legally flying in international airspace and that the EP-3 plane could not make sudden turns due to its large size. The *Times* presented the belief that the real cause of the collision was the Chinese fighter jet's continuous provocation of the U.S. plane and its dangerous maneuvers. After China announced the establishment of an air defense identification zone in the East China Sea in 2013, the United States sided with its allies of Japan and South Korea, accusing China of making provocations against the status quo in the Pacific region, and repeatedly stressed that the identification zone established by China had

---

[307] Hui-Hsin Huang, "Analysis of the News Frames of Controversial Events—Taking the 'Multi-level Management Issue of the Credit Departments of Farmers' and Fishermen's Associations' as an Example" (Master's thesis, National Taiwan Normal University, 2002), 9.

partially overlapped with those of Japan and South Korea and involved disputed islands; but the fact that the United States, Japan, South Korea and other countries had long established air defense identification zones was either not mentioned or it was downplayed; The analysis of the reasons for the face-off between Chinese and U.S. warships in the South China Sea was along the same lines as the coverage of the Plane Collision Incident: *The New York Times* emphasized that the U.S.S Cowpens was sailing legally on the high seas at the time of the incident; that it was the Chinese warship that used very aggressive tactics to force stop the Cowpens and almost caused the two ships to collide. *The Times* meanwhile deliberately missed the facts that the Cowpens was monitoring the training of the Chinese Liaoning aircraft carrier, that the Cowpens ignored the ban on navigation published on the website of the China Maritime Safety Administration, that the Cowpens broke into the "inner defense zone" of the Chinese aircraft carrier fleet, while proceeding forward when the Chinese warship sounded a warning whistle, and many other details.

Second, when *The New York Times* covered the crises in Sino-U.S. relations, it often conflated the events that led to the crises with other sensitive issues in Sino-U.S. relations. Sometimes it linked China's sovereignty with human rights issues, and sometimes it linked China's national security issues with Sino-U.S. economic and trade issues. It also had elevated long-standing territorial disputes between China and its neighbors to China's coveting regional hegemony. During the 1996 Taiwan Strait Crisis, *The New York Times* repeatedly mentioned human rights problems in China exposed by the Tiananmen Square incident in 1989, China's disrespect for intellectual property rights which was reflected by rampant piracies, and the sale of weapons of mass destruction by China to Pakistan, etc., saying that President Bill Clinton should impose economic sanctions on China. In the course of the crisis in Sino-U.S. relations caused by the Plane Collision Incident in 2001, *The New York Times*, in its explanations and analyses, combined the resolution of incident with U.S. arms sales to Taiwan, China's most-favored-nation trade status, China's accession to the World Trade Organization, and Beijing's bid to host the Olympic Games, etc. In 2013, in covering China's announcement of the establishment of an air defense identification zone in the East China Sea, *The New York Times* also analyzed the incident in tandem with China's human rights situation, its ambitions in the Western Pacific, and its rising domestic nationalist sentiment. During the newspaper's coverage of the following face-off between Chinese and U.S. warships in the South China Sea, the incident was compared with similar past incidents, including the Plane Collision Incident in 2001 and the U.S.NS Impeccable incident in 2009, emphasizing that these accidents were all caused by provocative and reckless actions of the Chinese aircraft or ships.

Third, the analysis and evaluation of Sino-U.S. relations and the U.S. policy toward China are an important part of the news frames of *The New York Times* coverage on the crisis in Sino-U.S. relations. Amid the three crises—the 1996 Taiwan Strait Crisis, the 2001 Plane Collision Incident, and the 2013 Sino-U.S. Maritime Rights Dispute, *The New York Times* always paid strong focus to the problems in Washington's China policy, for example, the Clinton administration's vacillation between "engagement" and "containment" of China, the Bush administration's lack of attention to China and high-level China experts in the core team, and the Obama administration's need to further clarify its Asian policy and its China policy thus to put Asian allies more at ease. In addition, during these three crises, *The New York Times* repeatedly mentioned the complexity and instability of Sino-U.S. relations, and showed disagreements with all of the characterization of the Sino-U.S. relations at the time, whether it was Clinton's "constructive strategic partnership", or the Bush administration's seeing China as a "strategic competitor", and not the least, the "new major power relations" proposed by President Xi Jinping.

Viewing from the news frames summarized above, it is not difficult to see that *The New York Times*' presentation of crises in Sino-U.S. relations is directly affected by national interest factors. Although in covering these three crises, *The New York Times* gave mixed reviews on the performance of U.S. presidents and their administrations, and sometimes even sharply criticized the government's China policies, in the eyes of the American media, the U.S. government is not equivalent to the national interests of the United States; sometimes the U.S. government is not even capable of endorsing and safeguarding national interests.

Therefore, *The New York Times'* criticisms of the U.S. government by no means conceal the newspaper's recognition and protection of U.S. national interests, ideology, values, individual rights, etc. in the report. It is known for its objectivity and fairness. During the crises in Sino-U.S. relations, *The New York Times* undoubtedly stood firmly on the side of national interests, and unconsciously acted as a microphone for the White House and the Pentagon. This shows that international crisis coverage is undoubtedly the type of international news reporting that is most closely integrated with national interests.

SECTION 2. THE FUNCTION AND ROLE OF THE MEDIA IN U.S. DECISION-MAKING PROCESS ON CHINA

As the author mentioned in Chapter 1, the research objective of this book includes two questions: First, what are the characteristics and patterns of American media's coverage during crises between China and the United States? Second, how does media coverage of the crises influence Washington's decision-making on China? Regarding the first question, this book takes *The New York Times* as an example and selects three typical cases for research; the summarized characteristics and patterns have been discussed in detail earlier. The relationship between media coverage and U.S. decision-making on China is also a key area to be discussed in this study. Due to the many practical limitations in research conditions, it is not easy to find the direct influence chain or the causal relationship. However, it is still possible to draw some conclusions when combining existing theoretical research results in the field of international news and international politics, and on this basis conduct analysis, reasoning, and summarization.

Media Functions in International Crisis Communication

Professor Liu Xiaoying has elaborated on the political roles and functions of international news in his book *International Journalism: Ontology, Methods and Functions.* He argues that the political functions of international news mainly include six aspects: First, by providing international political news, the media meets the audience's right to be informed; second, the media influences international public opinion through agenda-setting, and constructs the power of discourse; third, the media serves the state's global strategy and diplomacy, and safeguards national interests; fourth, the media supervises the government or the international community, and promotes people's political participation; fifth, international news shows "soft power" and constructs the national image; sixth, the media helps achieve social mobilization and political socialization.[308] These six points comprehensively summarize the political functions that international news can play. As a special form of international politics, international crises are often the subjects international media competes to cover. In the process of international crisis communication, the media undoubtedly also plays certain political functions. However, some of these functions are amplified during international crisis communication, and depending on the specific circumstances of each crisis, the media may also play some additional roles.

In international crisis communication, the function of the media to provide information and set agendas is more pronounced. Amid the international crisis, due to its uncertainties and potential serious consequences, the public's demand for information greatly increases. At this time, "if authoritative information is absent, gossip and various rumors will go rampant; on the contrary, the timely release of authoritative information will block the outlet of rumors."[309] Because media reports are the main information channel for the public to quickly and comprehensively understand the crisis situation, the media's judgments on the situation and the opinions expressed will have a greater impact on public opinion, and then it is likely to affect the government's agenda, and to a certain extent, its decision making.

The diplomatic and social mobilization functions of the media have also been demonstrated in the spread of international crises. In

---

[308] Liu Xiaoying, *International Journalism: Ontology, Methods and Functions* (Beijing: China Radio and Television Press, 2010), 260-273.
[309] Gao Xiaohong and Sui Yan, ed., *International Crisis Communication* (Beijing: Communication University of China Press, 2011), 71.

the intricate international crisis process, the media's extensive reports, interpretations and analysis of the crisis situation and situation, the government's diplomatic stance and decision-making can not only help the public understand the crisis situation and understand the country's foreign policy in an well-rounded manner, but also help the government gain more support and recognition, enhance the legitimacy of diplomatic decision-making, and ensure the smooth progress of diplomatic actions. As media reports on international crises continue to deepen, the patriotic enthusiasm, sense of social responsibility, and compassion of a country's audience are likely to be strongly stimulated by this cumulative effect, becoming a strong force of public opinion, and even directly translating into action. In this process, the media is not only the target of mobilization, but also exerts a powerful social mobilization function.

In addition, the media often plays additional roles in the spread of international crises, such as crisis warning and pacifying functions. Media reports during the incubation period of a crisis are likely to arouse the government, society, or individual's crisis awareness and activate an early warning mechanism because of the sensitive content or information involved. Some sudden international crises, due to their strong abnormality, destructiveness, and continuity, can easily arouse public speculation and social panic. During times like these, continuous and in-depth reports by the media can provide information while relieving these sentiments. This kind of psychological state can help the public stabilize their confidence, maintain calmness, establish a sense of alertness, and help them understand and support the government's foreign policy decisions.

The Role of the Media in U.S. Decision-Making on China

In the process of researching *The New York Times*' coverage on the crises in Sino-U.S. relations, the author found that in terms of source preferences, *The New York Times* to a high degree relied on information from the U.S. government, thus showing a tendency towards government-led news reporting. So, what exactly is the relationship between media coverage and U.S. decision-making on China? Is media coverage on Sino-U.S. relations largely controlled by the U.S. government? Or does the media actually serve as a tool for the U.S. government to promote its China policy? There are no obvious answers to these questions, and many scholars in China and abroad are constantly conducting in-depth research and discussions on them. Although it is impossible for U.S. media's coverage on Sino-U.S. relations to be completely separated from the control and influence of the U.S. government, nor are they able to guarantee absolute independence and objectivity, nevertheless, the U.S. media undoubtedly plays a certain role in Washington's decision-making process on China.

Regarding the roles of the media in the field of foreign relations, Cohen argues that there are mainly three aspects, namely: observer of foreign policy news, participants in the process of foreign policy making, and medium of foreign information.[310] According to Cohen, the media not only provides reference for the formulation of foreign policy, but is also an active participant in the formulation process. So what role does the U.S. media play in Washington's decision-making process on China? Based on the analysis of the U.S. media's coverage on Sino-U.S. relations crises in this book, and combined with the research results and views of some Chinese domestic and foreign scholars, the author argues that the roles of the U.S. media in U.S. government's decision-making process on China mainly include the following aspects:

First, U.S. media provides the government and the public with information and policy feedback from China's unofficial channels; Although the foreign policymakers of the U.S. State Department have their specific channels for collecting and obtaining information—official and unofficial—media reports often provide important information and angles of observation that are different from internal news. In addition, many mainstream American media organizations, including *The New York Times*, have sent reporters to China, who sometimes get information faster than through government channels. With the ever-changing international situation, grasping the news immediately as it happens is crucial for decision-making.

---

[310] Carol H. Weiss, "What America's Leaders Read," *The Public Opinion Quarterly* 38, no. 1 (Spring 1974): 1-22.

For those who are closely following foreign policy and international issues, most of the information they have got comes directly from mass media. [311] The American public is no exception; Their access to foreign information also relies on media reports. For those Americans who have never been to China or have experienced Chinese society firsthand, their basic impression of China is mainly derived from reporting in the American media, and they are practically ignorant of the tremendous changes that have taken place in China in recent years.[312] Due to the lack of necessary background knowledge, their views and attitudes on China's issues and understanding of Sino-U.S. relations depend on what issues the U.S. media pays attention or overlooks, and how the media describes China and evaluates China-U.S. relations.

Second, American media explains the U.S. government's China policy to the public and provides policymakers with a way to observe public opinion. Washington's China policy formulation or adjustment process is basically the same as other foreign policies; It is initiated by government entities such as the White House, the State Department, or the Department of Defense, and the news is then delivered to the media through press conferences and briefings. Media organizations will then report all or part of the information on China policy that the organization deems necessary, according to its own operational philosophy and values.[313] The special system of American democracy means that all decisions of policymakers need to obtain understanding and support from the public, and the China policy is no exception. The media happens to provide decision-makers with channels for them to introduce and explain various policies to the public, including the background of policy formulation or adjustment, basis of decision-making, expected effects, etc.; The media's editorials or column commentary articles also provide the public with diverse perspectives in policy analysis and evaluation. It is in this process that the public

---

[311] Charles W. Kegley Jr. and Eugene R. Wittkopf, *American Foreign Policy: Pattern and Process* (New York: St. Martin's Press, 1979), 229.

[312] Ezra Feivel Vogel, "Must We Treat China as an Enemy?," trans. Yang Xiuyou, *China Opening Herald*, no. 8 (1997): 25.

[313] Luo Juanli, "Tendency Analysis of American Media's Reporting on China Issues" (PhD diss., China University of Political Science and Law, 2013), 161.

establishes an understanding, judgment, and evaluation of the U.S. government's China policy, finally contributing to certain public discourse. The interpretation of the media will affect the political behavior of the government, for policy makers often accept the evaluation of the media.[314]

At the same time, the media also provides the government with feedback channels for the public's opinions and evaluations on various policies. In the United States, the role of public opinion in the field of foreign policy is critical, because the State Department must decide on the planning, formulation, adjustment, and implementation of any foreign policy based on public opinion.[315] Of course, government decision-makers can also understand the public's views and attitudes through public opinion surveys, but in comparison, media reports that reflect public opinion are a more convenient and effective way to ascertain the views of the people.

Third, the media assesses the U.S. government's China policy and affects public approval rate for the government and officials. Compared with domestic news, American audiences have always paid relatively low attention to international news. Due to the lack of knowledge of international affairs and diplomacy, the American public's understanding and evaluation of the U.S.'s China policy often comes directly from media reports. Within the framework of the American democratic system, the public has the right to supervise and question the government and officials, and the U.S. policy towards China is also under such supervision and questioning. Therefore, media coverage on Sino-U.S. relations and Washington's China policy will have a certain impact on the approval rates of government policies and individuals of the President and other officials themselves. In the United States, no government official or congressman will turn a deaf ear to the views of the media and public opinion reflected in the media.

Fourth, the media sets agendas for Sino-U.S. relations and builds public opinion environments for Washington's decision-making on China. The more the media covers a particular foreign affair matter,

---

[314] Doris A. Graber, *Media Power in Politics* (Washington D.C.: Congressional Quarterly Inc, 1984), 202.

[315] Lester Markel, *Public Opinion and Foreign Policy* (New York: Council on Foreign Relations, 1949), 29.

the more the government and the public pay attention to it, and they will consider this matter to be of importance and urgency. The continuous attention and intensive coverage of an event by the media may make the event a hot topic of discussion among government officials and the public, and then it may become an important foreign affair issue, even later transforming into a certain foreign affair action by the government. Not only that, in the United States, media consultants and public relations professionals directly participate in the formulation of foreign policies; government officials often consult them on a certain foreign policy and consider their opinions and suggestions.

In the process of formulating the policy toward China, obtaining public support to promote the smooth implementation of a policy is an important goal of the government, and "public opinion" is an important indicator that the government must consider in this process. Because the final implementation of the China policy must be supported by public opinion, the public's views, attitudes and opinions on related China issues, as well as their levels of understanding and support for China's policy, are all factors that the government has to consider and pay high attention to. American politicians always believe that the media can not only gain insight into the will of the people,[316] but also help the government create a favorable environment for public opinion. Through the media, the opinions and voices on China issues, Sino-U.S. relations, and U.S. policies on China, which are scattered in all corners of society, can converge into a force of public opinion and form a policy climate, be it favorable or not.

Implications to China's Diplomacy and International Communication Strategy

On the one hand, the American media can reflect the views and attitudes of the American people on Sino-U.S. relations and the U.S. policy towards China. On the other hand, it can pass public opinion to policymakers and participate to a certain extent in the formulation of

---

[316] Bernard Hennessy, *Public Opinion,* 5th ed. (Monterey, CA: Brooks/Cole, 1985), 249.

Washington's China policy. Because of the close relationship between the U.S. media and the government as it engages in international news reporting, and the media's crucial influence on the public's understanding and views on China issues and Sino-U.S. relations, the roles and influence of the U.S. media are elements that Chinese scholars must consider when conducting research in Sino-U.S. relations and international communication. China can not only observe the public opinion trends of the American people from media coverage, but through it can also predict the scope of adjustment of the U.S. policy toward China, as well as its future directions.

First, the American media often directly or indirectly displays negative positions and attitudes when covering China issues. We should treat such tendencies rationally, and respond actively. There are deep-rooted differences in political systems, ideologies, cultural traditions, and values between China and the United States. In recent years, as the pace of China's economic globalization has accelerated, the trade competition between the two countries has also become more intense. Therefore, the strategic competition and mutual suspicion between the two will exist for a long time, and the prejudices and negative attitudes towards each other may also continue to grow. The American media has an inherent instinct to chase negative news and has a long-standing stereotype of China issues; thus, we do not need to over-interpret, when to a certain degree there are objective reasons why American media is consistent with the U.S. government positions or sides with America's national interests, when it comes to Sino-U.S. relations and U.S. policy toward China.

Second, the Chinese Foreign Ministry can use American media coverage to ascertain and predict the intentions and goals of Washington's China policy, so as to buy time for China's foreign policy decisions and actions. The U.S. government has always been good at manipulating and using the media. The White House press conferences and press briefings are the main sources of political news in many U.S. media organizations. Washington's attitude and stance on Sino-U.S. relations, the formulation and adjustment of its China policy, etc., are communicated in advance through the media to test the waters of public opinion. The tendencies of public opinion which end up on mainstream American media may affect the China policy proposals by members of the Congress, as well as the policy adjustments of government policymakers. Therefore, China should pay high and close attention to this process, so as to anticipate the intentions and goals of Washington's China policy.

Third, China's management of foreign journalists in China should be more open and fitting. When studying *The New York Times'* articles on the Taiwan Strait Crisis in 1996, the Plane Collision Incident in 2001, and the Maritime Rights Dispute in 2013, the author finds that many articles mentioned the many restrictions and inconveniences foreign journalists have encountered when conducting interviews in China, making it difficult to get in-depth contact with interviewees or obtain true and comprehensive information; some articles on the Sino-U.S. Maritime Rights Dispute in 2013 also mentioned China's expulsion of foreign journalists, and expressed dissatisfaction. In recent years, China's management of foreign news organizations has become increasingly loose, but the degree of openness still needs to be improved. If foreign reporters stationed in China do not have access to more information in China, they will only use sources from U.S. officials, or experts and scholars, putting China in a disadvantaged position in obtaining the power of discourse; Foreign media's various kinds of complaints about China's press management system will further damage the image of China in the eyes of foreign audiences.

The media is the main wrestling area of China and the United States for discourse power and soft power. It is an extremely difficult but crucial long-term task to leverage American media coverage to enhance the American people's understanding of China's basic situation and social progress, change the American people's deep-rooted prejudices against China, and eliminate the suspicion and distrust between the governments of China and the United States. On the one hand, we need to observe and study the characteristics of the U.S. media's international news reporting in a more three-dimensional and in-depth manner, combined with an understanding of the mechanism and process of Washington's formulation of its China policy. At the same time, we should also improve the transparency of China's political life and society, strengthen information disclosure, and improve the spokesperson system, allowing more Chinese voices and opinions to be spread to the world more effectively.

SECTION 3. LIMITATIONS OF THIS BOOK AND FUTURE RESEARCH PROSPECTS

Taking the reporting of *The New York Times* as an example, this book studies relevant coverage on three cases of Sino-U.S. relations, namely the 1996 Taiwan Strait Crisis, the 2001 Plane Collision Incident, and the 2013 Maritime Rights Dispute (including China's establishment of the East China Sea Air Defense Identification Zone and the face-off of Chinese and American warships in the South China Sea). The way *The New York Times* presents China issues and the crises in Sino-U.S. relations are analyzed, with a focus on the newspaper's news frames on Sino-U.S. relations and the U.S.'s policy towards China.

Although *The New York Times* is highly representee of mainstream American media, the characteristics and patterns analyzed and deduced are certainly limited because only one media organization is used as the research sample. The issues involved in Sino-U.S. relations are numerous and complex, including politics, military, economy, culture, diplomacy, and many other fields. Although crisis is a special state in Sino-U.S. relations and the media pays high attention to crisis events, using crisis coverage as an entry point to analyze U.S. media's characteristics and patterns in reporting Sino-U.S. relations still risks over-generalization. Moreover, due to finite time and energy, in the research process of this book, the author has not used many foreign policy documents from the U.S. State Department and the Department of Defense as analysis materials, making it inviable to find a direct relationship between media coverage and U.S.'s China policy; this is a pity the author feels strongly.

Out of strong academic interest in this field, the author will continue to reflect on and explore this issue in future research work, drawing from the theories and methods of the discipline of international relations, and adding first-hand foreign policy documents and materials from U.S. State Department and the Department of Defense, etc. Under the new normal of Sino-U.S. relations, the author will deepen the query into the relationship between the U.S. media and Sino-U.S. relations, as well as

U.S. policy toward China, in view of the new situation and new issues in the relations between the two countries, in order to form a theoretical system that can guide China's international communication practice and serve as a reference for China's foreign affairs work.

BIBLIOGRAPHY

Almond, Gabriel A. *The American People and Foreign Policy.* New York: Frederick A. Praeger, 1960.

Arno, Andrew, and Wimal Dissanayake, ed. *The News Media in National and International Conflict.* Boulder: Westview Press, 1984.

Arquilla, John. *Louder Than Words: Tacit Communication in International Crises.* U.S.: Rand, 1993.

Babbie, Earl R. *The Practice of Social Research.* United States: Cengage Learning, 2013.

Becker, Neil Wu. "China and United States Press from 1949-1989: Critical Events Foreign Policy Analysis." PhD diss., San Jose State University, 1999.

Bennett, W. Lance. "Toward a Theory of Press-State Relations in the U.S." *Journal of Communication* 40, no. 2 (Spring 1990): 103-125.

Bennett, W. Lance. *News: The Politics of Illusion.* New York: Longman, 1988.

Benoit, William L. "Image Repair Discourse and Crisis Communication." *Public Relations Review* 23, no. 2 (1997): 177-186.

Berke, Richard L. "Now for Bush, A Novelty: Having to Face Novelty." *The New York Times*, April 5, 2001.

Bradsher, Keith. "Bolstering Military Ties, U.S. Gives Philippines Aid." *The New York Times*, December, 18, 2013.

Brecher, Michael. "State Behavior in International Crisis." *Journal of Conflict Resolution* 23, no. 3 (September 1979): 447.

Brecher, Michael. *Studies in Crisis Behavior.* New Jersey: Transaction Books, 1978.

Buckley, Chris. "China Claims Air Rights Over Disputed Islands." *The New York Times*, November 24, 2013.

Butterfield, Fox. "China's Demand for Apology Is Rooted in Tradition." *The New York Times*, April 7, 2001.

Chang, Tsan-Kuo. *The Press and China Policy: The Illusion of Sino-American Relations (1950-1984)*. New Jersey: Ablex Publishing Corporation, 1993.

Chen, Hanxi. "How the American Media 'Shaped' China's Image—Take the 'China-US Airplane Collision Incident' as an Example." *International Journalism*, no. 3 (2001): 5-12.

Chen, Weixing, ed. *International Relations and Global Communication*. Beijing: Beijing Broadcasting Institute, 2003.

Chen, Yinhua. "Media and China's Diplomacy: *Global Times* and *People's Daily* in Sino-US Relations." PhD diss., Communication University of China, 2014.

China Institute of Contemporary International Relations. *Introduction to International Crisis Management*. Beijing: Current Affairs Press, 2003.

Choe, Sang-Hun. "After China, South Korea to Expand Its Own Air Defense Zone." *The New York Times*, December 9, 2013.

Christopher, Warren. *In the Stream of History, Shaping Foreign Policy for a New Era*. California: Stanford University Press, 1998.

Chu, Shulong. "Sino-U.S. Relations Since the End of the Cold War." In *China and the United States—Opponents or Partners*, edited by Liu Xuecheng and Li Jidong, Beijing: Economic Science Press, 2001.

Chu, Yingchun. "On the Similarities and Differences of Sino-US Decision-Making in Foreign Affairs: Taking the Airplane Collision Incident as an Example." *China's Extracurricular Education (Theories)*, no. 2 (2007): 15-16.

Cohen, Bernard C. *The Press and Foreign Policy*. Boston: Little Brown Company, 1963.

Commercial Press. *Ci Yuan: Volume 1*. Beijing: Commercial Press, 1979.

Crossette, Barbara. "U.N. Mission to Haiti is Reprieved." *The New York Times*, March 1, 1996.

Dao, James. "China's Shadowing Had Annoyed U.S." *The New York Times*, April 2, 2001.

Department of Political Science at the University of Kansas, "Kansas Events Data System/Protocol for the Assessment of Nonviolent Direct Action (KEDS/PANDA) database." In *China and the World:*

Chinese Foreign Policy Faces the New Millennium, edited by Samuel S. Kim, 62. Boulder: Westview Press, 1998.

Deutsch, Karl W. *The Analysis of International Relations.* Englewood Cliffs, N.J.: Prentice-Hall, 1978.

Ding, Bangquan. *International Crisis Management.* Beijing: National Defense University Press, 2004.

Ding, Xiaowen. "Safeguarding National Interests in Crisis—A Study on China's Handling of Sino-US Diplomatic Crises." PhD diss., Peking University, 2005.

Dougherty, James E., and Robert L. Pfaltzgraff. *Contending Theories of International Relations.* Philadelphia: Lippincott, 1971.

Drew, Christopher. "Old Tactics May Pull the Rug From the U.S. Claim to Plane." *The New York Times,* April 4, 2001.

Elisabeth, Rosenthal, and David E. Sanger. "U.S. Plane in China After It Collides with Chinese Jet." *The New York Times,* April 2, 2001.

Erlanger, Steven. "Ambiguity' on Taiwan." *The New York Times,* March 12, 1996.

Erlanger, Steven. "Christopher to Meet His Chinese Counterpart." *The New York Times,* March 20, 1996.

Fackler, Martin. "Japan Rejects China's Claim to Air Rights Over Islands." *The New York Times,* November 25, 2013.

Faison, Seth. "Executives from Taiwan Worry, but Stay in China." *The New York Times,* March 20, 1996.

Fan, Shiming. "Why US Media is Hostile to China." *International Political Studies,* no. 3 (1997): 45-50.

Feng, Cunwan. "Modern International Communication and International Relations." *World Economy and Politics,* no. 12 (1999): 40-44.

Fink, Steven. *Crisis Management: Planning for the Inevitable.* United States: iUniverse, 2000.

Friedman, Thomas L. "Bending the Mountains." *The New York Times,* March 17, 1996.

Friedman, Thomas L. "Help Wanted: Deal Makers." *The New York Times,* March 24, 1996.

Friedman, Thomas. "One Nation, 3 Lessons." *The New York Times,* April 13, 2001.

Friedman, Thomas. "Sorry About That." *The New York Times,* April 6, 2001.

Fu, Ying, and Wu Shicun. "Sovereign Rights Dispute or Geopolitical Dispute? How Tensions in the South China Sea Evolve Step by Step." *People's Daily (Overseas Edition),* May 13, 2016.

Gans, Herbert J. *Deciding What's News: A Study of CBS Evening News, NBC Nightly News, Newsweek, and Time.* United Kingdom: Vintage Books, 1980.

Gao, Shiyi. "A Preliminary Study of Crisis Communication Research in the United States." Accessed September 24, 2020. http://cul.cssn.cn/xwcbx/xwcbx_cbx/201402/t20140211_961352.shtml.

Gao, Xiaohong, and Sui Yan, ed. *International Crisis Communication.* Beijing: Communication University of China Press, 2011.

Gargan, Edward A. "Chinese Missile Testing Fails to Disrupt Life on Taiwan." *The New York Times*, March 3, 1996.

Gargan, Edward A. "In Taiwan, Few Admit to Worries About China." *The New York Times*, March 17, 1996.

Gargan, Edward A. "Long-Term Forecast for Taiwan Remains Upbeat." *The New York Times*, March 23, 1996.

Gargan, Edward A. "Off China, Isle Waits Nervously." *The New York Times*, March 19, 1996.

Garver, John W. *Face Off: China, the United States and Taiwan's Democratization.* Seattle and London: University of Washington Press, 1997.

George, Amiso M., and Cornelius B. Pratt, ed. *Case Studies in Crisis Communication: International Perspectives on Hits and Misses.* New York: Routledge, 2012.

Gill, Bates. "China Policy, Without Regrets." *The New York Times*, April 12, 2001.

Ginneken, Jaap van. *Understanding Global News: A Critical Introduction.* India: SAGE Publications, 1998.

Gladstone, Rick. "Will Business Suffer in a China Stalemate?." *The New York Times,* April 8, 2001.

Global Times. "Inside Story of the Near Collision of Warships of China and the US." Accessed August 27, 2020. http://world.huanqiu.com/depth_report/2013-12/4664817.html.

Goldstein, Jonathan, ed., Jerry Israel, ed., and Hilary Conroy, ed. *America Views China: American Images of China Then and Now.* Bethlehem: Lehigh University Press, 1991.

Goodman, Robyn S. "Prestige Press Coverage of Us-China Policy During the Cold War's Collapse and Post-Cold War Years: Did a Deteriorating Cold War Paradigm Set the Stage for More Independent Press Coverage?." *International Communication Gazette* 61, no. 5 (1999): 391-410.

Graber, Doris A. *Mass Media and American Politics.* 7th ed. Washington, D.C.: Congressional Quarterly Press Inc., 2006.

Graber, Doris A. *Media Power in Politics.* Washington D.C.: Congressional Quarterly Inc, 1984.

Graham, Bradley. "U.S. Approves Arms Sales to Taiwan." *The Washington Post*, March 20, 1996.

Gu, Yaoming. *American Media in My Eye.* Beijing: Xinhua Publishing House, 2000.

Haass, Richard N. "Defining U.S. Foreign Policy in a Post-Post-Cold War." Remarks to Foreign Policy Association April 2002. Accessed September 12, 2020. https://2001-2009.state.gov/s/p/rem/9632.htm.

Hagel, Chuck. "Statement by Secretary of Defense Chuck Hagel on the East China Sea Air Defense Identification Zone." U.S. Department of Defense. Accessed August 25, 2020. https://archive.defense.gov/releases/release.aspx?releaseid=16392#:~:text=November%2023%2C%202013-,Statement%20by%20Secretary%20of%20Defense%20Chuck%20Hagel%20on%20the%20East,in%20the%20East%20China%20Sea.

Han, Xu. "On the Influence of Internet Media on China's Foreign Policy Decisions." Master's thesis, China Foreign Affairs University, 2011.

Han, Yugui. *Sino-US Relations After the Cold War.* Beijing: Social Sciences Literature Press, 2007.

He, Ying. *American Media and China's Image (1995-2005).* Guangzhou, China: Nanfang Daily Press, 2005.

Heath, Robert Lawrence. *Crisis Management for Managers and Executives: Business Crises, the Definitive Handbook to Reduction, Readiness, Response, and Recovery.* United Kingdom: Financial Times Management, 1998.

Hennessy, Bernard. *Public Opinion*. 5th ed. Monterey, CA: Brooks/ Cole, 1985.

Herman, Edward S., and Noam Chomsky. *Manufacturing Consent: The Political Economy of the Mass Media*. New York: Pantheon, 1988.

Hermann, Charles F. *Crises in Foreign Policy: A Simulation Analysis*. Indianapolis: Bobbs-Merrill, 1969.

Hermann, Charles F., ed. *International Crises: Insights from Behavior Research*. New York: Free Press, 1972.

Hilsman, Roger. *The Politics of Policy Making in Defense and Foreign Affairs*. New Jersey: Prentice-Hall, Inc., 1971.

Hoffman, Arthur S. ed. *International Communication and the New Diplomacy*. Bloomington: Indiana Univ. Pr., 1968.

Hou, Lijie. "Improving News Media's Communication Capacity in Crisis Communication." Master's thesis, Hebei University of Economics and Business, 2015.

Hu, Baijing. *Crisis Communication Management*. Beijing: Renmin University Press, 2014.

Hu, Fengying, and Wu Fei. *International News and Crisis Communication in the Era of Anti-Terrorism*. Taipei: Showwe Taiwan, 2006.

Hu, Ping. *International Conflict Analysis and Crisis Management Research*. Beijing: Military Yiwen Press, 1993.

Huang, Hui-Hsin. "Analysis of the News Frames of Controversial Events— Taking the 'Multi-level Management Issue of the Credit Departments of Farmers' and Fishermen's Associations' as an Example." Master's thesis, National Taiwan Normal University, 2002.

Institute of International Relations of Tsinghua University. "Database on China's Relations with Great Powers." Accessed September 25, 2020. http://www.imir.tsinghua.edu.cn/publish/iis/7522/index.html.

Jespersen, Christopher. *American Image of China*. United States: Stanford University Press, 1996.

Jiang, Changjian and Shen Yi. "Mass Media and the Making of China's Foreign Policy." *International Observation*, no. 1 (2007): 43-50.

Jiao, Shixin and Zhou Jianming. "The End of the Post-Cold War Era and its Significance to China." *World Economy and Politics*, no. 12 (2009): 40-46.

Jin, Canrong, and Liu Shiqiang. "Sino-US Relations since Obama Took Office." *American Studies*, no. 4 (2009): 39-50.

Jin, Canrong. "Supervisors Lacking Supervision—American News Media and Their Political Role." *World Knowledge,* no. 24 (1997): 16-17.

Jin, Hao. *"People's Daily* and China's Diplomacy: Analysis and Interpretation of the 'International Forum' Column (1994-2006)." Master's thesis, Fudan University, 2008.

Journalism Theory Research Office at Department of Journalism of Fudan University. *Introduction to Journalism.* Fuzhou: Fujian People's Publishing House, 1985.

Kahn, Joseph. "Standoff Brings Calls to Boycott Chinese Goods." *The New York Times,* April 11, 2001.

Kahn, Joseph. "Taiwan Arms Sales and China' W.T.O. Application Will Test a Relationship." *The New York Times,* April 12, 2001.

Kegley, Charles W., Jr., and Eugene R. Wittkopf. *American Foreign Policy: Pattern and Process.* New York: St. Martin's Press, 1979.

Kerry, John. "Statement on the East China Sea Air Defense Identification Zone." U.S. Department of State. Accessed August 25, 2020. https://2009-2017.state.gov/secretary/remarks/2013/11/218013.htm.

Kristolf, Nicholas D. "Off Taiwan, U.S. Sailors Are Unworried." *The New York Times,* March 19, 1996.

Lacey, Marc, and Steven Lee Myers. "With Crew in U.S., Bush Sharpens Tone Toward China." *The New York Times,* April 13, 2001.

Landler, Mark. "Biden Backs Ally Japan But Avoids Roiling China." *The New York Times,* November 25, 2013.

Landler, Mark. "Biden Urges Restraint by China in Airspace Dispute." *The New York Times,* December 5, 2013.

Landler, Mark. "Chinese Claim Forces Obama to Flesh Out His Asia Strategy." *The New York Times,* November 28, 2013.

Landler, Mark. "Standoff Worries U.S. Companies in China." *The New York Times,* April 6, 2001.

Leng, Russell J., and J. David Singer. "Militarized International Crises: The BCOW Typology and Its Applications." *International Studies Quarterly* 29, no. 2 (1988): 155-173.

Lewis, Anthony. "Molehill Into Mountain." *The New York Times,* April 7, 2001.

Li, Daojiu. *American Government and American Politics.* Beijing: China Social Sciences Press, 1990.

Li, Liangrong. *Contemporary Western News Media.* Shanghai: Fudan University Press, 2010.

Li, Shenming, and Zhang Yuyan, ed. *Global Politics and Security Report (2014).* Beijing: Social Sciences Literature Press, 2014.

Li, Xigen. "Effect of National Interest on Coverage of United States-China Relations: A Content Analysis of the New York Times and People's Daily, 1987-1996." PhD diss., Michigan State University, 1999.

Li, Xiguang, and Liu Kang. *Behind the Demonization of China.* Beijing: China Social Sciences Press, 1996.

Li, Xiguang, and Zhao Xinshu. *The Power of The Media.* Guangzhou: Nanfang Daily Press, 2002.

Lieberthal, Kenneth. "Domestic Forces and Sino-U.S. Relations." In *Living with China: U.S./China Relations in the Twenty-first Century,* edited by Ezra F. Vogel. United Kingdom: W.W. Norton, 1997.

Lin, Hongyu. "Where will Sino-US Relations Go in the Trump Era." *People's Forum,* no. 1 (2017): 108-110.

Lippmann, Walter. *Public Opinion.* New York: Harcourt, Brace and Company, 1922.

Liss, Alexander. "Images of China in the American print media: A survey from 2000 to 2002." *Journal of Contemporary China* 12, no. 35 (2003): 299-318.

Liu, Debin. "Speculation and Judgment of 'Post-Cold War Era'." *Journal of Social Science of Jilin University,* no. 4 (2002): 35-41.

Liu, Jinan. *Mass Communication and International Relations.* Beijing: Beijing Broadcasting Institute Press, 1999.

Liu, Liandi, and Wang Dawei. *The Track of Sino-US Relations—An Overview of Major Events Since the Establishment of Diplomatic Relations.* Beijing: Current Affairs Press, 1995.

Liu, Liandi. *The Trajectory of Sino-US Relations: An Overview of Events from 1993 to 2000.* Beijing: Current Affairs Press, 2001.

Liu, Xiaoying. "Archives and Records: *The New York Times.*" *International Communications,* no. 4 (2009): 58-60.

Liu, Xiaoying. *International Journalism: Ontology, Methods and Functions.* Beijing: China Radio and Television Press, 2010.

Liu, Xiaoying. *International News Communication.* Beijing: China Radio and Television Press, 2013.

Liu, Yin. "On the Influence of Internet Media on China's Foreign Policy Decision." Master's thesis, Xiamen University, 2011.

Livingston, Steven. "Beyond the 'CNN' Effect: The Media-Foreign Policy Dynamic." In *Politics and The Press: The News Media and Their Influences,* edited by Pippa Norris. United States: Lynne Rienner Publishers, 1997.

Longman, Jere. "Standoff Unlikely To Affect Beijing's Bid." *The New York Times,* April 11, 2001.

Lord, Winston. "The United States and the Security of Taiwan." US Department of State. Accessed September 25, 2020. https://1997-2001. state.gov/current/debate/mar96_china_us_taiwan.html.

Luo, Juanli. "Tendency Analysis of American Media's Reporting on China Issues." PhD diss., China University of Political Science and Law, 2013.

Malek, Abbas, and Krista E. Wiegand. "News Media and Foreign Policy: An Integrated Review." In *News Media and Foreign Relations: A Multifaceted Perspective,* edited by Abbas Malek. United States: Greenwood Publishing Group, Incorporated, 1996.

Malek, Abbas, ed. *News Media and Foreign Relations: A Multifaceted Perspective.* United States: Greenwood Publishing Group, Incorporated, 1996.

Marciel, Scot. "Maritime Issues and Sovereignty Disputes in East Asia." U.S. Department of State. Accessed September 25, 2020. https://2009-2017.state.gov/p/eap/rls/rm/2009/07/126076.htm.

Markel, Lester. *Public Opinion and Foreign Policy.* New York: Council on Foreign Relations, 1949.

Meritt, Richard. *Communication in International Politics.* Urbana: University of Illinois Press, 1972.

Mermin, Jonathan. *Debating War and Peace: Media Coverage of U.S. Intervention in the Post-Vietnam Era.* New Jersey: Princeton University Press, 1999.

Ministry of Commerce of the People's Republic of China. "Year-End Roundup of Business Work in 2015, Section 16: Deepening Win-Win Cooperation: Sino-US Economic and Trade Relations."

Accessed September 25, 2020. http://www.mofcom.gov.cn/article/ae/ai/201601/20160101245056.shtml.

Mitchell, Alison. "Anti-China Coalition in Congress Is Emboldened." *The New York Times*, April 5, 2001.

Mitchell, Alison. "Tempers Are Cooling, But A Cloud Remains." *The New York Times*, April 12, 2001.

Myers, Steven Lee, and Christopher Drew. "Chinese Pilot Reveled in Risk, Pentagon Says." *The New York Times*, April 6, 2001.

Ni, Feng. "The Foreign Policy Trends of the Obama Administration in the Second Term." *New Vision*, no. 2 (2013): 125-128.

Ni, Shixiong. *A Thousand Miles Can't Separate a Friendship Made with One Promise: 30 Years of Sino-US Relations in the Eye of a Chinese Scholar*. Shanghai: Fudan University Press, 2009.

Norris, Pippa, ed. *Politics and the Press: The News Media and Their Influence*. United States: Lynne Rienner Publishers, 1997.

O'Heffernan, Patrick. *Insider Perspective on Global Journalism and Foreign Policy Process: Mass Media and American Foreign Policy*. Norwood, N.J.: Ablex Publishing Corporation, 1990.

O'Heffernan, Patrick. *Mass Media and American Foreign Policy: Insider Perspectives on Global Journalism and the Foreign Policy Process*. New Jersey: Ablex Publishing Corporation, 1991.

Office of the Press Secretary of the White House. "Press Gaggle by Principal Deputy Press Secretary Josh Earnest — Los Angeles, CA." Accessed August 25, 2020. https://obamawhitehouse.archives.gov/the-press-office/2013/11/26/press-gaggle-principal-deputy-press-secretary-josh-earnest-los-angeles-c.

Padden, Brian. "Former US Envoy: Don't Expect Strategic Patience on N. Korea From Trump." VOA News. Accessed September 4, 2020. https://www.voanews.com/east-asia-pacific/former-us-envoy-dont-expect-strategic-patience-n-korea-trump.

Palmer, Jerry. *Spinning into Control: News Values and Source Strategies*. London: Leicester University Press, 2000.

Perlez, Jane, and David E. Sanger. "Bush Aides Saying Some Hope Is Seen to End Standoff." *The New York Times,* April 6, 2001.

Perlez, Jane, and Martin Fackler. "China Patrols Air Zone Over Disputed Island." *The New York Times,* November 29, 2013.

Perlez, Jane. "American and Chinese Navy Ships Nearly Collided in South China Sea." *The New York Times*, December 15, 2013.

Perlez, Jane. "Chinese Leader's Rise Came With New Attention to Dispute With Japan." *The New York Times*, December 3, 2013.

Perlez, Jane. "Powell Is in Driver's Seat On Plane Crisis Strategy." *The New York Times,* April 7, 2001.

Pew Research Center for the People & the Press. "Americans Spending More Time Following the News." September 12, 2010. Accessed September 29, 2020. https://www.pewresearch.org/wp-content/uploads/sites/4/legacy-pdf/652.pdf.

Qian, Qichen. *Ten Notes on Diplomacy.* Beijing: World Affairs Press, 2003.

Qian, Wenrong. "The US Election, Trump's Policy Trend, and Sino-US Relations." *Peace and Development*, no. 1 (2017): 1-16.

Qiao, Mu. *Dragon in the Eagles' Eyes: American Media's China Coverage and Sino-US Relations.* Beijing: CPC Central Party School Press, 2006.

Qin, Yaqing. *Rights, Institutions, and Culture—A Collection of International Relations Theories and Methods.* Beijing: Peking University Press, 2005.

Qiu, Meirong. "Crisis Management and Sino-US Relations." *Modern International Relations*, no. 3 (2005): 1-7.

Qiu, Meirong. "Review of International Crisis Research." *European Studies*, no. 6 (2003): 85-99.

Reston, James. *The Artillery of the Press: Its Influence on American Foreign Policy.* New York: Harper & Row, 1967.

Reuters. "China Announces Tests of Missiles near Taiwan." *The New York Times*, March 5, 1996.

Robinson, Piers. *The CNN Effect: The Myth of News, Foreign Policy and Intervention.* New York: Routledge, 2002.

Rosenthal, A. M. "On My Mind: Indicting China's Terrorism." *The New York Times*, March 12, 1996.

Rosenthal, Elisabeth. "Beijing Steps up Its War of Words Over Air Collision." *The New York Times*, April 5, 2001.

Rosenthal, Elisabeth. "China's Bonus: Attention, and Respect." *The New York Times*, April 12, 2001.

Rosenthal, Elisabeth. "Many Voices for Beijing." *The New York Times*, April 10, 2001.

Rosenthal, Uriel, and Michael T. Charles. *Coping with Crisis: The Management of Disaster, Riots and Terrorism*. Springfield: Charles C. Thomas, 1989.

Safire, William. "New Mandate of Heaven." *The New York Times*, March 25, 1996.

Safire, William. "The Politic of Apology." *The New York Times,* April 5, 2001.

Sanger, David E. "Bush is Demanding A 'Prompt' Return of Plane and Crew." *The New York Times,* April 3, 2001.

Sanger, David E. "Bush Team Is in Search Of Way Out Of Impasse." *The New York Times,* April 8, 2001.

Sanger, David E. "Delicate Diplomatic Dance Ends Bush's First Crisis." *The New York Times,* April 12, 2001.

Sanger, David E. "How Bush Had to Calm Hawks In Devising a Response to China." *The New York Times*, April 13, 2001.

Sanger, David E. "In the East China Sea, a Far Bigger Test of Power Looms." *The New York Times*, December 2, 2013.

Sanger, David E. "Powell Offers China Aides Outline for Standoff's End." *The New York Times*, April 5, 2001.

Sanger, David E. "Powell Sees No Need for Apology; Bush Again Urges Return of Crew." *The New York Times*, April 4, 2001.

Schlesinger, James. "Quest for a Post-Cold War Foreign Policy." *Foreign Affairs*. Published in Winter 1992. Accessed September 24, 2020. https://www.foreignaffairs.com/articles/1992-01-01/quest-post-cold-war-foreign-policy.

Sciolino, Elaine. "White House Snubs China Over Military Maneuvers." *The New York Times*, March 23, 1996.

Serfaty, Simon, ed. *The Media and Foreign Policy*. New York: St. Martin's Press, 1990.

Shambaugh, David. "No Easy Way Forward With China." *The New York Times*, April 3, 2001.

Shambaugh, David. *China's Future*. Germany: Wiley, 2016.

Shanghai Institute of International Studies. *Yearbook of International Situation 1996*. Shanghai: Shanghai Education Press, 1996.

Shanker, Thom. "Hagel Criticizes Chinese Navy, Citing Near Miss." *The New York Times*, December 20, 2013.

Shanker, Thom. "U.S. Sends Two B-52 Bombers Into Air Zone Claimed by China." *The New York Times*, November 27, 2013.

Shenon, Philip. "Gunboat Diplomacy, '96 Model." *The New York Times*, March 17, 1996.

Shinn, James. "Clinton's Gunboat Diplomacy." *The New York Times,* March 24, 1996.

Shu, Biquan. "Inhibitory Understanding: An Analysis of the Path of China and the US in Dealing with the Diaoyu Islands Dispute." *International Relations Research*, no. 6 (2013): 70-82.

Smith, Craig S. "China Releases U.S. Plane Crew 11 Days After Midair Collision." *The New York Times*, April 12, 2001.

Snyder, Glenn Herald, and Paul Diesing. *Conflict Among Nations: Bargaining, Decision-Making and System Structure in International Crises.* New Jersey: Princeton University Press, 1977.

Su, Ge. *U.S. Policy to China and the Taiwan Issue.* Beijing: World Affairs Press, 1998.

Suettinger, Robert L. *Beyond Tiananmen: The Politics of US-China Relations 1989-2000.* Washington, D.C: Brookings Institution Press, 2004.

Sun, Lu. "A Preliminary Interdisciplinary Approach to Communication and International Relations." *Journal of Hubei University of Science and Technology*, no. 2 (2013): 98-99.

Sutter, Robert. "Grading Bush's China Policy." *Pac Net Newsletter*, no. 10, March 8, 2002.

Tang Jiaxuan. *Strong Rain, Gentle Winds.* Beijing: World Knowledge Press, 2009.

Tang, Jiaxuan. "Recalling the 'Aircraft Collision Incident' Over the South China Sea in 2001 (Part 1)." *Party Literature*, no. 5 (2009): 15-23.

Tao, Wenzhao, and He Xingqiang. *History of Sino-US Relations.* Beijing: China Social Sciences Press, 2009.

Tao, Wenzhao. "How to Treat Sino-US Relations." *Contemporary World*, no. 8 (2015): 2-7.

Tao, Wenzhao. *American Policy on China after the Cold War.* Chongqing: Chongqing Publishing Group, 2006.

Tao, Ye. "Analysis of the Interplay Between Domestic Media and China's Foreign Policy Decisions." Master's thesis, China Foreign Affairs University, 2009.

The New York Times. "China's Coercive Play." November 26, 2013.

The New York Times. "China's Costly Rigidity." April 9, 2001.

The New York Times. "China's Military Power." March 17, 1996.

The New York Times. "Delicate Passage With China." April 3, 2001.

The New York Times. "Ending the Spy Plane Deadlock." April 12, 2001.

The New York Times. "In Statement Of President: 'It Is Time'." April 4, 2001.

The New York Times. "Managing the Spy Plane Incident." April 5, 2001.

The New York Times. "The Bludgeoning of Taiwan." March 8, 1996.

Tuchman, Gaye, and Barbara W. Tuchman. *Making News: A Study in the Construction of Reality.* United Kingdom: Free Press, 1978.

Tucker, Nancy Bernkopf, ed. *China Confidential: American Diplomats and Sino-American Relations, 1945-1996.* New York: Columbia University Press, 2001.

Tyler, Patrick E. "Beijing Steps Up Military Pressure on Taiwan Leader." *The New York Times,* March 7, 1996.

Tyler, Patrick E. "China Sends Taiwan A Dangerous Signal." *The New York Times,* March 10, 1996.

Tyler, Patrick E. "China Warns to Keep Away From Taiwan Strait." *The New York Times,* March 18, 1996.

Tyler, Patrick E. "China Warns U.S. to Stay Out of Taiwan Feud." *The New York Times,* March 12, 1996.

Tyler, Patrick E. "In Taiwan, a Mandate, but for What?." *The New York Times,* March 29, 1996.

Tyler, Patrick E. "Slogan for Many Chinese: Make Money, Not War." *The New York Times,* March 15, 1996.

Tyler, Patrick E. "Taiwan's Leader Wins Its Election and a Mandate." *The New York Times,* March 24, 1996.

Tyler, Patrick E. "TENSION IN TAIWAN: THE POLITICS; War Games Play Well for Taiwan's Leader." *The New York Times,* March 22, 1996.

Tyler, Patrick E. "War Games off Taiwan to Expand, Beijing Says." *The New York Times,* March 10, 1996.

Urano, Tatsuo. *Introduction to International Relations Theory.* Translated by Liu Suchao. Beijing: China Social Sciences Press, 2000.

Vogel, Ezra F. "How Can the United States and China Pursue Common Interests and Manage Differences?." In *Living with China: U.S./*

China Relations in the Twenty-first Century, edited by Ezra F. Vogel. United Kingdom: W.W. Norton, 1997.

Vogel, Ezra Feivel. "Must We Treat China as an Enemy?." Translated by Yang Xiuyou. *China Opening Herald*, no. 8 (1997): 25.

Wang, Guanghou, and Tian Lijia. "On the Characteristics of the Obama Administration's South China Sea Policy." *Southeast Asian Studies*, no. 1 (2015): 58-65.

Wang, Jisi. "U.S. Policy Toward China at the End of the Century—Background Analysis and Basic Judgment." In *Cross-Century Sino-American Relations*, edited by Zhao Baoxi. Shanghai: Oriental Publishing House, 1999.

Wang, Peng, Miao Xinping, and Zhang Qin. *A Brief Look into Air Defense Identification Zones*. Beijing: Military Science Press, 2014.

Weaver, David, and Swanzy Nimley Elliott. "Who Sets the Agenda for the Media? A Study of Local Agenda-Building." *Journalism Quarterly* 62, no. 1 (March 1985): 87–94.

Weiss, Carol H. "What America's Leaders Read." *The Public Opinion Quarterly* 38, no. 1 (Spring 1974): 1-22.

Wendt, Alexander. *Social Theory of International Politics*. United States: Cambridge University Press, 1999.

Williams, Phil, Donald M. Goldstein, and Jay M. Shafritz. *Classic Readings of International Relations*. United Kingdom: Wadsworth Publishing Company, 1994.

Wu, Jianmin. *Cases of Foreign Affairs*. Beijing: China Renmin University Press, 2007.

Wu, Xinbo, ed. *China-US Relations Strategy Report 2013*. Beijing: Current Affairs Press, 2014.

Xi, Laiwang. *Analyses of America's Decision-Making and China Policy*. Beijing: Jiuzhou Book Publishing House, 1999.

Xinhua News Agency. "Statement by the Government of the People's Republic of China on Establishing the East China Sea Air Defense Identification Zone." November 23, 2013.

Xiong, Zhiyong, Wu Xue, Li Qianyu, and Wang Jimei. *Lecture Notes on Sino-US Relations*. Beijing: World Knowledge Press, 2015.

Xu, Hui. *International Crisis Management: Theory and Case Analyses*. Beijing: National Defense University Press, 2011.

Yan, Lin. "American Journalists and Anonymous Sources." *International Journalism*, no. 5 (2000): 39-43.

Yan, Wenjie. "A Structural Analysis of the Changing Image of China in the New York Times from 1949 through 1988." *Quality and Quantity* 32, no. 1 (1998): 46-62.

Yan, Xuetong. "An Analysis of the Instabilities of Sino-US Relations." *World Politics and Economy*, no. 12 (2010): 4-30.

Yang, Jiemian. *Broadening of International Crises and China-US Joint Responses*. Beijing: Current Affairs Press, 2010.

Yang, Jiemian. *Sino-US Relations in the Post-Cold War Period: Theory and Practice of Crisis Management*. Shanghai: Shanghai People's Publishing House, 2004.

Yang, Yang. "Research on the Relationship Between China's International News Coverage and Foreign Policy—Taking Xinhua News Agency as an Example." PhD diss., Communication University of China, 2012.

Young, Oran R. *The Intermediaries: Third Parties in International Crises*. Princeton NJ: Princeton University Press, 1967.

Yu, Yanmin. "Projecting the China Image: News Making and News Reporting in the United States." In *Image, Perception and the Making of U.S.- China Relations*, edited by Hongshan Li and Zhaohui Hong. Maryland: University Press of America, 1998.

Zhang, Guizhen. "Mass Communication, Restricted by International Relations." In *International Relations and Global Communication*, edited by Chen Weixing. Beijing: Beijing Broadcasting Institute, 2003.

Zhang, Guizhen. *Perspective of Media in International Relations*. Beijing: Beijing Broadcasting Institute Press, 2000.

Zhang, Jiliang, *Introduction to International Relations*. Beijing: World Affairs Press, 1989.

Zhang, Jingjing. "Mass Media and International Crisis Management." Master's thesis, Shanghai International Studies University, 2005.

Zhang, Tuosheng, Michael D Swaine, and Danielle Cohen. *Managing Sino-American Crises: Case Studies and Analysis*. United States: Carnegie Endowment for International Peace, 2006.

Zhao, Xuebo, and Zhai Huixia. "The Philosophical Foundation of the Combination of Media and Diplomacy." *Modern Communication*, no. 4 (2005): 109-111.

Zhao, Xuebo. "Research on the Influence of Mass Communication on International Relations." In *International Relations and Global Communication,* edited by Chen Weixing. Beijing: Beijing Broadcasting Institute, 2003.

Zhao, Xuebo. *Visible Hands: Media in International Events.* Hefei: Hefei University of Technology Press, 2007.

Zhao, Xusheng. "On the International Crisis and Crisis Management in the Post-Cold War Period." *Modern International Relations,* no. 1 (2003): 23-28.

Zheng, Wei. *International Crisis Management and Information Communication.* Beijing: Central Compilation & Translation Press, 2009.

Zhong, Zhicheng. *For a Better World: Jiang Zemin's Foreign Visits.* Beijing: World Affairs Press, 2006.

Zhou, Qingan. "The Dilemma of International Crisis Communication: the Fukushima Nuclear Plant Accident." *International Communications,* no. 5 (2011): 15.

Zhou, Xinhua. "The Current Negative Influences of US News Media on International Relations." *Modern International Relations,* no. 12 (1999): 35-37.

Zhou, Yang. "International Communication Strategies in Incidents of Military Frictions—Taking the Sino-US Ship Confrontation on the South China Sea as an Example." *Southeast Communication,* no. 11 (2009): 12-14.

Zhu, Chongfei. "Information Game Between China and the United States Amid Two Taiwan Strait Crises." Master's thesis, Suzhou University, 2011.

Liu Wen, lecturer at the School of Television, Communication University of China. She received her doctorate in international journalism from Communication University of China in 2017. Then, she did post-doctorate work in drama and film at the same institution. Since December 2019, she is a visiting scholar at the University of Southern California. Her major research interests are international issues and news reports, international news and diplomacy, visual forms of film and television dramas and cross-cultural communication.

She took the lead in participating in the National Social Science Fund Project Research on the Mechanism of the Visual Forms of TV Drama Dissemination, and the Jiangsu Provincial Social Science Fund Project Research on the Law of Information Dissemination from the Perspective of Time and Space. She has successively published more than 10 papers in academic journals such as China Television, Contemporary TV, International Communications and News Front. She used to be the director of the programs Travel Around The World and Any Way Any Where on Travel Channel of China.

Printed in the United States
By Bookmasters